Also by John T. Kirk

American Furniture & the British Tradition to 1830
    (1982)

The Impecunious Collector's Guide to American Antiques
    (1975)

American Chairs: Queen Anne and Chippendale
    (1972)

Early American Furniture
    (1970)

Connecticut Furniture, Seventeenth and Eighteenth Centuries
    (1967)

The
Impecunious
House
Restorer

THE IMPECUNIOUS HOUSE RESTORER

Personal Vision
& Historic Accuracy

JOHN T. KIRK

Alfred A. Knopf   New York   1984

THIS IS A BORZOI BOOK
PUBLISHED BY ALFRED A KNOPF, INC.

Copyright © 1984 by John T. Kirk
All rights reserved under International and Pan-American Copyright Conventions.
Published in the United States by Alfred A. Knopf, Inc., New York, and
simultaneously in Canada by Random House of Canada Limited, Toronto.
Distributed by Random House, Inc., New York.

Library of Congress Cataloging in Publication Data

Kirk, John T.   The impecunious house restorer.

Bibliography: p.
Includes index.
1. Dwellings—United States—Conservation and
restoration. 2. Historic buildings—United States—
Conservation and restoration. I. Title.
NA7205.K57   1984   728.3'7'0288   84-47510
ISBN 0-394-53051-9
ISBN 0-394-72409-7 (pbk.)

Manufactured in the United States of America
First Edition

To Natasha

"It took so little effort to make changes for which people were grateful. You could show the good points with very little trouble."

—SAMUEL E. KIRK (B. 1904)

Contents

Contents

Color plates follow page 78.

x

Preface

It is arguable that I came to the reworking of early houses, and the creating of "appropriate" apartments, so that I could properly house the early furniture which has been my main concern for most of my life. But a large factor in my wanting to live in "early" surroundings was the influence of my father's work. I grew up in Pennsylvania, twenty miles west of Philadelphia, where he was a builder and contractor with a crew of six to eight men. Although he built new homes and maintained and added to many of the large homes that constitute the "Main Line," he was most interested when remodeling early buildings. Generally these were used by the owners, but often they were part of a large estate and had just been there when parcels were gathered as a setting for a grander house.

Old houses fascinated my father and he instinctively put back what was missing. If one room had lost most of its molding, he would take a remaining piece (or, if necessary, something from another room) to Mennonite woodworkers who ground knives to follow the sample. When adding to early stone structures, he dried mortar samples in our oven to ensure that the new addition matched the old in color and texture. This self-trained ability sprang from a natural, personal appreciation of the old, and from a concern to have new elements, small or large, live harmoniously with what they joined. The emphasis was always on quality and beauty of workmanship, and this established in me the authority of beauty and doing something well, if you did it at all. I rarely worked on these early buildings although I saw them constantly and heard detailed progress reports. I think the phrase that sticks most in my mind, and which I now appreciate fully, was the often-repeated "I'll get you in by Christmas, but I don't promise which one." As the introductory quote from my father suggests, a quick ripping out of later excrescences can produce amazing changes that delight the owner. But to reconstitute an early building that has not been properly maintained is to enter upon a voyage of discovery.

My involvement in bringing houses back to life began after deciding to concentrate professionally on early furniture. While a Yale graduate student focusing on the history of furniture, I purchased a house in Center Sandwich, New Hampshire, built about 1830 (see figures 47 through 49). I learned from it as I was learning from the early furniture at Yale. In 1975, I included in *The Impecunious Collector's Guide to American Antiques* a chapter entitled "Buy It Ratty and Leave It Alone." What is said there could be restated here, changing the examples from chairs, tables, and chests to the entire fabric of a building—floors, doors, moldings, paneling, plaster, and chimneys. In fact, Chapter 1 of that same book, "Perception Without Prejudice," is a tirade against sanding and varnishing floors and other wooden parts of a house to raw newness.

The present work is particularly concerned with the Daniel Bliss House in Rehoboth, Massachusetts. Making its particular character evident occupied me full time for a year and a half. The final result is a combination of what was there and what was brought to it. In other words, the taste and concerns of the person in charge of the restoration must be part of the final product. There is no way that the training and personal insight of the worker will not be apparent when the project is finished. It is, therefore, extremely important to have some knowledge of what you are after before you begin, for to review the history of any one preservation project is to trace endless compromises and personal judgments. Although it flies in the face of an American ideal of one right way, the perfecting of a single approach in restoration work is impossible. It is right to insist on the preservation of everything of quality—down to the smallest detail—but there is always a string of choices between two or more possibilities.

What this book is really about is learning how to develop a consistency of thought, a constant vision so that the finished environment, interior and exterior, will "work" for you. My desire in Rehoboth was to have the Bliss House as untouched as possible. Untouched except by time. This meant a series of changes based on my personal needs and feelings. Certain decisions drew

on advice from professional preservationists and architectural historians, but more often they resulted from my sense of beauty, informed by the training I had received. What I sought from the house were spaces that were viable for modern living while making vividly present its early character. I took it as a compliment when someone going through the finished house commented, "This house is spooky." What disturbed her was that the floors sloped too dramatically, the ceilings were low, the floors and many of the moldings were dark, the white walls were rarely smooth, and the furniture was quite ratty by her standards.

The demand for unaltered beauty—or as unaltered as one can leave it—may mean accepting inconveniences. Antoinette F. Downing is the architectural historian who has helped preserve much that is left of early Rhode Island and whose advice and energy were of critical importance in saving early Providence buildings. When I was working on the Bliss House, she brought a couple to see what I was doing and have me offer words of encouragement, for they were about to undertake the restoration of the Israel Arnold House (c. 1740s) in Lincoln, Rhode Island. That house had escaped heavy reworking since it was built. One of its glories was an original gambrel roof ell with a giant fireplace on the ground floor and a sleeping loft or storage area above. One access to the second floor of the ell was by a narrow staircase that twisted to the gigantic chimney stack which was flanked by small 4 over 4 sash windows (superimposed or double-hung sash, each containing four panes of glass). At the opposite end a doorway led to the second floor of the main house.

The side walls connecting the ends of the ell loft rose in giant facets created by the gambrel construction. Massive rafters crossing the room supported the boards to which the roof shingles were nailed. These nails penetrated the boards deep enough to be visible from inside, and the entire ceiling was layered with whitewash. The form of the ceiling was reminiscent of a barrel vault. As with similarly white and shadowed Cistercian abbeys, the space made one reverent for past glories and virtues, and still existing beauty.

The rest of the house retained much original woodwork of great beauty and importance, but this loft space had once held me transfixed. As the discussion with the new owners progressed, it seemed to me that although they cared very much about the house, they did not "feel" it. Their attitude toward the rarity and preciousness of what they had purchased was unaligned with my own. As the visit continued, communication crumbled. Finally, after they had finished discussing the rest of the house, they asked how they should make the second floor of the ell warm enough for their children to use as a bedroom. Its beautiful ceiling boards were not, of course, insulated, and only they and the shingles they supported provided a barrier to the elements. The owners wished to be encouraged to drop a new, warming ceiling below the rafters or to place insulation between them. My suggestion to insulate between the boards and new shingles was dismissed with disdain, but I refused to support changing the character of that important interior space. My final suggestion, which ended their visit, was: "Buy electrically heated sleeping bags." I long wondered whether they understood that I was not totally serious. Rather, I was stressing that while one has to find ways to live a modern life in old spaces, sacrifices must flow in both directions. I realize that not everyone wants their life conditioned by the integrity of what is beautiful and irreplaceable, but that is an essential requirement if you accept the claims of unique beauty.

This book has been arranged so that Chapter 1 moves briskly through the history of interiors, reviewing eighteenth- and nineteenth-century room arrangements and their influence on "colonial" installations in the twentieth century. It ends by contrasting "accurate" or "scientific" installations with more personal and idiosyncratic arrangements. To introduce the development of a personal approach, Chapter 2 reviews houses I worked on prior to the Daniel Bliss House, moves to views of that building after years of work, and ends with two lesser projects completed since. The body of the book uses the Bliss House to discuss the process of restoring an early structure step by step. Although the examples cited suggest a certain pre-nineteenth-century New England bias, the attitude is relevant when working on a building of any age and from any region. Chapter 3 covers looking for an early building, understanding what you see, communicating with real estate agents and architects, and beginning work.

Chapters 4 through 6 deal with the restoration of the Daniel Bliss House. Chapter 4 discusses the use of family and other records and then skirts around the outside of the main building while systematically discussing clapboards, doors, windows, drainage, roof, chimneys, paint, and landscaping. Chapter 5 begins by reviewing the basement and beams, sills, joists, corner posts, interior drainage, and heating. Then, moving sequentially through each room, it deals with particular aspects when they are first relevant: electricity, plaster, floors, paneling, moldings, doors, hardware, brickwork, and paint. The concluding Chapter 6 details the outbuildings and, in particular, the guesthouse made from an eighteenth-century slaughterhouse. The focus is on creating a new "colonial" environment.

Acknowledgments

First thanks must go to the buildings on which I have worked. Most are described here and I hope I have been honest where distance has shown my misuse of their qualities. From the dog days of graduate school, when all this began in earnest, I have counted on the assistance of one dear friend: with the condition that she be furnished with gallons of coffee and cream, Shirley Lear helped make many newly acquired homes—if not suitable yet for gracious living—clean and organized enough for rational restoration work to begin. During those beginnings the late Roger Bacon plunged me into appreciating untouched houses and furniture. Ruth Bacon arranged for Erica Kleine of *Colonial Homes* to provide the black-and-white photographs of the Bacons' Brentwood home, and Robert Mottley made available the color images of that house. Bill Hosley found the negatives and provided a print of the installation at the 1967 exhibition of Connecticut furniture. During early projects Denley Emerson was a helpful real estate agent; later, David Smith assisted with the Daniel Bliss House and Kenneth MacRae with the one on Beacon Hill. The Bliss

project could not have been done without the assistance of Bob Mende.

Various art historians provided guidance and encouragement. Antoinette Downing was a constant and generous source during the Providence–Rehoboth days, and since then I have counted on the knowledge and wisdom of Abbott Cummings, Richard Nylander, and Jane Nylander. Ellie Reichlin with good humor made photographs and records owned by the Society for the Preservation of New England Antiquities easily available, and Danny Lownes found in their archives photographs of nineteenth-century fences. John Sweeney and Florence Montgomery generously answered countless questions about the Stamper/Blackwell rooms at Winterthur, and Barbara Hearn and Frank Summer provided access to the Winterthur Archives. Barbara Ward sent information on the "frozen" rooms at Winterthur.

Hope Alswang read a version of the text on the Joseph Lloyd House. I am grateful to Janet Bliss Case for being willing to answer lists of questions about the Bliss family, particularly her father,

Richard Bliss, and for identifying family members in early photographs. She was assisted by her sister and brother, Barbara Bliss Coleman and Walter D. Bliss.

The book includes extracts from a daily working diary and periodic summations. These are edited selections from a much longer day-to-day manuscript I dictated to Elizabeth D. Kirk, and the summaries which she formulated. Further, the work could not have been conceived without both the casual and planned assistance of many camera enthusiasts; some took pictures, others taught the art of photography: Dick Benjamin, Norman Herreshoff, Bill Hole, David Hole, Chester Michalik, and Jackson Smith. Tom Lang printed my own often inadequate negatives with tender exactitude. And my parents were always an underlying part of each project. Realizing what they would say about a house helped clarify my thoughts.

Susan Montgomery has made clear various versions of the dictated, written, and typed manuscript, and has helped with research. Ann Armstrong, with awareness of homeowners' needs, created the bibliography. Jane Garrett has for fifteen years been the gentle but firm mover behind my publishing efforts. I am grateful to many at Knopf, particularly Bob Gottlieb, Betty Anderson, Virginia Tan, Nancy Clements, Ann Adelman, and Andrew W. Hughes. Trevor Fairbrother has been involved with recent restoration projects and photography, and he advised on the developing text.

This book is dedicated to Natasha. A good friend questioned the propriety of singling out a dog when discerning humans go unrecognized. But Natasha was a central figure during much of the creative time described and combined the aggressiveness and vulnerability I find necessary in any interesting original work.

The
Impecunious
House
Restorer

1

Use of Historic Objects and Spaces

Until recently, I had not seen a recreated room I believed to be historically accurate in arrangement of furnishings or mood, and had come to accept that it was impossible to create such a setting. To me the only believable rooms were those frozen at some point in their past, often because the owners had become impoverished and things remained fixed. When attempting to reconstruct an earlier period, it is impossible not to impose upon it one's own time's concept of a previous period. In museums and historic houses, countless period rooms arranged in the early part of this century—the first great period of gathering and displaying early American material—are now readily accepted as reflections of that phase of the colonial revival. In recreated living rooms of that era, forms such as high chests and wing chairs, which we now know were almost always part of bedroom furnishings, were prominently featured and sofas projected from fireplaces with tea tables before them. Today such historically inaccurate groupings tell us more about the rich collectors of the early twentieth century than about life in earlier times.

This strong criticism is not to condemn what was done, for the results were natural. Indeed, most periods have personal conceptions of what was important in the past. Fifteenth-century Italian architects and designers looked to ancient models to assist their designs, yet what they produced is part of their own Renaissance. In the seventeenth and eighteenth centuries English classical architects and Palladian furniture designers such as William Kent looked to both ancient and Renaissance Italian precedents: the new designs clearly communicate the time of their creation, rather than first- or fifteenth-century Italy. Many late nineteenth- and early twentieth-century American colonial revival architects and furniture designers thought they were being faithful to the past, but they were unable to escape fully the intellectual and artistic exigencies of the time in which they worked. Others, less exacting, saw their work as true to the spirit of earlier times without conforming exactly to the specifications of proportion and detail; as a result they produced freer, more spontaneous designs.

Although it is correct to admire those who

struggled to preserve and, in many cases, to make available to the public early rooms and buildings, it is continually proper to reevaluate what has been done and to find out how best to present those things we most admire, realizing that what we do will soon be inappropriate for another generation. Furthermore, a range of these early reconstructions should be kept intact to show each period's taste.

MUSEUMS

The options for a museum today include creating an accurate period room that reflects the date the room was first used, or showing how the room looked at some later date—whether at some other significant moment in the history of the house, when first installed in the museum, or at an even later phase of its life in that institution. Rooms with early woodwork can be used as appropriately scaled and detailed spaces where selected furnishings are placed like pieces of sculpture in an art gallery. A completely different attitude to object display is to place pieces in clear space, free from early room configuration and architectural details.

Virtually all of the architectural work shown in museums as "period rooms" has been altered from its original proportions and arrangement of parts. Available gallery space combined with a less stringent attitude toward preservation made this reshaping seem logical. Almost no museum room or historic house retains its original objects. In most cases they show the institution's collections, which are only rarely appropriate to the room in which they reside. Usually there are too many objects, or in rare instances, too few—as in the underdone Shaker rooms that ignore the greater complexity seen in early drawings, prints, and photographs, and suggest that these interiors alone anticipated modernistic sparseness.

Generally the objects come from many style centers, for that is what the donor or donors gathered. For example, the Winterthur Museum's seventeenth-century Oyster Bay Room (from Long Island) displays some pieces made in New York along with many from New England. When installing this room, Henry Francis du Pont created a beautiful colonial revival setting, with an Oriental carpet below superb early pieces within important woodwork. In the late 1970s it was decided to update the room to follow more accurately the pertinent contemporary room inventories. The Oyster Bay Room is now somewhat truer to the seventeenth century, but the collection does not have all the appropriate furniture forms or enough local work. What the room now exemplifies is a 1970s understanding of a compilation of seventeenth-century New York inventories, orchestrated with objects from various regions. Further acquisitions of New York pieces would bring it nearer the truth, but important New England material would then have to be taken from view unless new display space were found. Wisely, in 1975 Winterthur "froze" twenty-three rooms to show the original arrangements by Henry du Pont. Any changes in these must now be approved by the Board of Trustees.

This policy rightly preserves an exquisite and monied level of the twentieth-century colonial revival taste. It fixes rooms at a genuine moment rather than having them join those subjected to continuing curatorial vagaries as new ideas of the true past emerge. The decision, made some fifteen years after Henry du Pont's death, raises the question of whether it is appropriate to stop the rooms at the moment it was decided to freeze them, or to restore them to some point during du Pont's life. But should one choose the moment at which he considered the room finished, the date he gave his home to the public, or the date of his death? And should one restore family photographs and other personal items to the rooms in which he actively lived? Any choice other than the date at which it was decided to freeze would, of course, necessitate a restoration—the inevitable process of subjective judgments.

An alternative for museums, as opposed to historic houses, is to treat spaces with historic woodwork as sculpture halls (see figure 1), to present the woodwork as important and to install in it objects—furniture and other decorative arts—of similar character. Unlike rooms attempting to create the past, this allows a modern level of lighting and often greater access to the objects, for they can be arranged with the viewing public rather than a historic family in mind.

If the objects are of great quality it is tempting to stress the rightness of the sculpture gallery approach, but this too is not fully satisfactory either for the material or the visitors. In 1904, Charles Leonard Pendleton gave his collection to the Rhode Island School of Design, provided they agreed to place it in a fireproof building that looked like a private Georgian residence. The school copied Pendleton's Providence house, located just up the hill, and it was opened to the public in

1906. This first museum "American Wing" is an intriguing colonial revival structure, for the changes from the original were typical of the impositions then thought to be fair when inspired by an old building. The original house has a brick front overlaid by clapboard and wooden details. The museum's copy omitted the clapboard sheathing, and such details as the exterior window cornices were executed in stone. (Pendleton liked the stone Mount Pleasant in Fairmount Park near Philadelphia and the elimination of wood accorded with fire prevention efforts.) Interior changes include relocating the staircase from the rear left of the central hall to the right. In the new building one feels more like walking up the stairs than around them, perhaps because most people tend to think counterclockwise or in a right-handed direction. The dining room, located at back right, has a complex arcading not present in the old structure. The resulting building feels 1906, although this should not necessarily overrule the use of an early house inventory to help

1 Southeast parlor, Pendleton House (Museum of Art, Rhode Island School of Design; about 1969)

re-create a suitable arrangement. However, the kinds of objects in the Pendleton Collection do not allow this approach. Much of its furniture was made for bedroom use: chests of drawers, high chests of drawers, dressing tables, and chests-on-chests, and there is not enough first-floor furniture. Also, the collection contains a redundancy of forms, such as desks, that would normally make a single or at most a double appearance in any home.

If the decision is to forget historic arrangement and employ the sculpture gallery approach, new problems arise. The rooms are small and cramped and most lose two walls to a fireplace and windows. In the mid-1970s I was curator of the Pendleton Collection, and my first thought was to arrange the pieces sculpturally, take down the barriers, and let people get near these superior works of art. The public proceeded to sit on the chairs and to open the drawers to study the construction and interior woods—a commendable desire but hardly conducive to preservation of the material. When I asked people not to touch the furniture, the standard response was, "Oh, I have furniture at home." Since they had good furniture, they felt they knew how to handle pieces without hurting them. They did not normally touch the less familiar oil paintings. Unfortunately, it was necessary to place a barrier at the doorway of each room and turn the furniture to face it. When viewing the room (figure 1), it is difficult to see the great bombé chest of drawers at back left or the block front at right, but this unsatisfactory solution makes the pieces as available as possible in such a setting.

Since this American Wing is not appropriate for a "period" house arrangement or gallery spaces, a further option is to follow photographs of how Pendleton used the pieces in his own home. But this building does not exactly follow the early one, and such an installation will never feel like Pendleton's house. A somewhat more informative solution would be to attempt to put it back as seen when first opened to the public in 1906. This would tell us much about 1906 but make the pieces less visible. One member of the board of trustees of this museum, with more wisdom than seriousness, suggested letting the rooms become offices and moving the furniture to modern galleries.

Freed of period rooms, one can install objects as in figure 2 so that dramatic sculptural forms create thrilling patterns. This installation was part of a 1967 exhibition of Connecticut furniture held at the Wadsworth Athenaeum. The furniture was placed on high and low plinths, usually located some distance from the walls. True, this is not the way these pieces were intended to be seen by their makers or early users. Until the nineteenth century furniture was nearly always set back against a wall except when in use, and on the floor. Raising such pieces on high plinths changes the perspective: the feet are too near the viewer and thus too big in scale, while the backs are too distant. But for many visitors this exhibition and other installations that followed (such as the display at the Yale University Art Gallery created in 1973 which hangs chairs, chests, and tables from the walls) made people stop and say, "Look at those feet. What great shapes. It's like sculpture."

There is no perfect solution for museums attempting to show early rooms and furniture. The curator's role must be to choose the compromise that is best for his or her objects at that particular moment. Each installation will eventually be followed by a new interpretation and different compromises will be accepted. Whether any installation works depends on the curator having vast knowledge and an extraordinary eye. Some arrangements inspired by the Connecticut show and Yale installation, such as the 1977 display at the Philadelphia Museum of Art, lack their intriguing juxtaposition of forms. The ultimate questions are: what compromises are you willing to accept; what impact from the building and the arrangements within it gives you pleasure; and if

2 Installation at exhibition, Connecticut Furniture—Seventeenth and Eighteenth Centuries; *Wadsworth Athenaeum, Hartford, Connecticut, 1967 (Wadsworth Athenaeum)*

it is a public place, what will bring fresh insights to the visitors?

HISTORIC HOUSES

Unlike museum rooms, public historic houses can and probably should undertake the exacting and usually costly struggle to recreate an authentic statement of some point in their histories—although Drayton Hall (c. 1738) near Charleston, South Carolina, is successfully shown without *any* furnishings. If furnished, one should be able to expect to see it the way the house really was at the moment it claims to show. Then the rooms will, in most cases, contain things accumulated over time, perhaps family possessions handed down for their usefulness and as symbols of family longevity. Of course, some rooms and houses will need to be treated as they were when totally new: the moment the house was first used. This situation is less simple if some objects

were brought from one or more former residences. Certainly other rooms were done up afresh for a particular event: a wedding, new ownership, after the parents' death, or on receiving extra money.

Until recently, I had thought a recreated room could never successfully reflect the mood and arrangement of an earlier time, although I had once been convinced that the attempt should be made. This was the real need of a scholar in a related discipline: a historian of English literature who wanted to see a room in which Jane Austen might have lived and written. If she could see rooms as they were in rural England about 1800, she felt, she might more fully understand the author and her stories. But over the years the hope of such an experience dwindled.

Frozen in Time

Although it is difficult to find a recreated room in America that feels right, a few relatively undis-

7

turbed early settings do exist. One of the rare instances of a nearly intact survivor is the Jonathan Sayward House in York, Maine (figures 3 through 7). The building was described as "a New Dwelling House" when Joseph Sayward (1684–1741) purchased it from Noah Peck in 1720. Sayward had financial difficulties and perhaps to provide assistance, his son Jonathan purchased the house in 1735. After his father's death, Jonathan Sayward lived there. He probably added the paneling in the parlor and the room above it, and a small bedroom to the first floor. Except for these minor (essentially contemporary) changes, there have been no significant alterations to the building in the subsequent two centuries.

Jonathan Sayward was a successful businessman. When he died in 1797 at the age of eighty-four, he bequeathed the house to his eldest grandson and namesake, Jonathan Sayward Barrell. The only piece of furniture left to anyone outside the house was a bed he gave to his daughter Sarah, "to use and dispose of as she pleases." A few pieces of neo-classical furniture and other decorative arts were added, but Thomas Jefferson's Embargo of 1807 and the War of 1812 destroyed Barrell financially. A comparison of inventories from 1822 and 1889 indicates that very few items were added in the nineteenth century, most importantly, a sofa, a rocking chair, and stoves. During the middle of that century, the family proudly opened the house of their "venerable ancestor" to visitors.

Figure 3 shows it in about 1875. The chairs are covered with thin eighteenth-century silk (probably dress material) dyed green in the mid-nineteenth century. Pieces of the same material hung as curtains on the corner cupboard in the same room. A photograph of the room taken in the 1880s (figure 4) shows it garnished with family curiosities, including a fan above and a pewter platter and exotic shoes below the rectangular tea table. On the tripod table in the center stand a decanter, a large covered glass, a ceram-

ic mug, and another fan, and there are swords in the corner behind. It may be that the difference between these two photographs is that the second captures how it was shown to public visitors. Probably the room was little used in the second half of the nineteenth century except as a display area, for it did not acquire a stove. In contrast, another Sayward House room (figure 7) gained a heating stove and a more relaxed ambience.

In 1900, the house and its contents were purchased by Elizabeth Cheever Wheeler, a descendant of Jonathan Sayward. She added a porch and dormers and had the interior woodwork painted white, the walls repapered, and straw matting laid on the floors. The family used the house as a summer home (figure 5, taken about 1900–10) until 1977, when Mrs. Wheeler's children gave it to the Society for the Preservation of New England Antiquities. It was opened to the public in 1978.[1] A comparison of the parlor as dressed for the public (figure 4) and as it was arranged for the modern photograph in figure 6 makes evident how difficult it is to be faithful to an earlier time, even when original objects and photographic documentation of an early arrangement exist.

As the room now stands, two major features are inconsistent with the mood of the early photographic record: the very busy chinoiserie patterns of both the 1950s reproduction wallpaper and the carpet. These can be corrected. The large gilded neo-classical–looking glass at the left in the early photograph is no longer with the

3 Southwest parlor, Jonathan Sayward House, York, Maine, about 1875 (Society for the Preservation of New England Antiquities)

4 Southwest parlor, Jonathan Sayward House, 1880s (Society for the Preservation of New England Antiquities)

5 *Southwest parlor, Jonathan Sayward House, 1900–1910 (Society for the Preservation of New England Antiquities)*

6 *Southwest parlor, Jonathan Sayward House, 1979 (Society for the Preservation of New England Antiquities)*

building, although the cloth that draped its top is still in the collection and the nail from which it hung is still in place. More intriguing are the less apparent differences. There is no hearth rug. The large, wonderful family paintings which seem of amazing scale because the room is so small are now hung from the wooden casings of the girts as in the 1900–10 photograph. There are portrait miniatures on either side of a modest looking glass, whereas in figure 4 the large mirror echoed the scale of the oil portraits. The covered glass on the round table in the photograph is on the drop-leaf table. These and other small changes shift the mood perceptibly from the quieter and more casual earlier stance of figure 4.

In truth, the room as seen in figure 6 was a momentary arrangement for the photographer; normally, most of the small items live in cupboards to protect them from breakage and theft. The house is shown very much as it appears in figure 5 since it is now the Society's policy to freeze, more or less, a house at the moment it is given. But because the Wheeler family retained some items they had brought to the house, it does not reflect any specific historic moment. Since security precautions now keep smaller objects locked in cupboards, perhaps the installation should follow the scheme shown in figure 3.

In contrast to the Sayward House, most house curators are lucky to have an early inventory and perhaps a few family pieces; their problems are thus far greater. It is difficult to follow an inventory, even one that goes beyond a general listing of items and separates them into specific rooms. What is meant in a late eighteenth-century inven-

7 Southeast parlor, Jonathan Sayward House, 1880s (Society for the Preservation of New England Antiquities)

tory by "one old walnut tea table"? Is the top rectangular or round? (Both are shown in figures 4 and 6.) If rectangular, was it one of the few made during the William and Mary period or was it in the "Queen Anne" style with round feet (as in figures 4 and 6) or of the claw and ball foot variety? And where should it have been made? Was it one of the many tea tables imported from England, or brought from some distant American style center, or made locally? And once the objects that seem to follow those suggested in the inventory have been acquired, how are they to be arranged?

Copies

Acquiring appropriate early objects is difficult and usually expensive. Any tea table that fell under the inventory phrase "one old walnut tea table" could today be priced anywhere from $20,000 to over $100,000. It is therefore sensible to ask whether a restoration must always involve authentic material. When we discuss the illustrations of the Williamsburg room (see figures 25 and 26), it will be necessary to review the use of reproduction furniture in a reproduction building. Here, in considering an authentic ambience, are copies appropriate? Sometimes the pieces that once graced the house are known but not available. Should they not be copied and these used? Very few people are able to execute faithful reproductions, but it can be done. Up close they do not have the "feel" of an early work but from a distance they can be convincing. A few places, such as Mount Vernon, are now using copies of paintings that were originally in the house.

The grand John Brown House in Providence, Rhode Island, is the headquarters of the Rhode Island Historical Society and open to the public. Probably one of the designers of the house was John's brother Joseph. Today, John's great Newport block-and-shell desk and bookcase is in the Yale University Art Gallery. In its stead stands a related one made for Joseph. It is not identical to the Yale piece and it might be appropriate to have a fine copy of the Yale example made and placed in the house, which would bring the room nearer to the original truth. Since one cannot enter the room beyond a barrier—to protect the carpet and small objects placed about—only the most rarefied experts could tell the difference between a good copy and the original. (I do not mean to suggest that the public should not know the piece is a reproduction.) If the house were owned by an organization whose sole responsibility was this house, would it not be proper to sell Joseph's desk and bookcase to pay for the copy and any restoration work needed on the house? Indeed, the desk and bookcase would sell at such a price it could pay for a copy and restoration work, and still provide an endowment. Since the John Brown House is owned by a historical society where responsibility is statewide, and it has gallery space outside the house, the Joseph Brown piece might be displayed there where one could get near it under modern lighting.

Room Arrangements

During the eighteenth century even the rooms of the well-to-do were sparsely furnished, as inventories and paintings of interiors of that time show. There are very few pictorial records of American pre-Revolutionary rooms, but comparative analysis of inventories and other documentation indicates that they looked much like the rooms in English paintings of people of similar social and economic station. Upper- and middle-class English mid-eighteenth-century portraits often place the sitter (or sitters) in a large room on chairs either side of a table, with all three pieces of furniture standing on a small carpet. Even when the room is of considerable style, the rest of the floor is usually bare: the other chairs, perhaps a sofa, and a table or two line the walls. On very rare occasions, a large case piece is similarly marshaled. A typical American inventory of this sort reads:

Dorchester [Massachusetts] Jan.[ry] 11.th 1763[2]

Inventory of what Estates Real & Personall, belonging to Coll.[o] Robert Oliver [Esquire] late
of Dorchester Deceased, that has been Exhibited to us the Subscribers, for Apprizement. Viz.[t]

In the Setting Parlour Viz.[tt]

a looking Glass	£4. —.—
a Small Ditto	0. 6.0
12 Metzitens [prints] pictures Glaz'd @ 6/	3. 12.—
8 Cartoons D.[o] [Ditto] Ditto	4. —.—
11 small Pictures	—. 4.—
4 Maps	—. 10.—
1 Prospect Glass	—. 10.—
2 Escutchons Glaz'd	—. 4.—
1 pair small hand Irons [andirons]	—. 6.—
1 Shovel & Tongs	—. 8.—
1 Tobacco Tongs	—. 1.—
1 pair Bellowes	—. 2.—
1 Tea Chest	—. 2.—
2 Small Waters [waiters?]	—. 1.—
1 Mehogony Tea Table	1. —.—
8 China Cups & Saucers	—. 2.—
1 Earthen Cream Pott	—. —. 1
1 Ditto. Sugar Dish	—. —. 4
1 Black Walnut Table	1. —.—
1 Black Ditto Smaller	0. 6.—
1 Round painted Table	0. 1.—
7 Leather Bottom [seated] Chairs @ 6/	2. 2.—
1 Arm[d] Chair Common	0. 3.—
1 Black Walnut Desk	1. 12.—
1 pair Candlesticks snuffers & Stand Base Mettle	—. 4.—
6 Wine Glasses 1 Water Glass	—. 1.—
a parcell of Books	1. —.—
a Case with Small Bottles	0. 4.—
	22. 1. 5

The neo-classical style, and roughly contemporary social improvements stemming from the Industrial Revolution, effected major changes in room arrangements, which became more intricate and functionally complex. Beginning around 1760 in grander English houses, designers such as Robert Adam transformed earlier spaces and created new rooms with an airy classicism. A development of this new taste was broadcast to the upper middle classes somewhat later in London pattern books such as George Hepplewhite's *The Cabinet-Maker and Upholsterer's Guide* (1788) and Thomas Sheraton's *The Cabinet-Maker and Upholsterer's Drawing-Book* (1791–94). Because of the Revolution (the peace treaty was signed in 1783), and because it was for an upper-class audience, the classicism of Adam did not significantly affect American furniture designs. However, the advent of Hepplewhite and Sheraton's pattern books coincided with the end of the war, and they greatly influenced fashionable designs in America early in the 1790s. Once begun, the lighter, more novel and seemingly modern style swept fashionable American high-style centers and rapidly captured the more outlying areas.

The debate over the country of origin of a painting depicting a sitting room (shown as figure 8) demonstrates the close parallel between British and American rooms even before the nineteenth century. According to tradition, this is a painting of the Samels family. Although that is not certain, the real debate is whether it is an American or an English interior. In fact, it might just be a German room. The picture is signed "John Eckstein 1788." Johann Eckstein (c. 1736–1817 or 1822) was a court painter and sculptor in Mecklenburg, Germany. But probably while still based in Prussia, he had an address in London and exhibited there at the Royal Academy. In 1794 he settled in Philadelphia, and is recorded in the Philadelphia Directories of 1796–97, 1805–06, and 1811–16. He or his son was working in Philadelphia as late as 1822. The Historical Society of Pennsylvania has found no Samels family in Philadelphia wills, marriages, deaths, or other records.

In 1788—the date on the painting—Johann Eckstein was still based in Germany. However, the signature is the anglicized "John." The painting was assigned by an English owner to Christie's for sale in 1958, and oral tradition follows it back through a series of gifts to an English Samels family. It was purchased as probably American by the Museum of Fine Arts, Boston, in 1959. Sir Roy Strong, now director of the Victoria and Albert Museum, London, wrote in 1965 that the interior seemed English.[3] Quite possibly the artist executed the work in England while there on a visit from Germany. That the painting's origin is not *readily* apparent demonstrates the essential similarity of upper-middle-class taste on both sides of the Atlantic at the end of the eighteenth century. Although future understanding will make it easier to perceive subtle differences, the overriding impression is of a unified international approach impelled by the same modernizing spirit.

The painting shows parents and four children sitting in a corner against an unlit fireplace. The carpet is green with bright pink flowers; it is fringed, and not of the fitted, wall-to-wall variety. The pierced-splat "Chippendale style" chair at the left was made about 1750–85. The simply arched sofa and the armchair are of the neo-classical style, as suggested in such books as Hepplewhite's— published the same year the scene was painted. The upholstery is black with lines of brass nails. The circular, dish-top tea table supports a tray and tea set, including an uncovered silver sugar-bowl with blue glass liner and a silver creamer. The mantel is decorated with five ceramic figures. One wall has two oval portraits below a simple gilded classical sconce for one candle; it is placed high to reflect light across the room and since it is not in use, holds no candle. (Sconces, chandeliers, and candlesticks were cleaned up after use and paintings rarely show them holding candles unless they are alight.) The wall is painted or, more likely, papered a plain gray-blue. There is a patterned border edging the paneled dado and mantel.

While the original site of the international upper-middle-class room seen as figure 8 is uncertain, the location of the slightly later middle-class view in figure 9 is known. It depicts the family of Nathan Hawley, the jailer of Albany, New York. The painting was done by William Wilkie, an inmate, on November 3, 1801. Mr. and Mrs. Hawley are accompanied by eight children. In the first room, the floor (probably unpainted) has a stenciled, painted floor carpet. It could have been imported from Europe[4] or a distant American style center, or made locally.

The woodwork, chair rail, and area below the molding that extends from the uncushioned window seat are blue. The inner room has a paneled buff-colored dado above a red-brown base-board. All the plaster walls are white. The uncurtained

8 Probably the Samels family, probably English, inscribed "John Eckstein 1788" (Museum of Fine Arts, Boston)

9 Nathan Hawley and Family, by William Wilkie, dated November 3, 1801 (Albany Institute of History and Art)

10 *Sitting room and bedroom, a Folsom house, Dorchester, Massachusetts, about 1895 (Society for the Preservation of New England Antiquities)*

window may have folding shutters. The parents sit in painted slat-back fancy chairs with rush seats. The decorative pattern on the tapered-leg, drop-leaf table was possibly achieved by painted graining rather than veneer. The three landscape pictures (possibly colored prints) in narrow frames are hung high, each with two hooks. The inner room shows two portraits. The clothing of the family is fashionably neo-classical but not necessarily expensive. By 1800 more pretentious rooms in major style centers would have been considerably more complex. One would expect wall-to-wall carpets, wallpaper—both possibly with fancy borders—and curtains. Patterned veneer would be evident and there would probably be a sofa with cushions and upholstered mahogany chairs.

As the nineteenth century progressed, rooms became ever more complicated, with a greater variety of forms and specialized objects. Although not all reached the stereotypical "Victorian

clutter," the widespread use of machine technology allowed the less well-off to have the quantity of things they thought the upper classes had always possessed. What now seems redundant overlay, particularly in the use of textiles, became standard. Previously textiles had been very expensive, but in the nineteenth century machines could print or weave patterns that had formerly been the result of tedious labor. Now they covered floors, tables, mantels, and at times hung as drapes each side of a doorway. Small rugs were laid over larger ones and no longer just as protective hearth rugs in front of the fireplace. There was a conspicuous visual emphasis on things in general and textiles in particular.

The photographic view of a sitting room and bedroom (figure 10) in a Folsom house in Dorchester, Massachusetts, was taken about 1895. Fur rugs lie on a patterned wall-to-wall carpet with border. The chairs, sofa, mantel, wall bracket, and opening between the rooms are all draped. Patterns enrich nearly every surface. Pictures hang at an angle and one rests on another. There is a predominance of late nineteenth-century material—the most up-to-date furniture is of the Eastlake variety—but the assemblage was accumulated over time. The 1820–50 Windsor chair is repainted white with gold rings and decorated with bow knots on the top rail; it looks perfectly at home. One of the many items over the mantel is a larger lusterware pitcher. This too came from the earlier half of the century.

Figure 11 records the drawing room in Oak Hill before the early woodwork was moved to the

Museum of Fine Arts, Boston. In 1799, Elias Haskett Derby, merchant prince of Salem, Massachusetts, died leaving a tract of land to his daughter who had married Captain Nathaniel West. In 1800 they built Oak Hill near Danvers, Massachusetts. It is thought that the house was designed by Samuel McIntire and it is certain that his son, Samuel Field McIntire, was employed for at least part of the work, for in 1813–14 he billed "Madame Derby" West for carvings that included sheaves of wheat, urns, and eagles. The house was later owned by Mrs. Jacob Crowninshield Rogers (née Elizabeth Peabody) and figure 11 shows the drawing room as it ap-

11 Drawing room, Oak Hill, Danvers, Massachusetts, about 1915 (Society for the Preservation of New England Antiquities)

peared during her residency, about 1915. The floor is covered first with flat weave, wall-to-wall carpet on which lie a series of loose rugs, some overlapping. The lampshades are fringed and the fringed upholstery fills the room with plunging birds. Cushions appear on chairs, sofa, and floor, and the door drapes pile up on the floor. The tables are densely packed. A looking glass of about 1900, shaped like a Palladian window, covers the wall between the doors. When placed there it was probably seen as scaling accurately with the probably McIntire doorways and room cornices. Now, with even greater perspective on the *neo-classical* and this neo-neo-classical period, it looks inappropriately enormous, and the swags too repetitive, puffy, and overwrought for the early woodwork. The effect recalls the precious, lady-like attitude of such late nineteenth-century classicists as Ogden Codman. In 1921, St. John's Normal College purchased the house, which was later razed to make way for a shopping center. We shall return to this and other Oak Hill rooms when discussing recent attempts at period accuracy.

THE COLONIAL REVIVAL STYLE

It has become customary to see the conscious use of early American artifacts as beginning in the last years of the nineteenth century when the colonial style was reused by many prominent architects and designers. In fact, love and patriotic respect for the pre-Revolutionary period were naturally linked to America's first experience of a classical revival in the late eighteenth century. As in Europe, many sought to associate themselves with the first Republic and focused on Roman achievements. For example, when Thomas Jefferson was choosing a source for his Monticello, he used a Roman prototype. In the early nineteenth century the focus shifted to Greece, and pride in the New America joined the revival of Greek idealism. This vision of enlightened man-

kind produced an international style that was poignantly appropriate for the new nation. The eagles, swags, and urns of the classical ages became new national symbols of republican order. At the same time the founding fathers were idealized. George Washington was sculpted wearing a toga, and to encourage direct contact with the great man, quantities of his hair were preserved.

There was a growing awareness during the nineteenth century of the value of maintaining anything that recalled both the humble and the glorious past. Commemorative furniture was made from trees under which the gallant had stood. Cannonballs from a particular battle, or found in significant walls, were placed on special stands. The Rhode Island Historical Society has "the root that grew around the body of Roger Williams" and a partially filled bottle labeled "The supposed ashes of Roger Williams."

In some instances colonial domestic arrangements persisted naturally into the nineteenth century when people continued to live as they always had. This was true for the Sayward House, seen in figures 3 through 7, opened by the descendants in the mid-nineteenth century to show the home of their "venerable ancestor." Another example of the natural use of eighteenth-century forms and placement with nineteenth-century overtones is seen in the interior shown as figure 12—the room left to Zillah Walker Jennings (1766–1852) at her husband's death in 1813. The rest of the house was bequeathed to their son's family: Deacon Calvin Jennings, and his wife, Laura Hastings Jennings. Their daughter Marica Ann taught art and in 1863 married James Kilbourne. The picture is inscribed: "M. A. Kilbourn," and thus postdates both her marriage and her grandmother's death.

In this memory picture the floor coverings suggest the new century: the wall-to-wall striped, flat-woven carpeting is overlaid by a geometrically patterned doormat that may once have been a hearth rug, and two oval braided rugs dating after 1825.[5] The wallpaper of the first half of the

12 Interior of Joel Jennings Homestead, Brookfield, Massachusetts, *signed M. A. Kilbourn* [sic], *after 1863 (Old Sturbridge Village)*

nineteenth century continues onto the casings of the girts at the top of the room. The windows have roller shades (probably made of a textile and hemmed around a lath at the base) and there are transparent curtains. The early nineteenth-century clock is hung next to a window—undoubtedly to put its looking glass door near a source of light. The slat-back chairs could have been made in the late eighteenth century or in the first years of the nineteenth. One has rockers and arms, that at the foot of the bed a patterned seat. The desk and bookcase may date from the late eighteenth century. The new century is evident but the sparseness and general feel are from the previous one.

By the late nineteenth century there was a tremendous interest in earlier times. The Brooklyn, New York, Sanitary Fair of 1864 included a room with "treasures of the past" (a place for things belonging to events and heroes of distant lands) that included relics from America's beginnings, and there was a very inaccurate recreation of an early "New England Kitchen." Many of the Centennial celebrations stressed early material: the 1876 Philadelphia Exposition included another New England Kitchen, a Connecticut Cottage, and special collections of Washingtoniana.[6] These were picturesque minor delights among the vast displays of technical advancements, but they did help further the interest in American artifacts. At the 1893 World's Columbian Exposition in Chicago, early American materials were more in evidence, including a reproduction of Philadelphia's Independence Hall housing the original Liberty Bell.[7]

The late nineteenth-century interest in colonial materials developed two major attitudes. One connected the colonial heritage to the stringent and ordered aesthetic of the Arts and Crafts movement. In England, reformers like Augustus Pugin, John Ruskin, William Morris, and Charles Eastlake had come to value well-crafted, utilitarian objects as expressions of man's worth. In place of machine-made fancy goods they favored simple

13 Ready for Church, *photograph by Wallace Nutting, dated 1913 (Society for the Preservation of New England Antiquities)*

designs suited to the basic natural materials. In America, designers such as Gustaf Stickley followed their lead, producing objects and publishing designs for room arrangements that balanced honest oak, leather, copper, and textiles in modulated color relationships. The tendency was to sparseness, with pieces acting as sculptural forms in a unified scheme. This sensibility in its colonialist guise was manifested in the images created by Wallace Nutting (1861–1941), as seen in his commercial photograph (figure 13).

Wallace Nutting, whom many associate with his landmark *Furniture Treasury* (1928–33), typified this purer, less cluttered strain of the colonial revivalists. He owned early houses and large collections, particularly of American furniture. One aspect of his many-faceted business was the creation and sale of photographs of interior and exterior "colonial" views. He began taking interior shots late in the nineteenth century and early in this century introduced people in costume. Figure 13 is one of many hand-colored photographic prints Nutting gave to the Society for the Preser-

vation of New England Antiquities on December 1, 1914. The back is inscribed: "Ashland/Mass/ 'Ready for Church'/3268," and it is stamped: "From Wallace/Nutting/Framingham/Massachusetts." The lower left-hand corner of the front reads "©WN 1913." The scene projects a romantic vision of the past but it does not capture any reality except the time of composition. The figure wears an 1830s-style bonnet and sits in a vernacular "Queen Anne" chair that has lost its finials. At the right the slat-back chair with textile seat is without ring turnings or significant finials: this suggests a nineteenth-century date. The powderhorn, sword, and a probably nineteenth-century oval frame decorate the mid-eighteenth-century paneling, which is painted Greek revival white; and the hinges are black accents. In the eighteenth century the paneling and hinges would have been painted one color and almost certainly not white. The fireplace had an early crane but the andirons are later. Many Nutting interiors use circular or oval braided rugs. Although these became standard in col-

20

onial revival interiors, they were unknown before about 1825.[8]

The other important turn-of-the-century strain of interest in colonial achievements joined the mania for colonial materials to the still prevalent nineteenth-century taste for conspicuous abundance of possessions, often of a fanciful nature. The delight in a joyous proliferation of material goods was not limited to any social, intellectual, or economic group: it could be found in cosmopolitan settings and Alaskan Territory cabins.[9]

The room shown as figure 14 belonged to one of the most influential gatherers of American things. Like Wallace Nutting, he was passionate about early American material and he too conditioned how it would be viewed over the next sixty years. For this man, however, the emphasis was not on ordered and restricted arrangements but on elegant confections. Figure 14 shows a view of the apartment Henry Davis Sleeper (1878–1934) shared with his mother when they lived at 336 Beacon Street, Boston, about 1907 or 1908. In 1907, Henry Sleeper purchased just under an acre on Eastern Point, bordering the harbor of Gloucester, Massachusetts. He was then a wealthy bachelor, twenty-eight years old, who had studied architecture in Paris in the late 1890s, and his intention was to build near his friend, A[bram] Piatt Andrew. Just a year after acquiring the site,

14 Apartment of Henry D. Sleeper and mother, 336 Beacon Street, Boston, Massachusetts, about 1907 (Society for the Preservation of New England Antiquities)

Sleeper and his mother were summering there in a house of twenty-six rooms.

At first it had a shingled second story above a stucco first floor. Sleeper, who was not a practicing architect, worked with Halfdon N. Hanson, a local architect who had begun as a woodworker, carpenter, and handyman. Hanson became the protégé of Winthrop Sargent, who paid for his architectural training, and at twenty-three he joined Sleeper to produce one of the glories of colonial revival fantasy. The twenty-six rooms of Little Beauport (as it was first known) were only the beginning, for during the next seventeen years it would grow to about forty rooms (figure 15). Motoring through Essex County in the summer of 1907, Sleeper and Piatt Andrew discovered a disintegrating gambrel-roofed, two-story house which had been built by William Cogswell, probably in 1732 or 1739.[10] Sleeper fell in love with its paneling and wanted to incorporate it into his new house.

Andrew was a friend of Isabella Stewart Gardner, one of the great nineteenth-century gatherers of art and pieces of architecture. (In 1903 she had completed Fenway Court on the then western edge of Boston where treasures from distant lands were impressively combined in a grand and deliberately eclectic new work of architecture.) Andrew appealed to Mrs. Gardner for her approval to reuse fragments from an American building, and took her to see the Cogswell House. She enthusiastically gave her blessing: "What fun all this will be for me . . ."[11] Although the Cogswell paneling became an inspiration for the colonialized "cottage," Sleeper did not see the need to keep it intact. Rather, he put pieces where they fit and pleased his eye. Sections were used in at least two of the central rooms where they were joined by waxed brick floors, then seen as sympathetic to colonial wood.

Sleeper's design aesthetic was undoubtedly influenced by Indian Hill Farm, the home of Ben:Perley Poore (1820–1887), world traveler, historian, antiquarian, architect, and journalist.

Indian Hill lay in West Newbury, only a few miles from Gloucester and near the Cogswell House. By the 1820s, Ben:Perley Poore's father had begun buying furnishings and fragments from early buildings. He took his eleven-year-old son to Europe to visit English and continental houses, including Abbotsford, Sir Walter Scott's imitation of a Scottish manor. Upon their return, the senior Poore began turning what had been the Poore family house for six generations into an English Gothic manor house. His son avidly continued the transformation and by his death Indian Hill housed such disparate parts as a staircase from the Tracy House in Newburyport, paneling from the Province House and the John Hancock House (both of Boston), a fireplace from a New York Stuyvesant house, and another from a home of the first Napoleon.

What Sleeper produced in Beauport was indebted to the vision manifested in that fifty-year-old colonial revival stance mixed with European romantic ideals. Photographs taken in both homes show rooms with similar arrangements. Each had "period rooms." Others housed objects which related only in that they aesthetically complemented one another. Both arranged rooms around objects with historic association. Indian Hill had Napoleon's bed; in his Byron Room, Sleeper believed he had one that had belonged to the poet.[12] Comparison now must be by photographs of Indian Hill, for most of it was destroyed by fire in the 1960s.

For all his importance, Sleeper was but one force in a rising tide. In 1907, the year Sleeper purchased in Gloucester, George Francis Dow created just below him on the coast, in Salem's Essex Institute, what are among the earliest and perhaps most influential American period rooms. Dow was influenced by the Swedish Nordiska Museet, created by Artur Hazelius (1833–1901) in 1873, and as an antiquarian stressed age and authenticity over aesthetic value. The three rooms—kitchen, parlor, and bedroom—were gradually altered over the years but recently they

have been returned nearly to how early photographs show them. Soon after creating the period rooms, Dow added period buildings behind the Essex Institute, including the Ward House, and dressed guides in "period" costumes.

In 1909, American decorative arts were displayed for the first time at the Metropolitan Museum of Art in New York as part of the Hudson-Fulton Celebration. The Society for the Preservation of New England Antiquities was founded the following year, and in 1911 it acquired the first of what would amount to ownership of about sixty New England houses. Henry Sleeper became its honorary curator. The Metropolitan Museum's American Wing opened in 1924. During the years of preparation, curators spent some weeks at Beauport studying Sleeper's approach.[13] And the recreation of Colonial Williamsburg began in 1926.

From its inception, Henry Sleeper's Beauport drew the curious. In 1908, Sleeper added the Tower Wing in native stone, which houses a two-story cylinder library (at the right of figure 15). Here his play with dissimilar materials is perhaps the freest. The Gothic arch windows were inspired by one large and two small Gothic-shaped wooden hearse curtains he found in a Boston junk shop. The "beading" around the windows and the six statues on the walls of the window recesses are not three-dimensional but cut from a reproduction of a 1770s wallpaper in the Hancock-Clark House in Lexington, Massachusetts.[14] Mrs. Gardner quickly became a good friend who visited Piatt Andrew often and took a string of people to see Beauport. In 1908, she wrote Andrew: "I saw Sleeper. He had been *very poorly*—but he is an uncomplaining soul and works on for those he loves. I have *of course* taken people to see Little Beauport. That seems to be my mission in life."[15] (She also later—in 1911—took Henry James to see what was being wrought.)[16] In 1913, Sleeper removed the stucco sheathing from the exterior of the first floor (except where it did not show, near the kitchen) and replaced it with a four-inch brick veneer, laying it in the English manner with headers every five courses.

Piatt Andrew and Oliver Herford of New York established the American Field Service, a private volunteer organization providing American ambulances and drivers to the French Army shortly after the outbreak of World War I. Sleeper joined this effort and served as its director in Paris from 1915 to 1917, for which he received the Legion of Honor. His involvement continued for the next four years—the commitment drained him of health and much of his fortune. Since 1908 he had been advising as a decorator, but now necessity caused him to be more adventuresome, and he made a national impact working for such clients as the Vanderbilt family, Fredric March, Joan Crawford, and Douglas Fairbanks and Mary Pickford.

The colonial kitchen which Sleeper called the Pembroke Room was added to Beauport in 1917 (figures 16 and 17). The woodwork of the large L-shaped room came from a house in Pembroke, Massachusetts, built about 1650 by Robert Barker, an ancestor of Sleeper, and the bricks may have come from the ruins of a 1628 house. The Pembroke Room contains one of the most amazing collections of kitchen-related artifacts arranged for comfortable partying. The base of the L-shaped room has a large fireplace which is flanked at the right by an early curved settle and a modern one edging inside the fireplace at the left. Near it is a nineteenth-century rocking chair.

The socializing area in front of the hearth includes a "coffee" table, a mid- to late nineteenth-century hooked rug, and two modern wooden wing chairs with springs and linsey-woolsey covered cushions. These are separated by a convenient table and each chair has a footstool.

Such a comfortable and unkitchen-like setting would have been unimaginable in colonial times, but it became de rigueur in the twentieth century for those of the upper class with a colonial bent. The color scheme is predominantly the natural colors of wood and pottery glazes. There are two eating tables: a large one at the left in figure 17 and a smaller one in the large recessed part of the L extension, seen at the center of that illustration. (The end of the table and the back of one Windsor chair are just visible to the right of the corner cupboard.)

During one week in 1923 Henry Francis du Pont (1880–1969) made two visits that were to be of seminal importance to his future as the greatest collector of American period rooms. First he saw

16 The Pembroke Room, Beauport, about 1920 (Society for the Preservation of New England Antiquities)

Electra Havemeyer (Mrs. J. Watson) Webb's house in Shelburne, Vermont. (With other family members she would found the Shelburne Museum in 1947.) A few days later he journeyed to Beauport in Gloucester. The impact of the two houses crystallized his desire to focus his collecting on American material. Sleeper became du Pont's adviser, first for his home in Southampton, Long Island, and then as he began adding American rooms to his family home at Winterthur, near Wilmington, Delaware. Sleeper remained an adviser until they had a falling out in 1931.

Henry Sleeper's great ability was an eye that could create out of disparate elements a personal statement both elegant and delightful. He was willing to force materials beyond their original limitations and to use reproductions when they suited. With these he often changed the proportions from the originals so they would scale with their given space and the adjacent objects. The

two rooms seen as figures 18 and 19 show this imaginative flair. Because a church appears as part of the design in the wallpaper of the first, it was originally called the Chapel Chamber. Later it became the Paul Revere Room, for Sleeper's collection of Revere silver was displayed in a corner cupboard. (The silver is now in the Museum of Fine Arts, Boston.)

The room synthesizes elements that span two centuries. Exposed beams suggest the seventeenth century although they were at times used until about 1750. (Those in Sleeper's room are probably barn beams, chamfered to appear as house members.) The wallpaper was a commercial reproduction of an English 1760–80 paper found in the Boston Paul Revere House. The fireplace wall is placed at an angle and has an unusual pattern of four equally sized panels; its brickwork projects in a colonial revival manner. The 1900s braided rug and a single-width bed are modern notes. The room addresses no historic rightness;

25

18 Chapel chamber/Paul Revere Room,
Beauport, about 1914 (Society for the Preservation of New England Antiquities)

19 Belfry bedroom, Beauport, about 1914
(Society for the Preservation of New England
Antiquities)

rather, the parts create a charming and beautiful new unity.

The ceiling of the Belfry Bedroom shown in figure 19 slants at various angles, and the top of the door follows one of its lines. The ceiling paper is a modern copy of a Chinese non-repeat eighteenth-century wallpaper; its complex design grows from the paneled dado.[17] The intensity of pattern continues in the textiles: curtains, wing chair, and table and floor coverings. In lesser hands, there would have been riot rather than harmony.

All the arrangements at Beauport suggest relaxation and fun, playing at a historic mood but not at historic accuracy. A secret staircase links two bedrooms. The bedroom Sleeper created for himself in 1921, called Indian Room, is sheathed, ceiling and walls, with mellow pine boards. One wall lets onto both ends of a long balcony which hangs over giant rocks edging the water. Almost perversely it is lined with seventeenth-century New England turned chairs. Sleeper could, with enormous confidence, toy with things he loved, joining them to fashion fresh visual delights. Who else could with such serenity build a breakfast room with an enormous glazed window that can be made to disappear upward into the wall so you have an unobstructed view across rocks to the water, and then paint the furniture, including a fine New England Queen Anne drop-leaf table, flat sea green?

Henry Sleeper produced few areas that stressed period accuracy, but that approach became the intention of Henry Francis du Pont at Winterthur. As early as 1918, du Pont had purchased American pieces of furniture while concentrating on European examples. His 1923 visits to Electra Webb and Henry Sleeper turned him to acquiring American decorative arts while creating suitable rooms in which to house them, first in the Chesterton House at Southampton and then at Winterthur. In an interview in 1962 he recalled saying to his wife, "Why don't we build an American house? Everybody has English houses and

half the furniture I know . . . is new. Since we're Americans, it's much more interesting to have American furniture."[18] Although an authentic period room was a consideration, du Pont did not in fact step outside the need to have the room speak to his personal sense of aesthetics. He said: "Unless it looks well, then why have it? . . . It's one of my first principles that if you go into a room, any room, and right away you see something, then you realize that [it] shouldn't be in the room."[19]

Henry du Pont did not follow early inventories. Indeed, such an urge on a broad scale was about forty years distant from his initial efforts. Rather, his need was to create beauty with American and related materials, and his eye was the control. Heating ducts were adjusted so as not to ruin the first impression as you entered a room or hall, and if their placement would not fully conquer the outside temperatures, he used other rooms for intemperate times. "There will be a grill in one jamb of each window, preferably on the right-hand side of the window (or the north side) so that when you come in from the Reception Room you would not see the grill. I imagine that during zero weather these radiators will not bring the temperature up to 70°—but I simply will not use that room when it is too cold."[20]

The original dimensions and locations of features of early rooms were not the primary concern. Parts were adjusted to fit available spaces, or as they would create elegant arenas for living while housing his growing collections. In 1921 the house at 224 Pine Street, Philadelphia, built around 1764 by John Stamper and later owned by Dr. Blackwell, was demolished and its woodwork sold to several customers. Figure 21 shows the parlor still undisturbed in Philadelphia; in figures 20 and 22, some of the Stamper/Blackwell woodwork has been installed in the Rosemont, Pennsylvania, home of Mrs. Adele Leins McFadden, who used it to create a colonialized version of the grand manner which emulated English country house life. The late nineteenth-century

20 Stamper/Blackwell woodwork
in Rosemont, Pennsylvania, home
of Mrs. McFadden, about 1930
(The Henry Francis du Pont
Winterthur Museum)

21 Stamper/Blackwell parlor,
Philadelphia, Pennsylvania,
about 1921 (The Metropolitan
Museum of Art, gift of the estate
of Ogden Codman, 1952)

22 *Stamper/Blackwell woodwork in Rosemont, Pennsylvania; home of Mrs. McFadden, about 1930 (The Henry Francis du Pont Winterthur Museum)*

writings of Henry James frequently deal with American envy of European upper-class ease and confidence, but by the time of these McFadden photographs (at the end of the first quarter of the twentieth century), many Americans felt sufficiently assured to produce relaxed settings. This new confidence was reflected in Edith Wharton's collaboration with the Boston architect Ogden Codman, Jr., on *The Decoration of Houses* (1896).

In figure 22, the original Stamper/Blackwell parlor details are linked by new panel walls to create a rather opulent place for formal eating. But another McFadden room using other Stamper/Blackwell woodwork (figure 20) let asymmetry and informal placement establish a relaxed ambience watched over by a moose head. In 1936,

Henry du Pont purchased the woodwork from Mrs. McFadden and in 1939 additional Stamper/Blackwell architectural parts from the Philadelphia Museum. The McFadden wall panels were removed and the freer presentation tightened to a colonial setting for admiring Philadelphia rococo furniture (figure 23). Here one feels the desire for an accurate recreation overglazed by personal needs and taste.

Elsie de Wolfe is often credited with establishing the use of early, particularly French furniture in clarified settings. In the late nineteenth century she had been a society actress known chiefly for displaying chic Parisian gowns. Following the lead of Edith Wharton and Ogden Codman, de Wolfe chose to become the first important professional decorator. In France the dowager Marchioness of

29

Anglesey (formerly Minna King of Georgia) instructed her in French eighteenth-century objets d'art, and such fastidious collectors and arrangers as Comte Robert de Montesquiou-Fezesnac refined her decorating taste. Montesquiou was so exacting he could color an entire room in varying shades of dark gray.

Elsie de Wolfe emerged as a powerful arbiter of house fashions. Her first important commission was the Colony Club in New York, which opened in 1907, the year Sleeper purchased land

in Gloucester. Eliminating the musty side of Edwardian grandeur, she brought from country settings chintz and latticed interior walls to establish the fitness of light, openness, and visual clarity. Heavy chairs and tables, pillows and complex drapery were dismissed, and slender forms and pale colors, particularly beige, assumed authority. Where Wharton and Codman's publication was concerned with the estates of the wealthy, de Wolfe—although adoring high society largesse—wanted each American home to become

23 Stamper/Blackwell parlor, Winterthur Museum, 1980s (The Henry Francis du Pont Winterthur Museum)

tasteful. She wrote articles and published books to convert everyone to her point of view. Following the triumph of the Colony Club, she and Ogden Codman tore apart and redesigned a brownstone house on East 71st Street in Manhattan. The transformation was to demonstrate how everyone could move from the restraints of the previous century into the freedom of the present one by eliminating unnecessary remnants. That the du Pont rooms, and the dining room of Mrs. McFadden (figure 22), look more spaciously set than those in Beauport is probably due to the ideas of Wharton, Codman, and de Wolfe.

These three designers seem to have had the chief influence on the sophisticated restraint of the period room "look" that still permeates public and private institutions. This attitude differs from the Arts and Crafts strain of the colonial revival in continuing the Edwardian love of aristocratic posture, and glamorous objects remain the focus.[21]

Henry Francis du Pont embraced this attitude, and his vision of a gracious personal style of living controlled his creations. That he consciously played with architectural elements is recorded in a passage from an undated letter written to him by his architect Thomas T. Waterman: "If we could devise a good use for the Blackwell House pilasters it would be a good place to use them so near the other fine Philadelphia rooms. There are two pilasters and a [illegible word] fine *section of Doric cornice*."[22] In 1939, du Pont wrote about the Stamper/Blackwell material:

In reference to the Queen Anne Hall. I have enough of the Blackwell Room cornice left, and I shall use it here also, particularly as we are using the door trim from the Blackwell House which went from the hall into the room itself. As you will remember, this is the largest door of the three in the room. I think we had better have the same dado as in the Blackwell Room, but do you think that in this case we had better leave off the mahogany cap, in view of the fact that I am using some Queen Anne chairs and the "Papillon" wallpaper. The window door going to the Reception Room will have to be left the way it is, as I naturally do not want to change the effect from the Reception Room side. Whether to have a little trim in the Queen Anne Hall, I do not know: I will leave it entirely to you. Leslie will send you a drawing showing just how it fits into the wall. The window, I understand, is to be the same size as the ones in the Blackwell Room.[23]

What emerged (as seen in figure 23) was a wealthy man's concept of how an assemblage of sumptuous eighteenth-century material could look beautiful. Although the architectural parts were placed with some concern for historic record, there was little regard for early furniture arrangements. In the eighteenth century the wing chair was usually restricted to the bedroom where it provided comfort and protection from drafts, often held a potty under the seat cushion, and symbolized the aged. (Only two sitters were posed in wing chairs by the colonial painter John Singleton Copley and they were both very elderly women.)[24] But in Henry du Pont's Stamper/Blackwell parlor a wing chair graces the foreground as a post-Victorian symbol of comfort. Following an early nineteenth-century practice, a circular table holds the center of the room. Between the windows of the wall facing the fireplace is a table now recognized as not authentic but in the style of Philadelphia furniture of the third quarter of the eighteenth century. This is neither a comfortable twentieth-century room nor a recreation of eighteenth-century Philadelphia. Rather, it is a mid-twentieth-century collector's gallery of superior items. As such it should be frozen so that future generations may be able to understand this particular taste and attitude, which so strongly conditions how we now view early artifacts. Indeed, Henry du Pont is recorded as saying: "I want things kept as they are because in fifty years nobody will know what a country place was."[25]

Winterthur retains that otherworldly quality knowingly established by Henry du Pont. Stories told by Mary Allis, a dealer in primitives, particularly paintings, reveal what life was like when Winterthur was still a consciously colonialized home. Once, according to Miss Allis, a house-guest being taken through the rooms by Henry du Pont expressed pride in owning a few pieces like the small group of ceramics he saw in one cupboard. That evening the entire dinner table was set with the service. Miss Allis demonstrated what it took to stand up to this potentate. All the textiles in the rooms were original fabric—window and bed curtains, and upholstery on wing, side, and armchairs—and each had three replacements for seasonal rotation. When houseguests were assigned a room, the early fabrics were replaced by reproductions. During one of Miss Allis's visits, Henry du Pont said: "Mary, I know you love and understand old material and I have given instructions not to change your room to copies. I know when you go up to take your nap before dinner you won't touch anything. I've turned down your bed myself." When Miss Allis came down to dinner, Henry Francis hurried over and asked: "You didn't touch anything, did you?" "No, HF," replied Miss Allis, "I took those lovely large towels you have and lined the bathtub and took my nap there."[26] That the rooms still project a sense of "otherness"—removal from anything but a pampered life and the exquisite but ruthless eye of a great twentieth-century collector—is not surprising.

In 1950 the du Ponts moved into a smaller house nearby, furnishing it in part with pieces they had owned before amassing their American collections. A year later the Winterthur Museum was opened to the public.

To many, the 1924 American Wing at the Metropolitan, Colonial Williamsburg, begun in 1926, and the Winterthur Museum are the crown jewels of American collections. Because of the munificence of Maxim Karolik, the Museum of Fine Arts, Boston, is particularly strong in important early classical revival material. Probably the greatest teaching collection is at the Yale University Art Gallery, largely as a result of the generosity of Francis Patrick Garvan. He purposely assembled a collection encompassing a range of material that varied in quality so students might understand what produces superior designs. Most of the collection is housed like a library, in rows on shelves, imparting a flexibility that makes it easy to teach through the juxtaposition of varied material.

The twentieth-century collectors' monuments have had enormous impact on the taste and aspirations of collectors and house restorers of greater and lesser means. They have said how early materials, even reproductions, should look. Today, preservationists wishing to stress historic accuracy not only concern themselves with keeping the old intact but expend enormous energy campaigning to prevent reproductions from becoming gross versions of past achievements. At its best, the developing colonial revival zeal to do more period rooms can produce fine examples, such as those seen in figures 31 through 33; but in most hands, it sanctions such versions as that in figure 24, embodying the worst aspects of Philadelphia's Society Hill, Boston's Beacon Hill, or Providence's Benefit Street. The accent of the room is green: wall-to-wall carpet, painted 1820s woodwork, wallpaper, and bayberry candles. The mantel is centered by a basket of dried flowers. The rocker has lost its finials and the warming pan is situated to spill ashes onto the carpet. Too often such "restored" houses have kitchens with exposed brick hung with horse brasses or copper fish molds; many have reproduction Dutch tiles and nineteenth-century colored bottles. In such a house an array of small-patterned, pleated prints and various interpretations of the eagle abound. "Fun" extensions of this attitude are the "Colonial" and "Western" sections of Disneyland.

RECENT ATTEMPTS AT HISTORIC ACCURACY

In 1928 three rooms from Oak Hill (one seen in figure 11) were installed in the Museum of Fine Arts, Boston. Perhaps because of space restrictions or because a new sequence seemed more logical for museum viewing, the original arrangement of the rooms was not followed. Instead, they are strung out in a straight line and movement through the three spaces necessitates stepping though some doorways that were once windows. Between 1972 and 1980 these Oak Hill rooms had a major overhauling to create a more accurate 1800 aspect, although their spatial relationship was not altered. Since the museum owns Salem and Boston furniture—including pieces made by McIntire for the Derby family and other local patrons—it was logical to follow early documents and furnish the rooms as we now think they once looked.

The new arrangements appear somewhat stilted because they encompass the changing attitudes toward restorations prevalent during the years the project was under way. Initially, it seemed appropriate to have a fashionable textile and upholstery firm provide the draperies for the dining room and parlor. The textile was woven following a sample with a Salem history, but the drapes were cut and arranged with a twentieth-century perfection of line. Their visual firmness would have been less noticeable had it not been decided near the end to hang the bed and window curtains in the third room in a more original, less hard-edge manner. For this room, the fabric for the bed and window curtains and chair slip seats was copied from a sample once used in Danvers, Massachusetts—a printed glazed chintz of about 1815–20 with a pillar motif, an English fabric popular for bedroom furnishings. Following original bed hangings, the new ones are unlined, and festoons are created by cords attached to tapes sewn to the back of the material. When the cords are pulled, the drapery moves toward the tester to create bunched, uneven swags. The resulting somewhat disheveled look matches the appearance of beds in early paintings and the "feel" is wonderful.[27]

Since its inception in 1926, Colonial Williamsburg has been the leading tastemaker in the colo-

24 A Massachusetts bedroom, photograph 1972

nial frenzy. When Graham Hood went there as Director of Collections in 1971, he wished to change the interiors to show the past as accurately as possible. Realizing that he was about to disturb a sacred cow that could become a raging bull, he moved with caution. He began by studying appropriate local written material such as inventories, journals, and relevant pictorial sources with his staff. Gradual changes were noticed and not always liked by the visiting public. Particularly disturbed were those collectors inspired to follow Williamsburg's lead. For example, by the later 1940s the supper room, located just left of the front door of the 1934 reconstruction of Williamsburg's Governor's Palace, had become the modus operandi of those who could hope to emulate it (figure 25). The floor had an expensive carpet, and 1725–50 English chairs surrounded a contemporary English table. The silver chandelier is one of the rarest English pieces known. It was made in London by Daniel Garnier in 1691–97 for William III and is mentioned in a

25 *Southwest room of Governor's Palace, presented as supper room, 1948, Colonial Williamsburg, Williamsburg, Virginia (Colonial Williamsburg)*

26 *Southwest room of Governor's Palace, presented as steward's pantry, 1982, Colonial Williamsburg (Colonial Williamsburg)*

1721 inventory of royal plate: "One 10 nozzelled Branch . . . 730.0.0," placed "At St. James's In the Lodgings." In 1924, William Randolph Hearst purchased it at a Christie's auction and later sold it to John D. Rockefeller, Jr.

Such opulence has always been beyond most occupiers of this earth, and as a record of colonial Virginia it was woefully wrong. In the 1980s, after years of detailed research by the staff of Colonial Williamsburg, the Palace was thoughtfully reworked to accord with original room use and appearance. The former supper room became the steward's pantry (figure 26), a change that rocked the upper classes. Former generous donors who had helped to keep Williamsburg in the black needed stroking and the president opened Forum Weeks (one of the main attractions for potential donors) by explaining the value of historical truth over popular belief. He included slides of the backyard of the Williamsburg house he himself occupied, first showing it with the colonial revival planting, and then as it is now, with an unshorn lawn letting down to a brook crossed by a single plank.

In fact the first rumblings of dissatisfaction with Williamsburg's old approach had been reported by Ada Louise Huxtable as early as September 22, 1963, in an article in the *New York Times* entitled DISSENT AT COLONIAL WILLIAMSBURG. It began: "The preservation movement is at a crossroads in the United States, and to this observer is moving rapidly backwards." The complaints included Williamsburg's cut-off date of 1800, which was found to eliminate "any sense of reality, vitality or historic continuity. . . . The result has a tidy, if oversanitary and frequently suspect, kind of stage-set charm. . . ." Not only were later buildings eliminated, Huxtable lamented, but it was often difficult to tell which of those shown were old and on original sites, old and moved to old or new foundations, or new in an old or new position. Williamsburg was deemed ". . . a bore. And it is a dangerous bore, because it is largely responsible for the present widespread corruption of preservation practices at a time when the national architectural heritage is most seriously threatened." What concerned her most was the blanket sanction of replacing old buildings with recreations. As an example of this wrongheadedness, she cited "the corporation that recently tore down a 19th-century landmark to build a copy, not of a historic structure, but of the [twentieth-century] Williamsburg Inn."[28] The Colonial Williamsburg project was too wealthy to leave the good things alone.

In large part the new 1980s accuracy of the Palace reflects recent work done on the 1770 inventory taken on the death of Lord Botetourt, who had only recently arrived as Royal Governor. This document had been known since 1853 but its information was reevaluated, new material on the Governor's brief residency was found in England by Graham Hood, where it was housed with the papers of the Duke of Beaufort, a descendant of Botetourt's heirs.

The new restoration stressed the inventory over rarity, and copies of old objects are seen as correct tools of interpretation. For example, since chairs should appear in large sets, rather than joining small groups that were once part of larger sets, one or more original examples have been reproduced. Accurate copies are possible if the copyist has a good eye and superior hand skills, and stresses following an original piece without personal interpretation. They will not have an early surface and in time the new will become more noticeably unlike the original, as what is unconsciously added from our own time's concept of the past eventually stands out. Even now, some discrepancies in the recent Williamsburg reproductions are appar-

ent. One set of chairs copies an eighteenth-century wooden chair made to look like bamboo. The back has short pieces intriguingly arranged to a Chinese-type pattern between the posts. In the original, everything is a bit askew—the short parts that make up the pattern of the back do not all join others at right angles. This is because of shrinkage and a shifting over time and because they were put together by a pre-industrial eye that did not require precisely similar angles. It is just such variations that make the old look different from the new.

Using copies is a compromise, but restorations always involve a series of choices between not totally satisfactory possibilities. Trained minds must decide which strategies will come close to the desired end. To give just one example: early items are prized for their surface patina—original mahogany or walnut furniture should be mellow, and old painted furniture must have worn areas. Yet the reproductions and newly painted woodwork and walls will have new surfaces that must inevitably contrast.

How the Palace's stoves were reproduced demonstrates one choice between imperfect solutions. The inventory calls for a cast-iron stove in both the supper and the ballroom. Early examples could not be found, so copies of the one Botetourt purchased for the Capitol in 1770 seemed the obvious solution. An impression of the Capitol stove, now on display in Richmond, could have been taken and a casting made from it but the museum staff felt its surface was not sufficiently pristine to produce iron plates that would look as they did when new in 1770. Instead, new forms were carved following the old pattern, and the castings made from these. (The three-tier Capitol stove was reduced to two levels and the colony's arms on one side of the early example were replaced by Botetourt's own.) The resulting stove does look appropriately new, as though just purchased by a newly arrived Governor. But because the forms were carved by 1970s hands guided by 1970s eyes, in fifty years the piece will look like a 1970s concept of a 1770 stove. But then, so will the rest of the new work on the 1930s version of the 1706–20 Governor's Palace as refitted by Botetourt in 1770! Despite the obvious difficulties, the new Governor's Palace is the result of years of extraordinary effort by a large body of talented researchers. It would be difficult to conceive of a complex restoration arriving nearer a historic truth for the 1980s.

Since the present interpretation of the Palace uses much twentieth-century material, it is perhaps fitting that the normal guided tours (unless you choose a special tour to see objects) now take the form of role-playing experiences designed to make visitors feel eighteenth-century life rather than see eighteenth-century art. Of course, such a playing at life in the eighteenth century is yet another fantasy of how we today think it was. Fortunately, most of the "important" eighteenth-century works found inappropriate to the new Colonial Williamsburg are to be housed in a museum which will be chiefly underground. The story above ground will appear as a brick garden

wall, and visitors will enter through a reconstruction of an institution that once stood there: America's first building created solely to house the insane.

The rooms in figures 30 through 33 are recent installations of a more domestic scale than rooms in Colonial Williamsburg's Governor's Palace. The parlor seen in figures 29 and 30 is in the Joseph Lloyd Manor House (1766–67) on Lloyd's Neck, to the east of Oyster Bay on Long Island Sound, now owned by the Society for the Preservation of Long Island Antiquities. The first view shows it in 1920s colonial revival garb, which naturally included a spinning wheel, the ubiquitous icon symbolizing colonial achievement, industry, hand arts, and the woman's role. The walls within the arches to either side of the fireplace have been opened up to create a continuous space around the fireplace. (The restoration closed these—figure 30—but the Society, wishing to keep them flexible so the meeting room behind could

27 *First-floor plan, Joseph Lloyd Manor House, Oyster Bay, Long Island (Society for the Preservation of Long Island Antiquities)*

28 *Second-floor plan, Joseph Lloyd Manor House (Society for the Preservation of Long Island Antiquities)*

NORTH

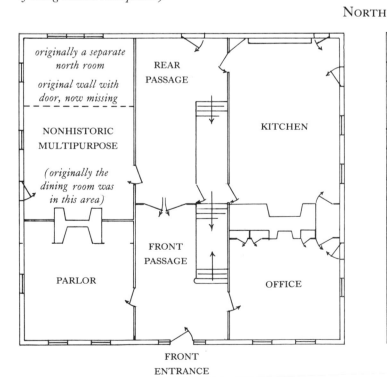

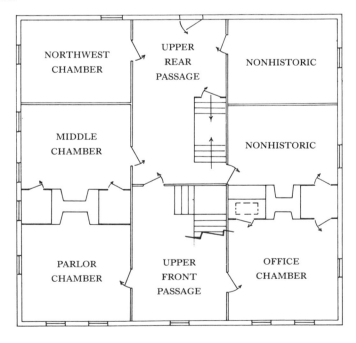

Scale ¹⁄₁₆″ = 1′

29 Parlor, Joseph Lloyd Manor House, 1920s (Society for the Preservation of Long Island Antiquities)

on occasion flow into the parlor, filled the arches with large, paired panels that can swing on hinges into the back room.)

During the late 1970s a group of restoration specialists worked to return the exterior and interior woodwork to an appropriate eighteenth-century aspect. In 1980, I was asked to assist with its furnishings, although the main effort on the arrangements has been carried out by Jane Nylander and the curator, Hope Alswang. When first approached, I was told that there was only a partial eighteenth-century inventory, and that the trustees of the Society had one stipulation: the house be manorial. They wished to make a statement about the life of an upper-middle-class, late eighteenth-century rural Long Island family.

The ground plans, figures 27 and 28, show both the historic and the modern use of the first two floors. Joseph Lloyd, the builder of the house,

bequeathed it to his nephew, John Lloyd II, in 1780, and the furnishings were to follow the inventory taken at John's death in December 1792. (The inventory is dated June 3, 1793.) To this was to be added what we felt was missing. Studying the inventory, I wondered whether it was incomplete, at least for the larger, easily listed objects. Did the John Lloyd II inventory seem partial because of a modern assumption that such a good-sized country house would be elaborately furnished with high chests, chests-on-chests, rugs, and many curtains? Indeed, if we sidestepped colonial revival grandeur, could the inventory be complete?

To help understand whether items might be missing, John's widow's 1818 inventory was studied to see if she had withdrawn her property prior to the taking of her husband's. However, it seemed to be a normal widow's portion of the

30 *Parlor, Joseph Lloyd Manor House, 1982 (Society for the Preservation of Long Island Antiquities)*

John Lloyd II estate and was included in his inventory. To corroborate that Lloyd's inventory was not improperly small for such a house, it was exhaustively compared with other Long Island inventories of similar size and value. Finally, we accepted that what we had was the full John Lloyd II inventory; although it did not seem to modern eyes manorial, if truth were to prevail it must be followed.

We tried very hard to break the inventory into logical room divisions. Assuming that the recorder moved from room to room while listing what he saw—even if he drifted out to a barn and then into another room—could we not divide the list by walking through the rooms and seeing where fireplace equipment, curtains, and beds broke the list into logical parts? But inventories are taken under a variety of circumstances, sometimes when furniture is jumbled rather than in

normal use, and the effort to see divisions in the Lloyd inventory was only partly successful. Therefore, division was in part based on room listings in other Long Island inventories. Although it seems fair to assume that generally the furnishing of one parlor, office, or main bedroom will be fairly similar to that of similar grandeur down the road, all houses are individual and each arrangement is to some degree personal.

To achieve a division that all of us on the committee could accept, we wrote each inventory item and its value on a separate sheet of paper. Then through one long and harrowing day, we forced ourselves to place each sheet in a room. (The inventory, possible room divisions, list of furniture, and initial room allotments are reproduced as Appendix 1.)

During paint restoration the woodwork of the parlor (figure 30) had been returned to what was in the eighteenth century called "stone green," a medium gray-green-brown. The plaster showed no evidence of color and probably originally had paper—either patterned or a solid color, but not white. The mantel is not from the first date of the room: normally it would be mounted on the rail below the large panel, and the present mantel covers the base of that panel, which retains original paint and early graffiti over its entire surface. The pulvinated style is of the 1780s. The flanking complex vertical moldings terminating in console brackets under the mantel shelf appear even later in style. The moldings were not returned to an earlier form since there is no evidence of their original shape and what we have is at least genuine. Also, the main additions are from about the date of the inventory followed.

The parlor windows have shutters that slide into the walls. Since the inventory lists only a few sets of window curtains, these were placed in the rooms without shutters. The ten chairs at 4 shillings each are represented in the parlor by ten chairs from nearly identical sets (six of them were owned by a local family and probably all were made in or near New York City). These pierced-splat chairs are lined against the walls with one of the two square cherry tables mentioned in the inventory. The wall opposite the fireplace has more chairs and the "old square [rectangular] tea table." A major looking glass, representing the one listed with a carpet at the high sum of £20, is hung between the front windows. The chintz chair covers use a reproduction of an eighteenth-century textile. Although its pattern does not follow any known to be used in America, the covers are shaped to follow a documented loose chair cover once used in the Van Cortlandt House at Croton-on-Hudson, New York. (That house is owned by Sleepy Hollow Restorations in Tarrytown, and the cover is in their study collection.)

One feature of the inventory is sixteen pictures, valued at a total of 30 shillings. These were deemed to be prints and two are seen to the left of the fireplace. When acquired, more will be added

to this room and others placed in the hall. Contemporary paintings of interiors show fireplaces with urns holding flowers and at times these or other images are depicted on fireboards closing the front of the fireplace. The placement of a bouquet within the fireplace on the day the Society first opened the house is appropriate, but the cleanliness of the brickwork within the fireplace is perhaps too pristine, although fireplaces were regularly freshened with whitewash.

The Lloyd inventory does not specify a type of carpet, but similar inventories list the Wilton type (the loops of the pile are cut) at about the same value as the best carpet in the inventory. It was thought proper to put this in the parlor. The carpet, made in 1981, was inspired by one that appears in the 1788 William Dunlap self-portrait with his parents (now in the New-York Historical Society). The pattern as executed is visually too congested: there are too many arabesques; also the shades of most of the greens and the red are rather Edwardian in tone. It was, however, proper that a rug be made for this floor (as for floors in Williamsburg's Palace where the colors are similarly off). The attempt was important, for only by taking such risks will we arrive at the methodology and resources that allow good recreations.

The Society, wanting to exhibit two important Long Island case pieces, compromised the inventory and installed a beautiful, recently acquired linen press and a locally made high chest with slipper feet in the style of Newport. Their use in this house, where evidence is against it, continues the desire to secure for America a past that is as complexly furnished as the heritage of Edwardian colonial revival taste dictates.

Where the Lloyd Manor parlor suggests a successful upper-middle-class family of the late eighteenth century, the parlor seen as figures 31 and 32 represents a more middling room of the second quarter of the nineteenth century. That in figure 33 is an even simpler setting of the same date. It was these two rooms at Old Sturbridge

31–32 West parlor, Stephen Fitch House, Old Sturbridge Village, Sturbridge, Massachusetts, 1982 (Old Sturbridge Village photo by Henry E. Peach)

33 Parlor, Freeman Farm, Old Sturbridge Village, 1983 (Old Sturbridge Village photo by Henry E. Peach)

Village that convinced me it was possible to re-create rooms that feel right.

In the fall of 1982 I walked into the Freeman Farm parlor (figure 33). Two young red-headed women sat sewing at the stand. One was working on what would be the hearth rug for this room. The stand was draped with a black textile printed with a red rococo pattern. (The red did not show up as a strong color but made the piece appear as though woven with a damask design.) On the cloth were items of sewing equipment, including threads of many colors. There were the small prints in grained frames to the right of a window, and a simple clock placed on a grained desk. Between the windows of the left outside wall (not visible in the photograph) a tiny mirror was placed high enough to be usable rather than aligned with the top of the windows. All this finally made me realize that it could be done.

The parlor in the Stephen Fitch House (figures 31 and 32) on the village green is equally con-

vincing.[29] That room mixes early nineteenth-century painted fancy chairs, a mahogany card table signed by the maker (c. 1815), Jonathan Fairbanks of Harvard, Massachusetts, and a slightly later horsehair-covered sofa. The turned-leg dining table of about 1840 is painted red. The fireplace has been closed and papered as the walls. The stove is set on protective metal. The reproduction ingrain carpet is based on one used locally—contemporary paintings of interiors show that some carpets had decorative borders while others were without them. The curtains are hung on strings which sag. I am less easy about the chairs drawn up to a cloth-covered table set for a family tea or supper. Rooms that have situation props make me wonder what is about to happen. Where are the people? Where the proper noise, movement, and smells? But at Old Sturbridge most such arrangements work, probably because they are done with a fine grasp of everyday events in the early nineteenth century.

PERSONAL VISION
OR HISTORIC ACCURACY?

Enough information exists today to make fairly accurate restorations possible. Although they will in time seem dated, proper research, the availability of appropriate early materials with perhaps the addition of adequate copies and a sensitive eye, can make this approach valid. The result differs from "Beacon Hill Federal" in not emulating some wealthy collector's dream but systematically following evidence. The question is, When is such exacting work and great expense appropriate? Certainly it is necessary if a public building is to be shown as representing an earlier time. But this is not the ambition of most homeowners. Rather, they wish to live in sympathetic surroundings. To demonstrate what may be the extreme of these two approaches—historic accuracy and personal style—I want to juxtapose the pre-

ceding "correct" rooms with interiors created by the late Roger Bacon.

Roger Bacon was a Maine farm boy who, as a leading dealer in vernacular furniture, showed many how to understand the aesthetic value of untouched furniture and old houses. He prized the ambience that worn beauty, whether architectural or on a smaller scale, could create. Bacon was one of the few people who, when a piece of textile with holes in it was held up at an auction, could see what was left rather than what was missing. His outstanding gift was his sensitivity to form, color, pattern, and surface; much of what I learned about early materials came from him.

Roger Bacon had a passionate eye and a single-mindedness that focused on what he liked rather than on what might sell, although he was a great salesman. The early house he used as a shop and home with his wife, Ruth Bacon, was built about 1705 in Brentwood, near Exeter, New Hampshire (figure 34 and plate 1). Historically, such a

34 Home of Roger and Ruth Bacon, Brentwood, New Hampshire, 1981 (Colonial Homes); seen also as plate 1

35 Pennsylvania Homestead with Many Fences, *anonymous, found in Pottsville, Pennsylvania, probably early nineteenth century (Museum of Fine Arts, Boston, M. and M. Karolik Collection)*

building would sit nakedly, without foundation planting. There might have been a large old tree and some youthful fruit trees, a small garden, and some fences as shown in figure 35, but no encroachment of untamed nature. Although this much fenced farmstead is from Pennsylvania and a hundred years later, it depicts the sparseness of American homesteads in the eighteenth and early nineteenth centuries. Only later in the nineteenth century did shrubs and other romantic paraphernalia creep toward the house. When I was director of the Rhode Island Historical Society, their great late eighteenth-century brick John Brown House had flounces of green "foundation planting." After these were removed, the bold, cubelike force of the brick house became evident.

The planting around the Roger Bacon house

was not historically accurate, but it was sensuously beautiful. When the Bacons moved in, there was little vegetation near the house or along the road bordering the property. Roger Bacon's recipe was "Stick in everything you can find." This meant things pulled from the woods and from neighbors and friends: sticks of mock orange, bits of lilac, evergreens, willow trees, anything that would grow. With surprising speed the house was screened and romantically encased. Now it has the beauty that developed around some artists' cottages planted in the 1920s. Different heights and colors of greenery nestle loosely around buildings and lawns. Pockets of grass are edged with ground cover that curves into the lawn.

The keeping room was to the right as you entered the front door. Partly because it was an antique shop, but more because this was how Roger

*36–37 Keeping room, Bacon House, 1981 (*Colonial Homes*); seen also as plates* II *and* III

Bacon wanted to live, the room was strewn with things appropriate to the seventeenth and eighteenth centuries, along with others that were made a hundred years later (figure 36 and plate II).

Although overpopulated by any historical standard, the room felt lived in because things were continuously being handled and moved. The right end of the fireplace needed rebuilding when the Bacons purchased the house in 1954 and that part may originally have held an oven. The amount of equipment Bacon placed in and near the fireplace was wildly beyond what any seventeenth- or eighteenth-century inventory suggests for such a house. But it appeared emotionally logical, for much of it was used or placed with a knowledge of use and a great eye had created a thrilling combination of shapes. There, as in the rest of the room, the continuing Edwardian sensibility linked beautiful but disparate materials through a personal style. Roger Bacon's "eye" was so firmly established that he could, with great confidence, combine many centuries. One of the most modern features is the colonial revival use of a thin cushion on seventeenth- and early eighteenth-century chairs. In that period cushions were puffy and provided comfort; now we prefer to see the lean structure of the chair. The only feature that seems completely foreign to the room is the reproduction chandelier and its regrettable flame-shaped bulbs. The Bacons said that they chose an obvious reproduction chandelier so it would not sell.

Turning from the fireplace, the sleeping area of the keeping room comes into view (figure 37 and plate III). Such rooms did contain beds, often without hangings in the summer, but no eighteenth-century bed was so surrounded. The wall arrangement of treen ware—and indeed the whole aspect of this room—reminds one of others created by such pioneer collectors as Edna Greenwood at Limestone Farm.[30]

As in the keeping room, the handling of space and objects in the parlor (left front room) was an extension of the vision that loved profusion over simplicity (figure 38 and plate IV). A comparison with the late nineteenth-century Boston parlor in figure 39 demonstrates this continuance. Figure 39 is an interior in the B. D. Greene House at 3 Mount Vernon Street in Boston, photographed before 1882. There is a similar piling up of carpets, table covers hung to the floor, and pictures placed everywhere. As in the Bacon House, some nineteenth-century rooms had pictures hung on doors as well as walls. In the Greene House they rest on tables, mantel, and floors, projecting a richness of images while simultaneously demonstrating wealth and social position. This was an international taste, for similar rooms were readily found in Great Britain and on the continent, from London to Russia. (A slightly simpler late nineteenth-century statement is seen as figure 10.)

Roger Bacon's sleeping chamber over the keeping room (figure 40 and plate V) again mixed furniture, ceramics, and carpets of various periods. On the table a seventeenth-century English slipware bowl rests on a 1790–1810 New England hearth rug. As a period restoration, this would be ludicrous. Instead, the Bacon rooms are a balance of pattern and forms combined by a personal love of beautiful things and a quite remarkable eye.

The photographs in figures 41 to 44 introduce a house with enormous possibilities. It is just up Homestead Avenue from the Daniel Bliss House that is the focus of the second part of this book—an eighteenth-century dwelling that was damaged by an interior fire when new owners began to work using inadequate extension cords. After the fire they were sufficiently discouraged to abandon the restoration project and build a brick house immediately behind it.

The front and west facades, as viewed in figure 41, are not particularly impressive; but from the other end (figure 42) the dropping of the ground, the old wall and steps, the potential of the overgrown garden, and the basement entrance all make one ache to mow a little here and adjust a little there so that the stone foundation, steps, and en-

*38 Parlor, Bacon House,
1981 (Colonial Homes);
seen also as plate IV*

*39 Parlor, B. D. Greene
House, 3 Mount Vernon Street,
Boston, Massachusetts, before
1882 (Society for the Preser-
vation of New England
Antiquities)*

40 *Keeping-room chamber, Bacon House, 1981 (Colo-ial Homes); seen also as plate V*

41–42 *House on Homestead Avenue west of Perryville Road, Rehoboth, Massachu-etts, 1973*

43–44 *House on Homestead Avenue west of Perryville Road, Rehoboth, Massachusetts, 1973*

croaching vegetation unite their beauty. The present state of the inside (figures 43 and 44) might seem an opportunity to introduce paneling and other spectacular features. It would be much grander to leave the open spaces marked with the early timbers and punctuated by rich brickwork. I am not proposing a high-tech, hard-edge, exposed brick aesthetic. Rather, there should be very little imposition of the new. The textures and colors necessary to achieve an elegant home are already present.

Whether in museums, historic houses, or private homes, historic objects can be placed in innumerable ways. The variety can range from stringently accurate rooms to a combination of personally loved items. In a personal arrangement such items need not be consistent in style and the twentieth century can be introduced with alacrity. The only mistake is for anyone to feel that they must march with the crowd, particularly when it follows a misreading of the past.

2

Establishing a Personal Attitude Toward Restoration

The visual aspect of any restoration results from the restorer's or curator's training, artistic sensibility, and innate concerns. Although there is nothing exceptionally unusual about my own approach to objects, I have included this chapter on personal projects in the hope that it may help others beginning the restoration process to be more quickly aware of their motivations and individual style by seeing where we differ.

After high school, I went to the Rochester Institute of Technology's School for American Craftsmen to become a journeyman cabinetmaker. I wanted the training so I might work with early American furniture. The main teacher was from Denmark and the style taught was Danish Modern. After World War II, this attitude toward design had swept the world, redefining the Arts and Crafts concern for quality workmanship and the visibility of materials used. Caught up in this approach to furniture, I then spent two years in Denmark studying furniture design with Kaare Klint, the leading figure of Danish Modern, and his life-long assistant Rigmor Andersen.

The emphasis was on materials, workmanship,

simplicity of line—an emphasis that would permanently condition how I look at objects, room arrangements, buildings, and things in general. The overly earnest modernist stress on lack of ornamentation developed during my Danish years was joined to an earlier love for Shaker clarity learned from such twentieth-century authors as Edward Deming Andrews. Perhaps unwittingly, he suppressed the more complex reality shown in early images of Shaker rooms.

Eventually I became a graduate student in art history at Yale University. The first large living space I was able to individualize was an attic apartment on the edge of campus (figures 45 and 46). The furniture mixed what I had brought back from Denmark, such as the Hans Wegner chair (1949) at the right of figure 45, and inexpensive early furniture, mostly acquired from local pickers. The Sunday morning adventure was to prowl the shops on State Street trying to find something nice for a few dollars. The apartment lacked insulation—it was freezing in winter and boiling in summer—but the resulting white walls, dark wood rafters and boards were important in

45–46 Apartment, Prospect Street, New Haven, Connecticut; about 1962

uniting objects that differed dramatically in date, style, color, and material. Pieces that might at first seem hard to associate aesthetically can often be harmonized by introducing one or more strongly unifying factors—carpets are particularly helpful in this role.

During the Thanksgiving recess of that first year at Yale, I was given a half-acre of land in Pennsylvania and its sale allowed me to purchase a summer house in Center Sandwich, New Hampshire, built around 1840 (figure 47). The window sash had been changed in about 1900 to 2 over 2 panes; formerly there had been 9 over 6 sash as seen by the original pair left in the gable of the barn. A porch with complex brackets had been added between the main house and the front of the ell, and the front door had been changed. The house had never had fireplaces but had been built with chimneys for stoves. There was a functioning three-seater privy in the back, left of the barn. The house was filthy from general neglect, not to mention the smoke from stoves which the owner had kept roaring even in the summer. Bedding was tumbled about and butter still sat on the table, left there since the owner had been institutionalized a year earlier. It did not occur to me to freeze this house at the moment acquired! Had I done so, it would have said something about the poverty level on the edge of a small New England town in the late 1950s. But I wanted to make it beautiful.

Of great importance to this house were the flowers which had taken over the yard at the left and rear. Eight kinds of old-fashioned roses sprawled about among ranges of iris and peonies. Interfering as little as possible with nature, it was only necessary to take a rotary mower and cut paths to see the stands of flowers.

I divided lengthwise a small room that made up the right half of the ell. In the front I put a small modern kitchen with sink and refrigerator and a tiny counter. I placed the medium-sized refrigerator on a shelf twelve inches from the floor and put a cupboard under it. This brought the refrigerator's spaces to eye level. Behind the kitchen I put in a bathroom. Placing all the plumbing in one area decreases the expense and disturbs the house less. The plumbing was done so that by unscrewing one plug and a tap on the hot-water heater, the system was drained for the winter. Any part with standing water, such as the sink traps, received a dose of permanent antifreeze.

The interior of the house reflected a Shaker-cum-Danish modern aesthetic. The dining room took up the left half of the ell and continued some ten feet into the main building. Figure 49 shows the left rear corner with simple modern shelves, nineteenth-century painted New England furniture, and the door to the attic. Rather than using small kitchen cabinets, I created a cupboard wall to the left of the attic door. It ran to the further corner, about ten feet away. The outer surface was entirely of new vertical boards, a practice which I continued later at Rehoboth. Instead of little cabinets there was a beautiful wall, and when a

door was open, access to everything from floor to ceiling. In the right end I made a built-in china cupboard by installing two old sash with early glass, one above the other (figure 49). They were hinged to the board end wall. I can now recall no early precedent for doing this. Early glazed cupboards are not uncommon, but combining vertical boards derived from a New England–Shaker aesthetic with a glazed window-sized sash was probably a personal choice. I planned, but did not execute, a screen porch across the back of the ell, for it is a great pleasure to be able to move from a kitchen directly to an exterior, bug-free space.

The Center Sandwich house was charming and produced excellent minimal spaces. But in my ignorance I undid some of its individual qualities. By the time I sold it a few years later, it looked as in figure 48. Unfortunately, the porch was gone; in its place is a stone terrace. The next owner turned the barn into a giant family room and made a large kitchen by pushing back the

47 House, Center Sandwich, New Hampshire, 1959

48–49 House, Center Sandwich, 1961

52

50–52 *Farm, Moultonboro, New Hampshire, 1963*

rear wall of the ell. When last seen, the front door was painted aqua and surmounted by a gold plastic eagle. After this I decided never again to return to a property I had owned. I appreciate that houses must stay alive by affording each owner an opportunity to express his or her personal taste, but I prefer not to see the next life of any building to which I have dedicated myself. I do not feel the same about museum displays, for there trained minds must continually update the installations and fresh, informed insights can be appreciated.

After a few years of working on the Center Sandwich project, my desire for an earlier house in a rural setting with more land led to the purchase of a hundred-acre farm in Moultonboro, New Hampshire (figures 50 through 52). The water supply was gravity fed from a well up the hill. It continually flowed through a pipe into a bin in the kitchen and the overflow entered a pipe that ran under the road to a watering trough near the barn. Although the house had few architectural features, all unnotable, it was serene both inside and in its setting. It would have been easy to ruin the ambience, for the beautiful, ordinary qualities were susceptible to "improvement." Indeed, a nearly identical house in the valley just to the north had been restored under the guidance of an "expert": all the interior tulip horizontal sheathing had been sanded free of its original paint and oiled so it was mat brown-green and the surface was always dusty.

The Moultonboro house needed its repose preserved. This is not to say that former owners had lived in it docilely. They had kept the wild roses mown flat and dark window shades were pulled down, for their distrust of nature and the elements was real. The woman of the house hated the influx of summer people and thought that laws applied to them and not to her. She drove a truck made by placing a wooden body on the chassis of a car. Feeling that she had the right to the road, she ignored stop signs and anything else impinging on her God-given freedom. Her husband sat in the passenger seat, turned sideways to face out—there was no door—so that he could jump free if she ran into something. To preserve their use of this house did not interest me. I wanted the beautiful bones of the structure and the bountiful unpruned nature to dominate. This meant removing the wallpaper that covered both the plaster and the simple board sheathing. It took careful cleaning to get the paper and paste off the woodwork without damaging the colors, which ranged from blue-green through red to a dark brown. The plaster was easier to clean and became dramatically white against the woodwork. (There was no evidence that it had originally been papered or painted.)

The furniture I used was the simplest early nineteenth-century New Hampshire type that could be purchased at local auctions: three-slat-back chairs, square tapered-leg tables, six-board chests, mid- to late nineteenth-century rag rugs and textiles. The concern was to have a minimum of objects so that they, the architecture, and the setting would play equal roles. It was in this house that I first understood the "reading" of architectural changes. For some years I had been working with early furniture and understood the changes that might occur to a piece—additions over time to an early form, the combination of two old parts to make one whole piece, the adding of new legs—but it had not occurred to me to look at architecture in this way, to see changes by looking hard at what is there to be seen. It was a friend, George Montgomery, with a summer house nearby, who said after the wallpaper had been removed: "Oh, there is a line down this [outside wall] paneling with no paint. That board wall must once have been over here." (There was an inch-thick board wall about two feet to the right of the unpainted line.) Instantly I saw how a building could tell much of its history.

The Moultonboro farm was sold to buy a house in Orange, Connecticut, southwest of New Haven. It is the oldest house standing in Orange and was owned in 1720 by one Richard Bryan. The photograph that appears as figure 53 was taken when the house was freer of lush planting and covered with shingles, although it probably originally had clapboards. Behind was a small, probably early nineteenth-century barn or shed. Figure 54 shows the house as purchased in 1964, enshrined in foliage. The shed was then open on the side facing the house and used as a two-car garage. The land between the house and this building was part of the driveway and had packed gravel. I closed the front facade of the shed and opened the side to the right. In closing the front, I placed a batten door at the left and tight against it a small window. The rest of the wall was of vertical boards. I find the early practice of a window right against a door visually exciting for it juxtaposes two rectangles—one solid and forceful, the other smaller and full of mysterious voids. It also has the practical advantage of letting in light on the inside of the door. The tradition is akin to that of placing a looking glass either next to or on a dressing table below a window. The gravel area was bulldozed and replaced with topsoil for lawn and gardens.

The plaster walls of the keeping room had a blue on white wallpaper copy of a French toile pattern; mantels of about 1900 capped the keeping- and living-room fireplaces. I removed both the wallpaper and the mantels. There was no evidence of a molding surrounding the living-room fireplace (figure 55), suggesting the old feather-edge boarding was added later. I copied a nearly contemporary molding used in a Connecticut room (now installed in the Yale University Art Gallery) and sent the design to my father. He took it to Mennonite cabinetmakers who ground knives and reproduced the shape. I installed the moldings incorrectly because I imposed my love of visible construction details. Instead of countersinking the nails and puttying over them before painting, I used large-headed, handmade nails and allowed their domed tops to be seen through the paint. Today, I would not waste the early nails I used, but would countersink modern nails and putty and paint.

The nearly nine-foot fireplace in the keeping room was of stone with brick ends (figure 56). At the right, a brick oven had a separate flue in front which led into the main fireplace flue. I not only removed the later mantel but took off the plaster covering the stone filling between the lintel and ceiling, in order to see the roughness of the material employed. I think the plaster was not original—there seemed to be whitewash under it—but in removing it I may have been imposing a mid-twentieth-century desire to see the units of construction.

The vertical boarding in the keeping room (wall at the right in figure 56) was covered with white enamel. I did not remove this for it was not thick enough to obscure the molded details. (When a chemical paint remover is used to get to the original coat, it usually leaves a muddy surface with the areas of worn wood tinted by the messed-about paint, an effect I particularly dislike.) I painted the sheathing a dark red-brown with oil-base paint. Then, to obviate the problem of furniture with early surfaces juxtaposed against freshly

53 *Richard Bryan House, Orange, Connecticut, about 1940 (published in Mary R. Woodruff's* History of Orange, North Milford, Connecticut *[New Haven, 1949], p. 54)*

54 *Richard Bryan House, 1964*

55–56 *Richard Bryan House, 1965*

painted walls, I washed the wall with a very thin solution of black-brown water-base paint—rather the density of an artist's watercolor wash. While it was still wet, I rubbed over the surface so that the darkness remained in the recessed areas. In short, I faked the surface to appear old.

Becoming director of the Rhode Island Historical Society took me to Providence, where I lived in an 1830s house. After leaving the Historical Society, I spent a year and a half full time putting the Daniel Bliss House in Rehoboth, Massachusetts, back together. The house was not exactly falling apart, but it did need a great deal of work. Each room had only a single light bulb in the center, the bathtub had a drain but needed hand-filling with a bucket, and there was no indoor toilet. The years I was involved with that house will be detailed in Chapters 4 through 6, but looking at the photographs, figures 57 through 64 (seen also as plates VI through XII), provides an opportunity to review what had by then become my philosophy of restoration.

A glance at figure 105 and then a return to figure 57 shows how much I thought it necessary

to impose privacy and create "natural" exterior beauty. Just in front of the bottom edge of the photographs is a small country road, Homestead Avenue, that curves back to the left and to the right, leaving the house projected slightly forward toward the T-junction with Perryville Road. This road comes up to the house in a long straight stretch (see map, figure 86). I sought greenery to shield me and the house, as well as a protective low stone wall. On both sides of the central steps I placed large stones excavated when the land behind the house was dug up. Although they provided an aesthetic flanking for the steps, their main purpose was to stop any car that might go out of control while moving toward the house. In front of the stone wall I planted myrtle—or periwinkle—taken from the knoll behind the house. It was so thick it could be taken up, moved, and put down as fully developed blankets of green. The property also supplied the peonies and wild roses that flowed over the wall.

Following Roger Bacon's advice on creating a screen of vegetation, I took everything I could find and stuck it in. For a while the neighbors thought the sticks would amount to nothing, but in three years' time the screen gave me privacy while psychologically moving the house further from the road. The main plants were dozens of lilacs, many quite large, that I pulled rather rudely from a quarter-mile stretch on a friend's property. They were moved with exposed roots wrapped in wet cloths during a hot summer. I mulched everything with sugarcane pulp, and have found that heavy watering for some weeks after planting saves almost anything. The lilacs at the center of the screen were chosen to cross over and provide an arch above the steps. Many wild cedars were added. These have long taproots and are difficult to transplant, so I moved three times as many as I needed and ended up with the right amount.

Inside the house there was no attempt to follow an inventory or place objects where they might have originally been used. Unless you already have a firm approach to room arrangements, it is often easier to know what to do with the building than the interior decoration. The house itself holds the key to any architectural changes; but unless you are doing a historic installation, the selection and arrangement of objects must be subjective.

I used the photographs seen here as figures 58

*57 Daniel Bliss House, Rehoboth, Massachusetts, 1975 (*The Magazine Antiques, *Helga Photo Studio); seen also as plate* VI

58–60 *Parlor, Daniel Bliss House, 1975 (*60: The Magazine Antiques, *Helga Photo Studio)*

and 59 in *The Impecunious Collector* (1975) to stress the sculptural potential of early pieces over a predominantly historic role. Both illustrations, and that seen as figure 60, are of the same corner of the Bliss House parlor. The rug remains constant while the objects change. In figure 58, the skimming bowl, brought from London, acts as a foil to the early English or continental iron rush and candleholder. The English portrait, painted about 1830, is signed "Larvey." In figure 59, the New England chest with drawer is accompanied by a Robert Natkin painting, a Sol LeWitt sculpture, and the safari chair designed by my Danish teacher, Kaare Klint.

Figure 60 shows the corner as it was more normally seen. The Robert Natkin painting and a colored drawing by Edward Koren provide the modern notes. A different skimming bowl is joined by seventeenth-century, probably continental brass candleholders. The table with original red-orange paint was found in the attic of the house and may have been there since house and table were made. The chair is probably from Connecticut.

The diagonally opposite corner of the parlor is seen as figure 61 and plate VIII. The Sol LeWitt metal sculpture is accompanied by a small Franz Kline collage and a probably nineteenth-century decoy of a golden plover with metal beak, button eyes, and spotted paint decoration (an inscription says it comes from Nantucket). The mid-eighteenth-century desk is painted red and was found in Gorham, Maine. The eighteenth-century miniature between the windows was purchased in England. The curtains are of early nineteenth-century material.

In this room there is no one period except the 1970s. The space has been used to arrange a personal selection of objects. To many the Sol LeWitt metal sculpture is the most surprising, but it is very like the room itself. I once explained it to my sister and her husband by saying, "How do you feel when you walk around the steel uprights of the George Washington Bridge? Doesn't the changing relationship of rectangular and triangular spaces, continually adjusting as you move, make it alive? The voids and solids are never static." Indeed, the LeWitt is like walking around a braced-back Windsor chair, where spokes play against spokes, never still, always intriguing. Beautiful objects in shifting relationships are important elements in good room arrangements. The same is true of exterior planting or a series of buildings. The enjoyment lies in seeing the adjustment between masses and colors, between one and several or several and a larger group. (The problem with reproduction furniture or houses is that they lack variations, individually and as a group.) Well-related parts are at times exciting, indeed thrilling; at other times they project repose.

61 *Parlor, Daniel Bliss House, 1975 (*The Magazine Antiques, *Helga Photo Studio)*

The keeping room in the Daniel Bliss House (figures 62 and 63, and plate IX) mixed one modern object with early pieces. The Frank Stella print at the right sets up an optical vibration not dissimilar to that created by the dots on the adjacent seventeenth-century hanging cupboard. There is a William and Mary turned leg and a late seventeenth-century turned foot on the rear half-round table. The use of Oriental carpets on tables was known in seventeenth-century America, but here, as an accent under an English brass bowl, the mood is nineteenth century at the earliest. Following historical tradition, I put candles in the chandelier only when using it. However, the double sconce, probably unhistorically, always held candles because I liked seeing the vertical thrust of their tapering off-white forms against the old tin color.

At the left—in the next room—the back of a bannister-back chair with its cut finials holding a horizontal rod (from when it was made into an upholstered chair) provides relief-like sculptural forms. (It is seen on a different wall of that room in figure 160.) The other end of the keeping room (figure 63) has a hollow log at the right with a board nailed across its bottom. This probably once held grain in a shed, but here serves as a wood bin. The door at the right leads to a hall off the parlor and the kitchen.

The stringent quality of much of the house is particularly noticeable in the photograph of the second-floor, southwest chamber (figure 64 and plate XII). The furniture, floor, and woodwork, which vary from red to dark red-brown, establish a harmonious scheme. The English painting at the left was bought as a pendant to that seen in

*62–63 Opposite: Keeping room, Daniel Bliss House, 1975 (*The Magazine Antiques, *Helga Photo Studio); figure 62 seen also as plate* IX

*64 Study chamber, Daniel Bliss House, 1975 (*The Magazine Antiques, *Helga Photo Studio); seen also as plate* XII

figure 58 signed "Larvey." The painting's dark intensity heightens the clarified aspect of the room. At the right is a watercolor signed and dated 1844 by John Kirk (c. 1823–c. 1862). He was born in England and came to America about 1841, where he was probably chiefly a line engraver. The back is inscribed: "Mrs John Grandville më Elizabeth West," and was purchased with a New Jersey history.

To create interesting and even intense moods, it is not necessary to have expensive items. Simple pieces such as the round wooden box and the chest

with one drawer in figure 64 are as artistically poignant as more developed and richly surfaced objects. Indeed, it is probably true that the achievement of quiet elegance is more difficult with forceful designs. Highly styled pieces (as seen in figure 1) demand greater attention; they do not as readily leave you alone. Forcing awareness, they announce a complex, expensive way of life. If you want aggressive, thrilling beauty, all of your choices must adhere to achieving that effect. At the other end of the spectrum is the stringency of over-idealized Shaker rooms. The Bliss House lies somewhere in between.

65–72 Apartment, Clarendon Street, Boston, Massachusetts, 1975

65

66

CREATING A NEW COLONIAL BOWER

Except for the first apartment, seen in figures 45 and 46, the living spaces in this chapter have been within eighteenth- and early nineteenth-century structures. The next project called for imposing my needs on less sympathetic rooms.

Before moving to Boston in 1976, I rented a dilapidated one-bedroom apartment there on Clarendon Street very cheaply. I was told that the same person had lived in it for about twenty years and had never cleaned it. During an excruciatingly hot August week, it was transformed by scraping and washing away the dirt, and painting everything in colonial colors, including the floors (figures 65 through 74). The sitting room (figures 65 and 66) received plain curtains hung on narrow tapes. A cut-down nineteenth-century bed with a nineteenth-century cover served as a sofa; it stood on a Gustaf Stickley rug. The rocking chair was an early nineteenth-century slat-back armchair converted later in the century to an upholstered piece. The "scrub top" table had a red painted base with square tapered legs. At the other end of the room (figures 67 and 68) I put an early nineteenth-century cupboard with decoys between two earlyish twentieth-century painted bentwood chairs. A similar transformation took

67

68

69

70

71

72

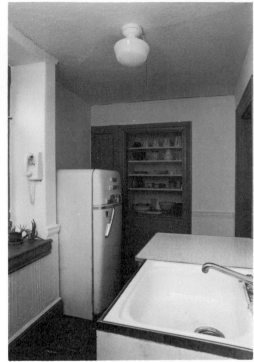

73–74 Apartment, Clarendon Street, Boston, Massachusetts, 1975

place in the hall and bedroom (figures 69 through 72). The hall window, which looked onto a light well, was covered to eliminate the feeling of interior containment. The kitchen (figures 73 and 74) needed only scraping and painting to establish a quiet, sun-filled area.

The reason for choosing to do this apartment was primarily one of economy, but if the rooms had not had acceptable proportions, the effort may not have been made. It took only cleaning, white walls, and deep-color woodwork and floors to transform destitute but well-proportioned spaces into a charming interior. Of course, the narrow hardwood floors were not originally painted and the mellow colors of the woodwork are wrong for the 1920s building.

After the Daniel Bliss House was sold I acquired a house on Boston's Beacon Hill, the central building with light-colored shutters and no visible roof deck seen in figure 75. The brick exterior had been painted gray. The spalling sandstone window heads and sills had been cut away to a depth of about two inches, rebuilt, and painted dark gray. The replacement shutters—

which are not really tall enough for the window opening—were off-white. (The house to the right probably has original shutters; those of the middle floor are in three sections, more clearly visible in figure 83.) The paneling in the recessed area of the front door had a light gray picked out in black. It looked a bit too "New Orleans Colonial" for my taste, but part of the charm of Beacon Hill is the changes made to the houses by a series of owners and I came to enjoy the colors on these terms. I find far less forgivable the scraping and varnishing of doors and entryways that were always painted. The area is now a historic district and permission is necessary before any changes are made to parts visible from the street.

The house was built about 1830, but some of its interior features had been obscured and a few eliminated. Originally, there were two rooms, front and back, on the second level. The dividing wall had been removed and the fireplace of the back room closed so its flue could be used for the furnace (figures 77 through 80). That chimney breast is now a plain projection into the room—to the right of figure 77. The doorway leading to the hall had gained louvered doors, and heavy

75 *House, Myrtle Street, Boston, Massachusetts, 1976*

76 *Plate 34 in Asher Benjamin's* The American Builder's Companion; or, A System of Architecture: Particularly Adapted to the Present Style of Building in the United States of America, *Boston, 1806 (Society for the Preservation of New England Antiquities)*

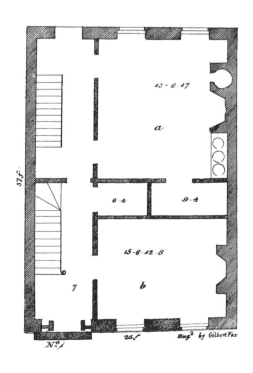

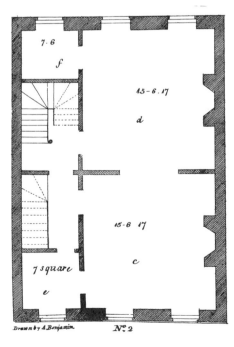

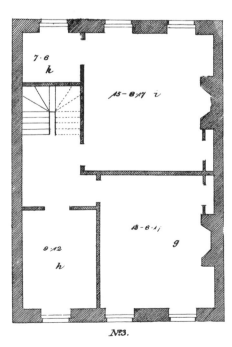

77

78

79

80

77–80 Parlor, Myrtle Street, 1976

drapes with deep pelmets hampered the influx of light. The remaining fireplace was crowned by a modern looking glass in the Federal or Adamesque style. The spaces between and flanking the chimney breast were filled with mid-twentieth-century bookcases above cupboards. These were useful but not completely sympathetic to the building or to the objects I would use. The relationship of the bookcases' thin cornice to the more majestically scaled cornice at the top of the room was particularly unhappy.

When the pelmets and curtains were removed, I discovered that the original window cornices were missing. They had been used in the hall when each story was divided from the others by new doorways in order to make apartments. New cornices were made (figures 78 and 80). The gilded looking glass was sold. The louvered doors were put into the basement and a heavy drape used in

their place during the winter. The useful bookcases were not removed but their noisy mustard yellow was quieted to a warm, light gray and the presence of strong furniture and paintings made them almost completely disappear. The third-floor front room (figures 81 and 82) became a study. The hand-printed mid-twentieth-century French wallpaper was removed.

Figures 77 and 81 show the simple 1830s marble mantels—bold, dark statements calling for some continuation above. The airiness of the neoclassical looking glass in figure 77 was too delicate for this role. It was replaced by two stacked *Airplane* drawings by Edward Koren. In the study, the pair of dark background paintings by Larvey extended upward the dark mass of the mantel. The combination acted as a central force in the middle of a room filled with disparate objects.

Although I did not intend to reestablish early room use, it is helpful in understanding a house to appreciate how a contemporary architect understood such rooms at the time they were first used. Figure 76 is Plate 34 in *The American Builder's Companion; or, A New System of Architecture: Particularly Adapted to the Present Style of Building in the United States of America* by Asher Benjamin, architect and carpenter (first published by Etheridge and Bliss, Boston, 1806). The plate is entitled "Plan and Elevation for a Townhouse." Drawing N°. 1, in the lower left-hand corner, is of the basement story. Its dimensions, as with each room, are given in feet and inches. Space *a*, to the rear, is the kitchen; *b*, at the front, the breakfast or counting room. Drawing N°. 2, at the center, is the parlor floor and has the tallest windows. The parlor and dining room, *c* and *d*, are each 15 feet 6 inches by 17 feet. Space *f*, at the upper left-hand corner, was the china closet; at the front left, *e*, the library, was 7 feet square. Drawing N°. 3, at the bottom right, was the chamber or bedroom floor; *g*, at the front right, was the spare chamber; *h*, at left front, a small bedchamber; *i*, the lady's or gentleman's bedchamber. Off it at left rear was a dressing room.

On this plate the use of the fourth level was not designated, but a similar building (Plate 33) describes that top level as "Upper chamber floor." The text details the windows: the glass of the basement story of figure 76 was 11 by 17 inches, with "six lights to each window," meaning three panes in one sash and three in the other. The "Principal floor" had panes 11 by 16 inches in 6 over 6 sash. The first chamber floor had glass 11 by 15 inches in 6 over 6 sash. The upper chamber floor used 11 by 15 panes in sash of unequal size, six panes in one and three in the other. Perhaps to intensify the stripped-down look that Asher Benjamin championed, the window sash were not delineated in the drawing. Nor are shutters present. These began to grow in popularity from 1800 and were common by the 1820s; if during its

history the Boston house had been more seriously altered, such a document would be invaluable, providing an owner wanted to restore original features.

The sense of the out-of-doors was completely absent from this house. When I bought it, there was a small roof deck about fifteen feet square, but it was in poor condition and the possibility of having ample out-of-door space made a full deck inevitable. Since this necessitated adding something visible from the street, plans for the changes had to be submitted to the Beacon Hill Architectural Commission. Confronting such a group can be ominous. The committee I approached, which has since changed, was comprised of people who cared very much about "The Hill," but some were

81–82 Study, Myrtle Street, 1976

83 Proposed roof-deck fence, Myrtle Street, 1976

84–85 Roof deck, Myrtle Street, 1980

not as knowledgeable as they should have been. One member suggested that the edge of the roof deck be a "Chinese Chippendale fence," that is, a lot of uneven members arranged in a geometrical pattern and probably painted white. The suggestion was not pushed after it was pointed out that the house was several styles later than "Chippendale" and such fencing not practiced after the 1780s.[1] To find an appropriate fence design, Danny Lownes at the Society for the Preservation of New England Antiquities generously provided Xeroxes of photographs of fences used in early Boston. Some were of vertical boards and a few of these even appeared on rooftops. The Asher Benjamin illustration (figure 76) shows above the cornice a set of vertical lines that probably signaled a balustrade but they are not unlike vertical boards! The photograph with the penciled-in fence seen as figure 83 was submitted to the commission and accepted.

Rough pine boards were used for the fence and the planting boxes. The floor was of redwood. The earth was brought from Rehoboth, with some favorite flowers and herbs (figures 84 and 85). The small black roof seen in figure 84 covers the stairwell that has the door through which you arrive at the deck. After a few years the board roof on either side of it was added to provide shade for the people and the house plants summering there. Figure 85 shows the view from under that roof looking toward the Charles River. On the Boston side is the "Hatch Shell," where outdoor concerts are held in the summer and on the Fourth of July a barge is moored nearby from which fireworks shoot heavenward.

As with the other buildings and apartments in this chapter, this one has been personalized. The fabric and details have not been altered; everything except the roof deck can be changed by a new color of paint. New owners will temporarily impose their needs. Probably in this preservation-conscious era, little will be done of a permanent nature, although one can never be sure about that. Part of the initial push to make Beacon Hill a historic district was because an owner of a similar house took out the two first-floor windows and the bricks between them, and installed in the opening a plate-glass window for a ranch-style living room. Fortunately a different owner has recently restored the original fenestration.

3

Looking, Evaluating, and Buying

After three years in Providence, I simultaneously resigned as director of the Rhode Island Historical Society and developed house disease—the desire to organize a living space. I craved an early house in need of considerable work. In part the labor was to serve as therapy, working long hours away from people, but also such a structure would be less expensive. For about a year I had, in a desultory way, been looking for an early house in Rhode Island; as the director of the state historical society, it would have been considered heresy to look in a neighboring state. Now I was free to turn to Rehoboth, Massachusetts, which many had praised for its rural homes.

The town lies halfway between Providence, Rhode Island, and Taunton, Massachusetts, and still feels like a farming community, although business people and faculty from Brown University and The Rhode Island School of Design have joined the descendants of early settlers. It is a proud town, conscious that it was first settled in 1643 and immediately originated free education. To gain a sense of the community and its homes, I spent some days slowly driving every Rehoboth

road. Late in that venture, I was headed west on Homestead Avenue where it curves north and is joined in a T from the south by Perryville Road (see map, figure 86) when I saw the Bliss House as shown in figure 105. (The photograph is taken looking up Perryville Road.) The shades were drawn and it had an unlived-in, scruffy look; the chimney was the right size and the house was sufficiently ratty to produce goosebumps. It was too close to the road and too large—but I wanted it.

LOOKING

Clearly, the initial step in finding the right house is a vision of what you want as an end result and some understanding of what you are willing to go through to acquire it. If you can afford to have all the work done, you face finding people who can do it in a way that will satisfy you. If you are to do much of the work yourself, a fairly clear understanding of the scope of the job is essential. Consider whether you want a house that although beautiful is basically a convenient "machine for living," or a place you can make personal and glorious. If the latter, then you should be very sure the situation is free of features that would daily drain you, such as visible supermarkets, gasoline stations, constant noise, traffic, or street lights that shine in your windows. To understand living there it is important to see the house at times throughout the day, and find if weekends differ from weekdays. Is there heavy traffic during rush hours or on beach days, for example? What will snow and ice or the hot months mean? You cannot do this for all the seasons of the year, but you should attempt to envisage them.

The importance of careful scouting was brought home to me when, after purchasing the Bliss House, I drove to it for the first time after nightfall. I had expected to see it tucked in rural darkness, a light or two illuminating one or more windows, while the mass merged with the surroundings. What I found was a super-powerful electric light on a telephone pole flooding the entire house front. It was placed to illuminate the junction of Homestead Avenue and Perryville Road. It depressed me, for one of the aspects I thought I was purchasing—a subtle fusion into the landscape—was missing. After negotiating with the authorities, they directed the light away from the house; it might even have been possible, although I did not do this, to insist upon a shield that would keep the light from illuminating the land. For some owners the presence of a strong light would be an asset, for it discourages burglars, at least on that side.

I find that purchasing houses is like buying early furniture or other art objects. *Do not do it if you can walk away from it.* With furniture it is rarely satisfying to hunt for something that is just the right width to go between two windows, for the correctly sized piece may prove to have little intrinsic interest. Also, such looking curtails the discovery of unexpected greatness. Similarly, do not talk yourself into a house or go

looking with unnecessary blinders. In deciding whether you have found your place, the important thing is to have the "bones" of the house feel right. This is true for urban as well as rural properties.

Outside, does the house you are considering have the right scale and juxtaposition of parts? What is the setting of nearby buildings? If they are on "your" property, how does one building relate to another? Will you join them, tear any of them down, turn one into a guesthouse? How do they fit into the grounds, how do the grounds work for you, as they are now and as the basis of what you will bring to them? How do the buildings on this property relate to the neighbors' buildings? Indeed, what are the neighbors like? Do you want to know them? Do they want to know you?

At Rehoboth, I always worked in a T-shirt, blue jeans, and sneakers. (If you step on old nails, tetanus may ensue; tetanus shots should always precede such projects.) During the tearing-out stage I was always distinctly filthy. One day, when my grubbiness was enhanced by a kerchief sweatband and a carpenter's apron, a long green Cadillac drove into the drive announcing a courtesy call from very proper neighbors. They described how they had redone a similar eighteenth-century house just down the road and actually said: "We did it as they would have done, with our taste." And they meant it. Any worn areas had been replaced with their fresh versions of the past, and the original doors and floors had been bulldozed into the ground with their personal bulldozer. This proved their only visit and shows that being dirty can be a means of keeping such attitudes at bay.

Take the time to find the official who can tell you about local zoning. Would you be allowed to subdivide the land or house and sell part of it to help with the costs, or after children are gone? Can you change or add to the exterior without permission from a historic agency? Could your neighbors change their buildings? How close to the property line can you build? Check the property line carefully. I learned the value of this when I purchased the hundred-acre farm in Moultonboro, New Hampshire (figures 50 through 52). I did not walk the lines prior to purchase and was eventually surprised to find how close the eastern border was to the field behind the house. The real estate agent should provide you with a plot map or description and help walk it. This is as true of a city dwelling as a rural place. What are the bus, subway, and school bus routes? Where are the stores you need, and the library, police station, firehouse and fire plugs? (The nearness of the last two could affect the cost of the house insurance.) Acquire a map of the area and see if it has features you want for swimming, golf, or jogging.

Inside, take an ice pick and see if you can drive it into the beams, particularly in the basement. But remember that some degree of rot may not be a serious problem. Many houses have had bug damage or dry rot, but most early houses were overdesigned, and the beams were often much thicker than they need be to support the weight they carry. Therefore, a partially destroyed member need not necessarily be replaced. As we will see when discussing the cellar of the Bliss House, people too often tear out and replace parts with new materials quite unnecessarily.

Do not be shy about running taps, flushing toilets, searching inside closets. Lift the corner of linoleum or wall-to-wall carpets and check what is underneath them. Are moldings on the surface of the plaster or embedded into it? If the former, they may be later and easily removed. If the latter, they may well be original and removal means the plaster will have to be patched. Make a list of what has been changed: floors, moldings, plaster, mantels, and so on through the house. (Helpful checklists are available—see the Bibliography.)

All of this builds knowledge that may either diminish your emotional involvement or heighten it. You can change the details: add them, remove

them, drape them, paint them out, or otherwise camouflage them. But the basic masses, shapes, and spaces must be there or their addition feasible. This understanding is both intellectual and emotional. For me the important first reaction is that what I am looking at is "right." The second stage is blocking any emotional involvement and becoming solely analytical. From that stage until you own the building, and perhaps for some time after, it is an intellectual pursuit. I felt "right" about Rehoboth when I first saw it. Then, through the analyzing period, that belief became an act of faith—that it would eventually work. After some weeks of laboring I had brought the parlor to the state seen in figure 143. I placed within it, among shavings, an early carpet and a blue painted chest over drawer and "saw" how the room and the house would eventually look (as it does in figure 61).

REAL ESTATE AGENTS

Good agents can answer most of the obvious questions, but they make a living by providing a service. As in all fields they vary in degrees of honesty and dedication to the customer, themselves, and the seller. I was told by one real estate agent that a particular well was just fine, only to discover later that he had lent the owner milk cans for hauling water during a recent drought. But after I bought a house through him he lent me a truck without charge for taking stuff to the dump. Do not count on what an agent says when normal pressures may make it difficult to carry out the promise. The agent for the Bliss House said he would call me as soon as it went on the market. He called others first, and only because of my persistence did I learn when it was available.

Normally one sees a building for the first time with a real estate agent. My relationship with the Bliss House was the other way around. I had been seduced by the front and when some days later I saw inside with the agent, I fell in love with the back hall. The floor had once been painted blue-green and now the dusty, worn oak boards were mostly visible through it. The plaster above it had great character: it was rough and personal, as seen in figure 149. The quality of this rather rudimentary space gave me confidence that the rest of the rooms might be similarly beautiful if the few intrusive features were removed. In fact, there were very few modern excrescences. Some moldings had been changed and cupboards had been built here and there in the nineteenth and twentieth centuries. The electricity was minimal and the plumbing basically nonexistent. Most of the rooms were hard to "read" because of accumulated stuff that obscured features, but they felt right. It was what I wanted: a Chinese puzzle to be maneuvered, a tangle of intellectual, emotional, and aesthetic problems to be thought through and solved.

The rooms had furniture so their size was fairly easy to understand. It is difficult to judge the size of an empty room, how it will look when furnished. Empty rooms often look smaller than they are, and in some instances, larger. (That is one of the reasons it is normally easier to sell a house furnished.) When looking at an empty room, imagine your sofa, a piano, or certain large objects you can picture and pace out. Mark their size with bits of wood or paper. In planning furnishings I always lay out each room on graph paper, letting each square represent a foot or an easy unit of a foot: two, three, four, or six inches. Then I cut graph paper to the size of the large objects to be brought to the house. These are moved about on the drawings until it is possible to believe that everything will fit.

DOCUMENTATION

Hunting through courthouse records and inventories to learn more about a house before purchase may prove useful in your decision about buying.

It will certainly prove helpful as you work on a building. The courthouse or another municipal building should have the names and birth and death dates of the family members who lived in the house; their neighbors and business relationships will be seen in wills, deeds, contracts, foreclosures, land plots, civil and criminal contests, tax records, and commissions. Among the finds may be the longed-for early inventories that tell you what was in the house, and perhaps the rooms where the items were located. Early newspapers will describe daily events that occurred at the time. The town, county, or state in which your property lies probably has a historical society as well as local history "nuts" and neighbors who have information about the house. It may be discussed in a bicentennial handbook or listed in the local or national historic house surveys. If you are very fortunate, there will be photographs of this or similar buildings in your house or among neighbors or members of the owner's family. Some societies, such as Boston's Society for the Preservation of New England Antiquities, have thousands of photographs organized for finding views of early buildings by regions and, within them, by towns and then streets. Such organizations can guide you to architectural handbooks and other means of learning who may have built your house, lived in it, and what roles it may have played in the past. (For further guidance, see the Bibliography.) Early descriptions and photographs will give the obvious help of showing what has been removed and added, but they can also help establish the mood of an earlier time that might influence your plans. In the attic of the Bliss House were albums of late nineteenth- and early twentieth-century family photographs. Some showed features or buildings that were now missing. Most important, they projected a rural attitude I wanted to capture. I could see that quality in the buildings and land, but to have pictures helped clarify my instinctive reactions. Many of the photographs are included in the following chapters.

WORKING JOURNAL

(Selections from the daily journal kept during the restoration of the Daniel Bliss House are included to show the kinds of excitement, involvement, and work accompanying such a project. The entries appear in shaded boxes so readers may skip to more recent thoughts. Passages from the day-to-day diary are dated; summations made from time to time are not.)

Friday, May 22, 1970. House finally on the market (had driven past it but not been inside). Saw house in the afternoon; several other couples milling around. Long conversation with Mr. Bliss—born 1884, married four times. Grew up here. Milk route to Pawtucket—2 hours, seven miles. As a child of seven his father would load a wagon with wood and he would drive it to Pawtucket—his father would then ride in and unload it and he would drive it back, stopping to buy a big piece of cheese and five cookies for 10¢ (?) and eat them on the way back. They had a surrey, a buggy, a "democrat wagon"—with "two seats"—and farm carts— two horses for milk route, two for the farm, one gentle for his mother to drive. At 19 (?) told farm would go to *younger* brother, so he got a job with jewelry firm in Providence—accounts—and soon became their New York manager. He eventually became an insurance adjuster. Stayed in New York until after brother died and until his first wife died. Then in 1914 he came back to Rehoboth. Chicken business. Milk—23 cows and five horses in barn. Chicken business began to lose money, so he went to work for a dairy. Was on Board of Education and put through Rehoboth's first consolidated school—instead of 16 one-room schoolhouses.

He built the glass-door cupboard in the kitchen and put the concrete floor in the "piazza" which his father had built around 1908 with a wooden floor. The "chicken barn" [*eventual guesthouse, figure 211*] had once been a slaughterhouse and larger.

House being sold with contents, largely junk of all ages, but a few interesting things in the furniture line. The land included 3½ acres, all north of Homestead Ave.

Phoned parents to ask Dad to come and look at it and assess construction. Sills and beams in cellar very bad—dripping wet and pulpy, and some members visibly gone.

Saturday, 23. Brought Bob Mende [*builder*] out in the morning to give estimates on structural work; once he grasped how much I would really do, very helpful. In afternoon parents arrived and came out again. Dad and I spent 2 hrs. or more going over everything. He feels it is manageable if I realize what an operation it will be, and if I don't try to go too far in redoing everything puristically at once. Made offer of $20,000—with explanatory sheet of expenses.

Sunday, 24. Mr. Bliss accepted offer if I will pay the realtor's fee. In the afternoon went out to see the house and sign the Purchase and Sale Agreement. The Bliss family, assembled for Mr. Bliss's 86th birthday, came by to see the house once more. Ceremonial welcome. Mr. Bliss, who is worried as I about someone breaking in, says I may start working, may sleep here, and may take key objects back to Providence for safekeeping. Came back later that night and took back Queen Anne table [*figure 60*] from attic—got it into the VW somehow—and started to work on it. One leg had split at top and was nailed with five 19th-century nails. One hinge gone and that leaf nailed to side of leg to keep it on. Removed nails, reglued, washed and put in a new hinge next to broken one.

Monday, 25. Put 10 Arnold Street on market. Went to bank about financing.

To help understand what was involved in saving the Bliss House, and because I would need his help, I asked advice of Robert Mende, who, like his family before him, had been responsible for some of the best restoration work in Providence. It was easy to discern that he was awed by the amount of work the Bliss House would entail. It seemed hopeless, just a huge project beyond most people's means. When I said I was going to work on it full time, if he would do certain things I found too large to handle easily, he became encouraging. My father, who had worked on early houses in Pennsylvania, came to give advice, and we spent a delightful afternoon discussing problem after problem, but always with a sense of "Wow, you could do this," or "You could do that!" His only fear was that I would do too much, take it back too completely—spending too much time and money. Clearly the attitude of both of us was positive and joyful, for the real estate agent said: "I don't know if they're going to buy it or they're just having fun."

BUYING

The Daniel Bliss House was owned by Richard Perry Bliss, who had lived there all his life, except when as a young man he was employed in New York. He decided to sell the house after he married his fourth wife for, as he said, "She had a bathroom and I moved in with her." The house had been in his family since it was built but his children did not want to face what was involved in bringing it to modern standards. An offer was made through the real estate agent, some-

what lower than the asking price, with "honest money" (also called "earnest money"), a small amount usually of about $1,000 indicating that you are serious. I submitted with the offer a list of what the major improvements would cost: a well, heating, plumbing, electricity, and structural work.

Mr. Bliss accepted the offer on condition that I pay the real estate agent's fee rather than having it come from the amount of the offer. I signed a Purchase and Sale Agreement, which regularly requires 10 percent down payment. This is normally lost if it is the buyer's fault the deal does not go through. However, you should place in the P and S Agreement conditions allowing you to withdraw if certain standard problems arise. One is that you are unable to obtain a mortgage. The P and S should state how long you have to achieve this, perhaps thirty days. Another regular condition is that the house will be inspected and if not found free of termites or other infestation, the seller will correct this at his or her expense. If that is done, the sale must take place unless the P and S says differently. If bugs are to be killed by chemicals, be sure they are biodegradable; some retain their strength for years and are known to be harmful to animals. Their effect on humans is not yet certain. It is also important to add the right to have the building inspected for unexpected major structural problems and that you can back out if these are found.

In most areas there are professionals who, for a comparatively small fee (usually under $200), will walk through the building with you for a couple of hours, pointing out every problem they see. Starting generally in the basement, they discuss the sills, basement walls, furnace, heating, plumbing, electrical units—the viability of everything they can show you. You will learn how the heating system works, whether it can have such items as moisture control or air conditioning added. Then you move up through the house, looking at the stove, dishwasher, sink, windows, et cetera. Finishing in the attic, you inspect the insulation, evidence of leaks, and chimney(s). Outside, perhaps with binoculars, the building is looked at for sagging and other problems. Even the condition of the grass and shrubs can be reviewed. If you are not knowledgeable in these areas, get an expert who is.

The seller also places in the P and S Agreement features such as the time when the sale will take place, amounts to be paid to the seller and the agent, and may list objects that will not stay with the house. Each region has different rules for what normally stays and what is taken, but any seller can take anything he or she lists, such as a well-loved light fixture or particular or even all of the garden plants. Normally those things attached to the structure stay, for example, electric fixtures, gas stoves, curtain rods, picture hooks, and wall-to-wall carpets. Detachable items like refrigerators and curtains are usually automatically taken.

The mortgage man from the bank joined the growing number of those appalled by the Daniel Bliss House. Probably it was only because of preservation connections in Providence that I acquired money for the mortgage and a second loan for improvements. Years later, when I saw that person again about some other matter, he visited the house in a finished state and said: "How did you know it was going to look like this?" I wanted to answer: "A professional should be able to tell."

As part of securing a mortgage, the bank will do a title search, at your expense; they want a clear title if they need to foreclose. They make certain that each time the house was part of some transaction, it was done properly and you are buying it free from any unexpected conditions; that no one, unless you have been so informed, owns part of it; that there is no right of way across your property; and so on. Part of what came with the house in Providence was a right of way through the yard of the neighbor to the east. It was "narrower than a carriage for two horses." In the nine-

teenth century an owner of the house I was buying sold the land on that side for the construction of a new house. This left no outside way to my backyard except through that property. The "narrower than a carriage" defined that it was a walkway, rather than a driveway. Part of what the new house builder acquired was the right to have a heavy cornice of the taller, Italianate house project over the older one.

It is rare to have a house sell without a mortgage, in part because payments are tax deductible, but if you are buying the house without one, you should have the title search done by a good lawyer. It is worth what you have to pay—within reason! The Beacon Hill house (figure 75) had once been sold by people who took a first and second mortgage on the property from the new owner. He did not pay them or the house taxes, and they had to foreclose and resell the property (to me). My lawyer found that the foreclosure had not been advertised in the newspaper in the manner prescribed by law. To keep the title clear, he had the owners go through another correct foreclosure procedure.

It is usually worthwhile covering the amount of the mortgage by a term life insurance of the length of the policy or some other means to secure that the death of the mortgage payer will not necessitate the sale of the property. Also, consider whether the seller has enough insurance on the property to cover your involvement up to the point of acquiring it. After the P and S is signed, it may be partly your loss if the house is damaged. If you own a house and it has not sold by the time you buy the new one, you may need a swing or bridge loan, often a mortgage on one or both properties. In some cases I have been able to sell a house a few days before buying the new house, and for a nominal fee rent back the former place for a few weeks. (I put this in the P and S Agreement.) This gave me the capital to buy the new property without a bridge loan, as well as time to paint and move to the new place.

ARCHITECTS AND BUILDERS

What you do or do not do to the building will affect how easy it will be to sell. If you leave such idiosyncrasies as crooked floors, the majority of those who consider purchase will react like the person who said of Rehoboth: "This house is spooky." Also what you add, because of personal peculiarities, will affect the sale. One house I considered in Providence had been reworked by a couple who were both over six feet four inches tall, and for their convenience they had placed the kitchen and bathroom counters at unusually high levels—unusable for those of more normal height. Such additions can in turn be altered, but changes to early features are much more serious. All occupancy is temporary. Others will follow, and what you have done will condition whether future sojourners will have a vital experience. A building must not be seriously diminished by any passer-by.

Few architects are trained to work with old buildings. Most who do are insensitive to them and have a sentimental and inaccurate view of the past. Often what they suggest is either overly romantic or too designeresque; exposed brick easily became a must. In the 1970s there was too much high-tech imposition on early spaces. One small house supervised by an architect for a collector in Providence placed light switches halfway between any two architectural features. For example, a switch was centered between a doorway molding and the parlor fireplace mantel, making it impossible to hang a painting there. If you want professional architectural guidance, see finished examples of the architect's work. Ask a lot of questions: What are the basic problems I face? What are the basic advantages to an old house? Play dumb if necessary and ask big, generalized questions as well as specific ones. But remember even if the architect is good with old houses, he or she cannot understand a building quickly. Each place has unique

problems or variants of known ones, but the general approach and an estimate of costs should be established before proceeding.

If you plan to have some or all of the work done by a builder, find a first-class one whose work on other projects you can inspect. Most are used to replacing everything that is worn, totally changing the character of the structure. Usually, these changes are *not* necessary. If a builder is not sympathetic to what *you* like about the building, he or she is not likely to change in attitude while working with you. My caution is: do not believe a builder who has no experience with such projects and no sympathy with your likes and wishes, for it is all too easy to make irreversible changes.

Experienced people should be able to give you a ball park figure for all major work; doing a bathroom, for example, might average $2,500 or $3,000. They know the average cost of a tub, shower, toilet, sink, and plumbing and wiring. The same is true of a basic kitchen. Even though the cost of different cabinets varies, you should be able to know basically what you are getting into before you begin. When discussing costs do not accept, "It's an unknown quantity." Anyone used to such a job should be able to estimate the parameters of your financial involvement. Of course, there are always the unknowns. When we pulled the corner boards off the Bliss House, the corner posts inside were found to be rotted up to four feet. The old pieces had to be trimmed and new pieces inserted under them. Such problems should, however, be anticipated—not necessarily the particular ones, but the general number of them, and cost estimates should be nearly correct.

Usually even experienced restoration builders want to work without estimates, surely not a written one. Some may work by the hour, plus costs, and if they are skilled this might be a satisfactory solution. One of the many extraordinary things about Bob Mende was that in estimating the cost of his work on the main house and again on the guesthouse, the final bills were *under* what he said they would be—and not because he had inflated the estimates.

You should be able to get from an architect or a builder statements in writing that include: the exact changes which are to be made; the quality of the materials; that they take responsibility for all work conforming to building regulations and planning requirements; that they will acquire the approval or releases necessary to do the work; and that the work should be satisfactory on completion and should remain so for six months at least. If possible, you should have a starting and finishing date. I know this is virtually impossible and repeat here my father's oft-given answer: "I'll get you in by Christmas, but I don't promise which one."

The agreement should also include terms of payment. You may want an agreement that withholds a certain percentage until the work proves satisfactory. You should receive a price list of individual parts and have an agreement as to how to handle extras. These can mount quickly if you suddenly decide that you have to have something just seen or heard about, particularly if what you formerly wanted is already completed. The builder should be able to agree that above the estimates only extras and variations agreed to in writing will be paid for by you. There should be an arrangement as to what happens to the materials that are taken out, such as slate, marble, copper, lead, and even early glass windowpanes. What you want to know is all costs and the basis for them: what the total will not exceed. This is hard, because the costs of building materials can change in surprising ways. When working on Rehoboth, contrary to the traditional pattern, it was more expensive to use plywood than 1″ × 12″ pine boards because Japan had just bought most of America's plywood. Be sure you keep a copy of all memos of understanding, the original agreement, and any that develop during the project. Many factors cause problems with builders and those who subcontract from them. For example, topsoil is often scraped back in order to work on founda-

tions and put in sewer systems; this has at times been sold off and only enough for a thin layer put back after construction is finished. Topsoil, if indeed it must be moved, should be scraped back with great care so that it is not mixed with subsoil.

While others are working on the site, visit it often. It will look rough and new possibilities will occur, but do not change your mind easily. If you do, speak to the person in charge and let him or her give directions. Conflicting instructions add to the expense and create counterproductive tensions. Realize that delays will happen. Sometimes these are unavoidable and upsetting, but far more frustrating are the contractors who take the easy way out and tell you what is not true. The plumber in Rehoboth would call and say, "I'll be there on Monday," and he must often have said the same to at least one other customer. How he chose which place to go on Monday I do not know, but I suppose such behavior keeps other jobs from going to another plumber. Once he said, "I'll be there on Monday," and it turned out he was leaving the Sunday before for a week's vacation. I had subcontracted him through Bob Mende, who took most of the brunt of this unsatisfactory behavior, but I too knew that he was supposed to be there on the Mondays he did not show up.

Do not let your plumber or electrician choose the fixtures for you. Go to the suppliers' displays and look at and touch each item. Try the bathtub to be sure it is long enough, and sit on the toilet to be sure it is comfortable. Pretend to wash your hands at the sink. Is it wide enough, deep enough? Is the medicine cabinet flanked by the kind of lights you really want? A light above is not bad for people with beards, but those who shave or want to see under their nose and chin benefit from side lighting. The contractors may receive a percentage of what you pay if they do the ordering or you purchase where they send you (they buy at wholesale and sell it to you at retail), so they may want you to shop where they have an understand-

1 *Home of Roger and Ruth Bacon, Brentwood, New Hampshire; seen also as figure 34*

II *Keeping room, Bacon House; seen also as figure 36*

III *Keeping room, Bacon House; seen also as figure 37*

IV *Parlor, Bacon House; seen also as figure 38*

V *Keeping-room chamber, Bacon House; seen also as figure 40*

VI *Daniel Bliss House, Rehoboth, Massachusetts; seen also as figure 57*

VII *Daniel Bliss House; seen also as figure 131*

VIII *Parlor, Daniel Bliss House; seen also as figure 144*

IX *Keeping room, Daniel Bliss House; seen also as figure 62*

X *Parlor chamber, Daniel Bliss House; seen also as figure 183*

XI *Study chamber, Daniel Bliss House; seen also as figure 185*

XII *Study chamber, Daniel Bliss House; seen also as figure 64*

ing. You should feel free to look in any store that may sell what you want. Be specific, even to the type of toilet-paper holder that you want. You will have to live with all these things until you move or tear them out. (See the Bibliography under Catalogues.)

I have always insisted upon using the best materials so they would last and not just provide a cosmetic effect. This means the paint has outlived my occupancy in virtually every house I have owned. Probably my stress on quality stems in part from the fact that I did not know I was going to move and thought, "One should do it once and get it done with." But more important is the feeling of living with something that has integrity.

In short: what you need is, first, a great deal of planning, and second, to try to stick to the plans; but you will, of course, realize new possibilities and want to get them right. Remember you will see other things once you are living there and may want to make changes in a year or two. Not everything needs to be done at the start. One of Roger Bacon's best bits of advice was: "You won't really understand the building until you've lived in it."

BUY IT RATTY
AND LET IT TALK

When T. S. Eliot was asked, "What is your method?", he answered, "The only method is to be very intelligent." The same is true from the moment you begin any changes to a house. Once you have begun, you almost immediately reach the point of no return. Not only does one change affect others, but the house is possibly unsalable until you have finished. When you do not know what to do at any particular moment, it is better to do nothing than to end up living with a mistake that is not easily undone. The best general advice is to disturb the fabric as little as possible, particularly the early features. Whenever you disturb one element, you are selecting something other

than what you already have. Not everything old is good, but the replacement you use will not *necessarily* be better. You should know by now whether you are doing a conversion or a restoration. Are you mostly imposing your own taste and time, or are you seeking to make useful a period house?

Before you tear anything off, invest time letting the house talk. It is possible to recover from a bad start but it is expensive, both emotionally and financially, to put back or recreate something that should not have been removed. Recently the Museum of Fine Arts, Boston, restored their early library. Not long before, they had thrown out the original lighting fixtures because there were no plans for a restoration. Now they have had new fixtures made, following the original design.

If not already done, this is the time to check closely the walls, ceilings, floors, moldings, doors, and paneling for hooks, nails, holes, and patching in the wood or plaster that may show where something was once attached. These may indicate later additions since removed, or they may have held original shelving, lighting, or fireplace equipment. For example, when the plaster ceiling was taken down in the keeping room of the Bliss House (figure 170), there were nails in the beams that must once have been used for hanging baskets and other kitchen equipment. These were carefully noted on a diagram; any additional nails used in that ceiling were of the modern variety, which could be distinguished from the early. Such an investigation in the John Brown House in Providence during one of the restoration phases found under the electrical conduit attached to the surface of the room a half-inch-wide strip of wallpaper. Its vivid blue color and paper type matched one of the eighteenth-century rolls of wallpaper left over when the house was first papered. Until that point, it was not known in which room any of the original examples had been used.

Have you established a cutoff date or are you working by the features you like and do not like? As we move around the Bliss House, we will see that the original building, about 1742, had parts added in the late eighteenth century and the mid- and late nineteenth century. Consider leaving things that you find ugly at this point, if they can be removed later, particularly if they are not so much ugly as from a period with which you are not yet sympathetic. Verandas in the right place can be a godsend in August, even if they were not part of the original structure. The rear doorway of the main house of the Bliss homestead probably once had a solid door. In the mid-nineteenth century that was replaced with one that had a glazed upper half, allowing useful north light into the rear hall.

By now you should have knowledge from written or pictorial sources of similar local buildings to guide your changes. What you are after are the right proportions, the right feel. Do not exaggerate: do not put in beams that are bigger than they would have been at the period, for instance, simply because size seems to some to denote importance. Let what you add move with the old. When my family bought the house that had been in the Kirk family for some generations, there was no mantel over the kitchen fireplace. My father put one in, using a level to make it perfectly horizontal. It always looked new and people commented on the crooked mantel. In fact it was the floor and ceiling that sloped. In this instance my father was insensitive to the room in which he was working. Tipping that mantel down at one end would have made it look level and pass as original.

Additions will probably look new when you add new woodwork, particularly outside, for they will not have an eroded surface. You can help correct this by using a wire brush with the grain, digging out some of the soft part of the grain. I happen not to mind, in most instances, letting new wood look new against the old, particularly if both are to be painted the same color. Certainly buildings had such mixtures as they were maintained through the years. Do not work in the opposite direction and remove patina from the old, filling in chips or eliminating the very character that makes it interesting. Presumably, this is the reason you made the purchase and are going through this exhausting process. A patch, looking like a patch, can be part of what makes a wall, a floor, a space, a building, look marvelous. (I do not feel this way about pointing areas of brickwork with too wide mortar.)

If you are going to remove paint, use chemical removers and hand tools that will not eradicate the old marks in the wood. Sandpaper, heavy scraping, and sandblasting destroy old surfaces. On bricks, such harsh treatment removes that outer, heat-strengthened surface that shuns water. (See the Bibliography for suggested manuals on finishing surfaces.) Remember that today almost everything old can be fixed. Unlike twenty-five or thirty years ago, it is possible to impregnate damaged areas with new synthetic materials. Recently an inept restorer worked on the important New England Fairbanks House (c. 1637) in Dedham, Massachusetts. Its top front plate had been made of pieces joined with a complex bladed scarf joint, and is now famous among scholars of seventeenth-century New England architecture. By the 1970s that area had become punky; but instead of firming it up with consolidants or patching it carefully, the restorer cut out the entire area and threw it into the woods behind the house. To further the crime, the manner of putting in the new piece did not follow the historic precedent. Fortunately, what had been removed was found by a person who understood its historic importance and it now rests in the office of Abbott Lowell Cummings, director of the Society for the Preservation of New England Antiquities. Beside soft beams and posts, areas such as door bottoms and columns may now be saved and holes filled and plaster firmed with resins: acrylics, epoxies, polyesters, alkyds, et cetera (see Bibliography).[1]

The value of an archaeological investigation should be considered. You may want to do it yourself, if you have the proper skills, or can work under professional direction. Often local groups or college courses can provide interested diggers and guidance, or they may undertake all the work as a class project. The state preservation agency or the National Park Service should know where to look for help. What you are seeking, if you are trying to do a full restoration, is anything that people threw away or lost. Often the holes of abandoned privies were used as a place to throw broken ceramics, glass, and other articles, once a new hole was dug. In the eighteenth and nineteenth centuries, pits for receiving trash were dug and cellar holes were used as a place to discard unwanted material. Things fell into wells: silver, glass, ceramics, iron, and so forth. In the seventeenth century, a means of disposing of broken items was to cast them out through a door or window or just generally spread them about outside—perhaps down a bank. This material is now called "sheet refuse" by archaeologists. Trenches may disclose much about what took place in the house. Often small items have fallen between the floorboards or been carried there by rats: buttons, coins, and bits of textile may inform you of former occupants and life within that structure. Historical archaeologists—those who deal with both the written record and the material underground—can be of great assistance in making intelligent decisions about your undertaking.

BEGINNING

If you have a neighbor who is more knowledgeable than you are about all this, hook up a walkie-talkie or some way of achieving constant communication. When I worked on my first house, in Center Sandwich, my next-door neighbor, Peter Lear, was one of those do-it-yourself geniuses and he convinced me I could do the plumbing. It had to be all new work as the house had not had any plumbing before. He guided me through ordering, cutting, and soldering copper pipe—everything except the drainage for the toilet. (Now it could be done with plastic pipes, far easier to work.) I had tried to establish a good relationship with the community, which usually disparaged

summer people. I dug the septic hole by hand, hauled my own rubble, and avoided naive and thoughtless questions like "What do you do here all winter?" The value of community acceptance was made apparent when I turned on the water for the first time after finishing the plumbing. The only thing that leaked was the kitchen sink faucet, which had been ordered from Sears. The sink was cemented in place and the nut I had to tighten was up behind. I needed a kind of wrench that I did not own. I rang Peter on the walkie-talkie, who phoned the friendly real estate agent, who called a friend in a neighboring town. He took the special wrench to the postman, who dropped it off at our central store where I picked it up. One turn of the wrench and the job was finished; the wrench then went back through the same line of supportive people.

Do not follow good advice blindly. When I was about to cover one wall of the Center Sandwich study with bookcases, Peter suggested aggressively that it should be insulated first, for then I would not need to remove the bookcase when I insulated the house. I spent an entire Christmas vacation taking down the plaster and lath, installing insulation, and putting up plaster board. Building the bookcases took one day. Of course that wall is the only one in the house with insulation.

Do not yourself throw trash out the doors and windows: it will ruin the lawn and other plants. Large barrels (the thick cardboard type are lighter) should be constantly available. Cover the floors, if you want to protect them, with heavy building paper obtainable at any builder's supply. This will spare you endless hours of cleaning up bits of wallpaper and save the floor from being marked. (It is not advisable to put down building paper if you are using steam or water in removing wallpaper; it will remain wet too long and may mark or even warp the floor.) Building paper may seem a nuisance as it becomes scuffed, but you will be glad later.

I find it helpful to use a notebook and enter in

it each evening everything you have learned that day and speculations as to what it means. These notes will be corrected as you proceed. Such a record helps you write up the project later should you choose to do so; more important, writing and reading it will assist you in understanding what you are doing and how to plan the rest of the work. Record each room systematically: what was done and in what order, then what still has to be done and what remains undecided. List all major features such as plumbing and electrical work as well as what seem like minor changes, problems, and thoughts. The process clarifies the thinking.

A last piece of advice: sit in each room and imagine using it. How many hours will you spend facing which way? Toward the fireplace? The picture window you feel you need? The sunniest side? The kitchen stove? Flowing with this knowledge will allow you greater future rapport with what you are creating.

4

Restoring the Bliss House – Outside

THE BLISS FAMILY

The Blisses, among the earliest settlers of Rehoboth, Massachusetts, were descended from Thomas Bliss of Devonshire, England. The houses they built, or with which their families have been associated, dot the town. Most of them are to the north of Route 44, the old road that linked Providence, Rehoboth, Taunton, and Plymouth. The first purchase of land *recorded* by Daniel Bliss was on October 14, 1727, and the description includes: "on the Easterly Side of Palmer River Near the House of ye said Daniel Bliss Containing by Estimation thirty two acres. . . ."[1] Clearly Daniel already occupied a house nearby. Throughout his life he was to record a total of twelve purchases and in a deed of October 28, 1751, Daniel and his wife, Ide Bliss, purchased "about 100 acres" below Homestead Avenue and near Wolf Pond. (A transcript of portions of the deed from Ephraim and Hannah Chaffee and further Bliss family documentation are included as Appendix 2.)

In 1759, Daniel Bliss gave part of the hundred acres and an adjacent three and a half acres north of Homestead Avenue to his son Jacob Bliss. On the land north of the road was a "Dwelling house." The deed indicates that Jacob was already occupying the house and that his father lived elsewhere. It is, however, uncertain when Daniel obtained this small parcel of land and when it acquired a building. Family tradition states that Daniel built the house in 1742. At his death in 1807, Jacob divided the house between his wife and his daughter, Lucy. His son Asaph was to have his mother's two thirds at her death, and to consolidate the house, Asaph purchased his sister's share in 1813. Jacob Bliss's 1807 inventory is preserved and constitutes the first known listing of objects in this home. An 1862 inventory of Asaph L. Bliss records its contents in the middle of the nineteenth century (the inventories are included in Appendix 2). Various sales and bequests separated much of the original land from the house, but these were to a large extent reunited by J.[ames] Walter Bliss. He bequeathed the house and nearly all the land to Richard P. Bliss in 1921. Richard Bliss gave the land to his children and

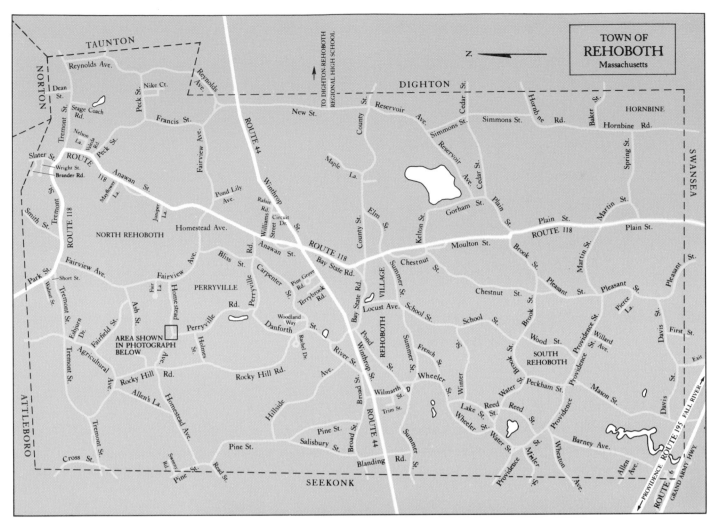

86 Rehoboth, Massachusetts
(Town of Rehoboth)

87 Aerial view of Daniel Bliss
house lot (left) and Bliss school
(right), about 1960

in 1970 sold me most of the original house lot of three and one-half acres.

The left of the aerial view in figure 87 shows the basically triangular piece I purchased. From the bottom edge came Perryville Road, which terminated in Homestead Avenue. Just to the north of that junction was the main house with an ell extension to the right, or east, and from that a shed went north. The front of the house still had a full-length porch. Heavy shadows to the rear make it difficult to read the back line. Behind the shed extension was the "chaise house." The light-colored building behind and to the left of that, seemingly with two chimneys, was the slaughter–chicken house that would become the guesthouse. (The three buildings can be seen in figure 129.) To the right was the long barn—a circular area near the left front corner was the old silo base. Just above the right end of that barn was the remains of the blacksmith shop mentioned in Ja-

cob's 1807 will. Richard Bliss said it had been moved there at some later date.

During his youth Richard Bliss had been interested in photography and in the attic were his photograph albums along with pictures by professionals and other amateur photographers. There were negatives—some corresponded to the photographs in Richard Bliss's albums but others did not have prints. All the negatives were cleaned and reprinted and the images provided visual evidence of earlier moods and physical changes. Fortunately, Richard Bliss and his children were able to date most of these.

The view up Perryville Road (figure 88) was taken about when Mr. Bliss was born, in 1884. There are tall pine trees inside a picket fence. (Seen also in figure 107, these were gone by the time of the next photograph, figure 89.) The picket fence is recessed at the left of the house. Behind it a large tree stands on a knoll. A week after

88 Daniel Bliss House, 1880s

89 Bliss family, Daniel Bliss House, about 1896

90 Richard Bliss and mother, about 1905

signing the Purchase and Sale Agreement, before owning the property, I was sitting in the kitchen when two thirds of that tree split off and crashed to the ground. It did not damage any building but I was glad that I had increased the insurance over what Mr. Bliss had on the property. The building roughly in the center of the photograph, just to the right of the ell, is the chaise house. It had white doors crossed with dark moldings. Behind it is a giant oak (figures 217 and 218), which I immediately had cabled, joining the larger branches so that in heavy winds all the branches helped stabilize one another.

At the right of the photograph is the large barn. The right third was a later addition: the

cupola marks the center of the original building. Toward the viewer from the left end of the barn is the ice house, which was gone by the time I purchased the property. Shutters had been added to the main house in the nineteenth century, and by the time of this photograph the windows had been changed from small pane to 6 over 6 sash. The front door and its flanking sidelights were probably added in about 1840.

By about 1896, as seen in figure 89, which shows the Bliss family, the pines were gone and foundation plantings nestle the house. These bushes are seen again in figure 90, taken about 1905 of Richard Bliss, his mother, and their dog standing at the corner of the picket fence, which had a molded top rail, a deep base, and was still in the barn in 1970. It has since been reused by a neighbor. In most of the early photographs some of the shutters are closed, particularly those on the window at the center of the second floor that let onto the upper front hall. Perryville Road and Homestead Avenue were still dirt with a grassy island where they met when recorded about 1911 in figure 91. Mr. Bliss said that his father added the "piazza," or porch, in 1907 or 1908, and recalled it as "the pleasantest room in the house, always cool and breezy." He slept there in hot weather and it had bamboo shades and screens. (The screens were still in place in 1970, figure 105, and the shades were in the large barn.) Because of the closeness of the road, the piazza was the social center during the summer. One could wave and chat with neighbors as they walked or rode past.

Behind the curving part of the picket fence was a glider swing and a hammock (figures 92 and 93). The porch had fairly comfortable wooden chairs, probably most of the rocking variety. Figure 94, taken in 1924, shows a baby buggy next to a screened baby crib. The grass is rather coarse and Mr. Bliss said nice lawns developed only after the advent of the power mower. Indeed, sumptuous lawns were until then only available to the wealthy. In front of the porch is a stone step which was pushed to the front of the house during

91–92 Daniel Bliss House, about 1911

restoration to serve as a stepping stone for the main doorway (figure 115). It appears in that position, with a low board step in front of it, in a pre-porch Bliss photograph. Other Bliss photographs show croquet being played between the porch and picket fence.

The porch originally had a wooden floor (figure 94). When this rotted, Mr. Bliss replaced it with a poured concrete slab, which is long-lasting but when placed next to wood can cause the wood to rot. Moisture entering between the two materials dampens the wood and the concrete prevents the movement of air that would dry it out. One of my first decisions was to remove the porch. It kept the front from an eighteenth-century aspect and the first-floor front rooms from sunshine. When the bulldozer began to break up the concrete slab and push parts of it about, a corner jutted through the front wall.

The family photograph (figure 95) was taken about 1892, when Richard Bliss was eighteen. He appears in the back, just to the left of the window. Across the front row from left to right

are: Richard Bliss's mother, who had been a Perry; Warren, his younger brother; Mabel Perry, his mother's sister, sitting in a Windsor-type chair with a broad top rail attached to the front of the back posts and probably original red paint; cousin Edgar A. Perry stands next to his mother, Mrs. Edgar Perry; and Dr. Edgar Reed Perry finishes the front row. (He is seated in a chair with the top rail between the back posts; chairs from both sets remained in the attic and appear in figure 197.) Moving across from top left we see: J.

87

93 Richard Bliss and unidentified woman, about 1911

94 Barbara Bliss [Coleman], 1924

Walter Bliss, Richard's father; Dr. Arthur R. Perry, Richard's mother's brother; Richard P. Bliss; and his sister Mildred [Waite]. The two smaller children are, first, Harold Perry, and then his sister Esther [Patton]. The family was photographed behind the house, with the shed as the background. (The main house is to the right and they are placed about where the bird feeder appears in figure 201.)

That the pace of life was once slower, if not less busy, is recalled in the following photographs. Figure 96 looks from the Bliss House down Perryville Road. The horse and buggy were, according to Richard Bliss, "the first Rehoboth RFD, about 1912, with Mr. Small driving." Beyond the child's head is a small, flat building. Each

year a similar structure was built of rather rough lumber and in it slept the migrant strawberry pickers while they worked on the farm. Then the structure was taken apart and the wood used to repair the farm buildings during the following year. That everything was put to use, where much that happened involved personal labor, is shown by the entry in Richard Bliss's diary for Tuesday, May 4, 1915: "Weather clear, wind—north, temperature 75. I cut piano box in two and made chicken coop of lower half. John harrowed, the plowed part of the potato piece with wheel harrow, zig-zag, then with spring tooth and bush. Father and John marked it out. Hogs[:] Grain 16 qts. Poultry[:] Grain 40 qts[;] eggs laid 82."

The large tree in figures 97 through 99 and 107 stood on Homestead Avenue to the right of the drive as you entered the property. By 1970 it and the ice house behind were gone. Between the tree and the ice house is the well. There was a concrete slab around it and perched on top a little wooden house with a crank to bring the water to the surface. This wooden structure had been placed in the barn, probably after water was pumped by electricity directly into the pantry. Behind and to the left of the ice house is the silo with the main barn behind it. The children in figures 97 and 98 are on the dirt drive at the base of the giant, protective tree. The picture evokes fun, relaxation, and hopefulness.

The figure at the base of the same tree in figure 99 may be pensive, but probably what we see is loneliness. This is Cora Bliss, the first wife of Richard Bliss, whom he met and married in New York on August 9, 1911. She died there on March 12, 1912, of tuberculosis. If we had only this photograph, Cora Bliss might be read as a nervous and camera-shy person; but others record her, even when turned out in elaborate bonnet and coat, as withdrawn behind worried eyes. This is not part of what one normally wants to restore. It is more heartening to think of personal growth and health, and the rich, renewing earth; yet loneliness and often fear are a large part of the

95 *Bliss family and relatives, about 1892*

96 *View down Perryville Road with Helen Morse [Femly] (Richard's stepdaughter through his first marriage) and Mr. Small (driving), about 1912*

97 *Phyllis Waite and Dorothy Waite, about 1923*

98 *Walter D. Bliss, 1919*

99 *Cora Bliss, about 1911*

past. The first house I owned, in Center Sandwich (figure 47), had padlocks on every door. As the owner moved from room to room, she unlocked and then locked each door behind her. Many of the doors in the houses I have owned have at one point been smashed, had hinges ripped off, latches torn, panels, stiles, and rails broken. A standard expression still viable in snow-bound areas is "cabin fever," when after a long, hard winter, rage and fear are difficult to control.

Preferable to loneliness is the relaxed aloneness shown in the photograph taken of Richard Bliss with scythe about 1910 (figure 100). This active but less frenzied existence is further recalled in a passage from Richard Bliss's diary for Tuesday, January 11, 1916:

100 Richard Bliss, about 1910

Cloudy cool wind south. I discovered that the hot water boiler at the house was frozen. Lit oil stove beside it and thawed it out. In P.M. father & I went to Swanson's and got his pig crate. Telephone men put up new wires on poles and in house. Gave us the old wire. I went to Attleboro in evening and saw Josephine. [*His second wife, Josephine M. Drahorad, who was in the hospital with the new baby, Walter Drahorad Bliss.*] We unloaded coal at bungalow.

A 1917 entry for Friday, February 2, reads:

Clear cold wind N.W. We got in our ice about 30 tons. Bowens Anderson & Father drew ice. Swanson worked on pond. Whittaker helped in ice house.

The bottom of the page records "39 eggs." The elements—particularly sunlight—had long controlled life. In the Bliss House attic there was an eighteenth-century sheet of paper with a letter written on one side; it had then been folded and the address put on the outside: "Mr. Aseph [sic] Bliss, In Rehoboth" (figure 101). The letter reads:

Rehoboth December ^th^22^nd^ 1797 Mr Bliss Sir I Now Set My Self down to write a Few lines to You to in form You of a Dance Next Thursday Night At the Hous[e] of Mr Thomas Carpenter ^the^ [4s?] If fare

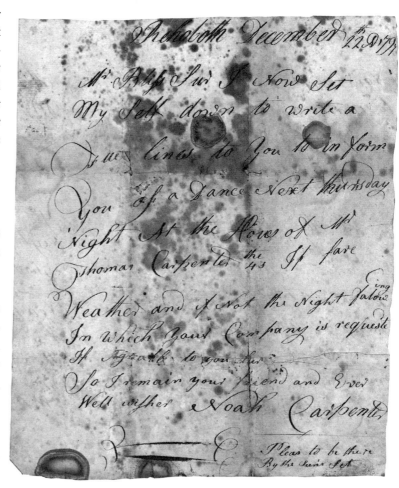

101 Letter from Noah Carpenter to Asaph Bliss, dated December 22, 1797

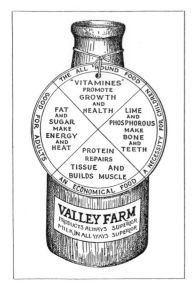

102 Advertisement for the Valley Farm, 1920s

1970) continued an American way of life that reached back to the founding settlers; he was Rehoboth and Massachusetts, New England and America. He farmed family land, and his concerns were those of his ancestors, particularly those involving education. Rehoboth is proud of its schools, boasting that it was the first town to introduce free education and did so in its first year, 1643. The Jacob Bliss will dated 1806 left to Asaph a share in the local schoolhouse. On an 1850 map the building is to the west of the Bliss House, while an 1895 map has it moved to the eastern side. During one visit, Richard Bliss said the school had stood to the west of the house; but Reuben Bowen, the neighbor to the east, complained that his children had to walk further than J. Walter Bliss's, a matter of about three minutes. When this became a serious contention, each family gave a small piece of land where their properties joined and the school was moved down the road and placed on the new site. (Figure 104 shows it in late nineteenth-century garb; in figure 87 it is the smallest of the four buildings grouped to the right—the ridge of the roof runs back from the road.)

During another visit, Mr. Bliss recalled that in 1920 there were sixteen one-room schoolhouses in Rehoboth. He saw in *Country Gentleman* that consolidated schools were being tried in the West, so he "read up on it and went to Town Meeting and proposed it." The chairman asked, "Does anyone want to vote against this?', and when no one leapt up, they declared it passed." They put Mr. Bliss on the school board and gave him $200 so he could consider the possibilities and develop and present a plan. "The anti's fought it again in Town Meeting, but there was a tie so the earlier vote held."

The plan was for a six-room school. The Selectmen told Richard Bliss they would not oppose it if it was reduced to four, so he accepted that compromise. In a year the new school, complete with busing, was such "a howling success that Central Rehoboth wanted one. Then even North

Weather and if Not the Night following In Which Your Company is requested If Agreeable to you, Sir. So I remain your friend and Ever Well wisher Noah Carpenter. Pleas[e] to be there By the Sun's Set.

After his return to the farm from New York in 1914, Richard Bliss tried chicken and dairy farming. The image in figure 102 is from one side of a 1920s handout advertising Valley Farm, as the Bliss homestead was then known, and milk. A commercially available advertisement was personalized by each farm owner. On the reverse side, paragraphs describe the virtue of milk under such headings as: MILK IS OUR BEST FOOD; "VITAMINES" [sic] NECESSARY FOR OUR HEALTH; PASTEURIZING OF MILK DESTROYS VITAMINES. The last includes a statement that "Valley Farm milk is clean milk. Valley Farm milk is NOT pasteurized. Valley Farm milk is whole raw milk.—Nothing is added—Nothing is taken from it." Further paragraphs define the dangers from bovine tubercle bacilli and the safety gained by testing cows for tuberculosis. But the farm proved to be an unreliable source of income and Mr. Bliss went to work for a dairy.

Richard Bliss (figure 103 as he appeared in

103 Richard Bliss, September, 1970   *104 Bliss School House, 1880s or 1890s*

Rehoboth, which owing to population leaving because of some financial disaster, hadn't enough children still wanted it and children had to be bused in. The original four-roomer is still a part of the big school complex, recently built for one million."

BEGINNING

WORKING JOURNAL

(Selections from the daily journal suggest the intensity and complexity of an active restoration project.)

Wednesday, 27. Mowed grass (towing after handle broke), and began sorting, cleaning out center back [*keeping room*] which now looks much bigger, and investigating the fireplace in front left [*study*] a little. There is clearly something back of the present

bricked up fireplace, maybe there are two rebuildings.

Thursday, 28. Continued cleaning out downstairs, and sorting into piles: keep, auction, and dump. Norman [*Herreshoff*] came to photograph house. Weeded a little. Mr. Bliss came with surveyors. It seems windows in slaughter–chicken house and shed—12 over 12, and 12 over 8 sash—are the 1780s main house sash. Most of the old glass intact and sash salvageable. Began on right front upstairs [*parlor chamber—from this point I have changed the entries to reflect my later room designations as used on the drawing in figure 132*]—took up linoleum and found 1940 newspaper.

Friday, 29. Trip to hardware store. Took off storm windows (20—numbered from front kitchen door around counterclockwise). Cleaned out cellar. Almost everything punky and rotted at least halfway up. Canned pickles, pickle relish, peaches, bottled beverages most gone bad. Barrels with hoops rusted. Jelly cupboard with bottom half rotted. Box of sand. Bin made of center-grooved boards lined with tin—must have been for water or to keep animals out. Water line on walls shows water must get 1 foot deep in cellar. Removed partition of center-grooved boards between cellar of ell and main house cellar. Much more light. There was a screen top for tin-lined bin. Five or so good cider barrels left. Cellar still needs raking. Set up fan blowing out, to pull air through basement. Beams are already drying out—visible moisture gone. Sorted upstairs, too. Plumber came and failed to make pump work. Cellar stairs began to collapse—patched them and relaid one step of stone stairs under bulkhead. Took out wicker chairs—sat in sun. After 2:00 lunch sorted back rooms of 2nd floor—made piles, not carrying. Future bathroom full of clothes (including home-dyed black), Xmas tree ornaments, poultry magazines, sheets, mostly torn. "Man-handled" one pink mattress and box spring down front stairs and sunned them on lawn. Put glass pane in one window. Merrill Cornell phoned about mortgage, etc. Manageable. Will start sleeping in house—plan is: back to Providence each night: wash and dry clothes, bath, dinner, then return to house for night on pink mattress and next day.

Saturday, 30. Finished cleaning out basement. Worked on cleaning out second floor. The [*Daniel*] Robbinses arrived and had lunch. Obvious most of chimney brickwork mixes used and unused brick. Went into keeping room and began with cold chisel opening bricks inside "Franklin."

Monday, June 1. Completed brooming and vacuuming attic, except under stoves east of staircase.

Tuesday, 2. Telephone replaced with new one. Found cooking fireplace and beehive oven. Bought industrial vacuum cleaner for $50. Re-vacuumed attic. Then decided to clean out kitchen and moved all I could out. Cleaned the shed—broomed floor, walls and ceiling—moved things to corner—took out chest of drawers from future laundry. Told David Smith [*real estate agent*] would like to buy 4 acres across road. Took down mantel in parlor. Made hole in south wall, found later sawn lath and plaster covering remains of wallpaper, but no evidence of paneling. Probably originally a thinner plaster wall.

Tried to open peekhole [*to area between chimneys*] above 4th step of front staircase—had been too damp to open before—it opened and saw back of beehive oven intact. *Beautiful* between chimneys—layers of board platforms mount upwards for standing on when building chimneys.

SUMMARY

Condition of House [*Summation made prior to beginning carpentry work, using Journal entries.*]

Cellar: Visible joists and sills pulpy and dripping wet. Seemed at first as if everything would have to be replaced, but as I get things cleared out and drier, and can see better, there is enough left that supplementary support alongside may do it. Cellar obviously sometimes floods. Dirt floor. Complicated by house having been shut up tight a year. Major problems: water from lack of gutter and downspouts gives nowhere for water from back roof to go except cellar; also, land behind house slopes toward it. Crawl space area under west half of house seems better, because drier and work was done behind clapboard when first-floor level of main house studded. Bugs obviously active throughout, and may necessitate some small repairs as well as major extermination job, but damage seems pretty slight, though pervasive.

Outside: Early clapboard, mostly salvageable (except behind piazza and perhaps lower half of sides of main house). Windows vary. A few have original beautiful cornice and/or sills—worth eventually having copies milled and put in throughout, but at a later stage. Frames seem to be right size except east window of parlor (where sill has been lowered to level of ell front windows) and four back windows. Seams in cornice and clapboard, and ground plan suggest west half of house built first. [*This was the opposite of the truth.*]

Back mostly shingled and in bad condition, clapboard area—from the west corner to door—in better state. Victorian back door—tatty and not handsome of its kind. Ugly modern metal bulkhead. Shed has asbestos shingles west and north and concrete base up 1½ feet.

Chimneys: Should be taken down to roofline, and relaid with same brick. Only shed one is urgent. Need dampers eventually; stuff with pillows or leaf-filled trash bags in the meantime. Flashing of later chimneys needs attention.

Propose at present:
1) move 1780s sash from shed and slaughter–chicken house into front of main house

2) put the only 1740s sash—now in upstairs back hall—in the upstairs front hall
3) shorten east parlor and second-floor study windows
4) not to eliminate the hodgepodge look of the back wall with its irregular fenestration and even (probably) replace rotting back door with another glazed one
5) remove the porch and eventually find a correct front door (1740–80)
6) keep the present 1780s fireplace wall of keeping room
7) not to change the ground plan

The idea is that both as a house and as a mode of survival for the present, I will change nothing unless some really worthwhile feature which is actually there, not hypothetical, can be restored by so doing, or there is some real disadvantage to leaving it. This holds up to 1900 or so.

THE EXTERIOR WORK

One of the most pressing needs was to dry out the basement under the east half of the house and ell. (The west half had only a crawl space.) I immediately made two small openings in the cellar foundation walls, and pushed air out the bulkhead with a fan. I closed the space around the fan to pull drier air more efficiently through the new openings and down from the house. The droplets of moisture on walls and wooden members quickly disappeared. Eventually the openings in the foundation were fitted with frames and sash with four lights in a row.

A new well was drilled approximately where the pile of rocks appears to the left of the house in figure 106. Since well-drilling is paid for by the foot, it is always a tense time—the parameters of what a well might cost are helpful but uncer-

105–106 Daniel Bliss House, 1970

tain guides. When the drilling reached the greatest of the estimates, the flow was not enough to run a modern house with a laundry, dishwasher, and two bathrooms. I had to decide whether to drill further in hopes of obtaining a stronger flow or to "work the well"—make what water there was flow as fast as possible in hopes new fissures would open and increase the amount available.

It was decided to go further and the bill for drilling was $1,000 beyond the original maximum estimate. The flow did become stronger but

it was still not up to modern standards. The drilling was halted and during the summer the water was run as much as it would flow: I left the sprinkler on and the fissures gave up silt and sand, repeatedly clogging the sprinkler and the dishwasher, but the amount did increase until it was more than adequate.

The old stone wall, at the right of figure 105, was to be carried across the front. Since the house sits at the end of a straightaway, I placed two giant stones either side of the stone steps where they acted as barriers. In time the wall was completed to the left (see plate VI).

The first changes to the exterior of the building were to remove the 1907–08 porch and check for rotten structural members, clapboards, and boarding. The emphasis was on replacing only what was unsavable. Since the house had stood without many structural features the inexperienced might think essential, I felt it would continue to do so if only the totally useless members were replaced. The rotten parts were cut away and new timber spliced in. What could be saved of the old corner boards was put back. Where new pieces were needed, the proper large bead molding was run along the edge of one board, and its back rabbeted to receive the other board with no molding (figures 109 and 110).

Wiring

I wanted the new electric meters to be placed inside the shed so those bulbous glass protuberances would not disturb any exterior wall. However, recent new rules made it necessary to have them outside so meter readers need not enter the house. They were placed on the back wall where it meets the east side of the shed. When I mentioned their ugly appearance to the installer, his comment was: "Oh, no one can see them from the road." So that *I* did not have to see them, I planted in front of them an old-fashioned rose, guaranteed to grow twenty feet high. Before replacing clapboards, I ran electrical and telephone wires

107 Daniel Bliss House, 1880s

108 Daniel Bliss House, 1970

between the boarding. Television or burglar alarm wires could also have been installed at this time. This is much easier than snaking them through plaster walls. Trenches dug to the well and septic system can be used for the main electrical and telephone wires to the house and outside electrical lights. (See Bibliography for more detailed discussions.)

Clapboards and Shingles

The basic house construction was of large timbers covered with heavy vertical oak planks that rose from the ground to the cornice. Holes were cut for doors and windows. The outer surface received clapboards or shingles and the inside split lath that held the plaster. When purchased, the back of the main building was mostly shingled but it had an area of clapboards (figure 122). The front of the large barn and the back and west of the house shed were covered with asbestos shingles. It was some time before I realized that the main walls visible from the road originally had clapboards: the front and ends of the house and ell, and the fronts of the chaise house and large barn, those less visible from the street, had all been shingled. (In 1970 the east side of the house

shed had clapboard [figure 120] but in an 1880s photograph [figure 107] it is shingled.)

The clapboards on the first floor of the front and ends of the main house were more widely spaced and of heavier material than those on the second story and ell (figures 105 and 108). Upon investigation, I found that the lighter clapboards were applied to original heavy *vertical* planking while the heavy clapboards were nailed to horizontal planks. Simultaneously, I discovered that the interior side of all walls with wide clapboards had new plaster on later sawn (rather than the earlier split) lath and that lath was attached to new studs applied to the planks (figure 143).

In the late nineteenth century, before the porch was added, the ground-floor level had been cut away and studding introduced. On the outside, this was covered with horizontal planking and broad clapboards; inside, the studs received new sawn lath and plaster. This rebuilding increased the thickness of the walls and the window frames had been made deeper. Also this diminished the amount of corner post projecting into the rooms. I decided not to rebuild the walls to their original thickness and to leave the wide clapboard on the end walls. To achieve an early feel on the front of the house, I removed the broad clapboards and

109–110 Corner boards and clapboards, 1970

put on narrow ones. To eliminate drafts through the uninsulated walls, heavy paper was placed over the planks before the new clapboards were applied.

The original clapboards had been about five feet in length. The ends of each had been skived (cut to long bevels); when in place they overlapped at the top, bottom, and each end (upper half of figure 111). I did not use short lengths or skived ends when installing the new clapboards because of the expense of extra installation time, and because I do not mind leaving evidence of changes for the discerning as long as the general impact is right. For the clapboarding and shingling I hired a young man without much experience at carpentry. I asked him to space the clapboards so they overlapped considerably near the ground; then, moving up the wall, to increase the amount of clapboard exposed. This early spacing puts a thick layer near the ground. Besides the gradual spacing, I wanted each clapboard to show a slightly uneven increase from those below and above, rather than a regular 2½, 2¾, 3, 3¼, and so on, so that it would look put up by eye rather than ruler (figure 115). Further, because the left end of the front facade was a foot and a half taller, the clapboards had to fan, showing greater width of surface at that end. The carpenter was loath to follow these directions, feeling that potential customers would think he could not measure. Yet the final effect achieved the subtlety of eye-controlled handwork—and looking at it always gave me great satisfaction.

The Front Door

The front doorway was an 1840s addition of little interest or merit; in fact, it seriously diminished the looks of the building. For a replacement it would have been possible to copy one of two fine 1780s Rehoboth doorways. The Colonel Thomas Carpenter House, seen in figures 112 and 113, was built just south of Route 44. (The door had two panels removed and glass inserted.) Also

111 Clapboards, 1970

nearby is Rehoboth's Old Parsonage with an entrance of the same date and design (figure 114). Such locally available precedents certainly encouraged copying one for the Bliss House. But if such a dramatic feature was once present, it seemed unlikely the Bliss family would have removed it, and there was no evidence of a pediment having been attached to the original planking under the center window of the second floor. So I judged it best to install a minimal doorway—one that would provide enough focal interest while not allowing a new feature to dominate the facade. I was given as a present a broad mid-eighteenth-century door with a wonderfully weathered paneled exterior

112–113 Colonel Thomas Carpenter House, Rehoboth, Massachusetts, built 1780s (Society for the Preservation of New England Antiquities)

114 Old Parsonage, Rehoboth, Massachusetts, doorway added 1780s (Society for the Preservation of New England Antiquities)

and vertically sheathed inner (figure 155). The surrounding architrave was based on the front-door of the Lincoln, Rhode Island, Israel Arnold House, and used molding details from parts of the Bliss House. The trim boards had bead run on their inner edges and cyma moldings attached on the outer (figures 116 and 117). Six lights capped the door, and the whole was topped by a crown molding following the original ones over the windows (figure 118). The window moldings are discussed further when the back of the building is reviewed.

The Ell

The first-floor level of the ell had heavy oak framing that perhaps predated the original part of the main house. It may have been an original structure on this property or another that was pulled up against the main house when the addition was put on in the nineteenth century. The upper level is of nineteenth-century construction. The ell chimney never serviced a fireplace but was installed for a stove. To clean that chimney and prepare it to take the furnace flue, I opened its base, where I found about four inches of sand with three clay pipes (seen on the table in figure 82) in the middle. They had not been smoked;

115 Front door, 1975

116 New two-part outside molding

117 Detail of front door, 1975

118 New window and door cornice molding

their stems were broken off to about five inches from the bowl, and they were all stamped: MCDOUGALL and GLASGOW. (The bowl of one is stamped TD and the spur under the bowl has a cast W; the other two spurs have a cast M.)[2] Above the sand was soot. Probably the pipes were placed in the chimney to ensure that it would always draw properly.[3]

The pre-porch view (figure 107), taken in the 1880s, shows a slightly disheveled fence still enclosing three large trees. In a view of the corner between house and ell taken about 1905 (figure 119), Richard Bliss on the right is holding a bunch of flowers while a cousin, Elmer Colwell, chastises him for getting his feet and the bottom four inches of his trousers wet. There were then

119 *Elmer Colwell (Richard's cousin), left, and Richard Bliss, right, about 1905*

wooden steps to the ell door. By 1970 these had been replaced by poured concrete steps and dampness between them and the sill had caused the latter to rot (figure 108). The late, wide clapboards are visible above the cousin's back.

The Shed

The shed points north from the ell of the house (figure 120). As seen in figure 107, it once had a shingled east wall and probably then did not have the small tool room on the north end. (Figure 107 shows it with one window to the north of the door; figure 120 with clapboard has a longer wall with two windows.) Mr. Bliss had poured a concrete floor and bracing walls that angled outward. The shed had been used for dairy and farm functions (separating milk and working with eggs). The small pane sash found there were exchanged with larger pane sash from the main house. I painted the clapboard east wall and all the exposed concrete dark like the clapboards of the house and ell. The asbestos shingles on the north and west

wall were replaced with cedar shingles (figures 121 and 124).

The Back

The lower level of the northern facade of the main building, to the west of the back door, had been treated like the rest of the main house: cut open, studded, and closed in with wide clapboards on horizontal planking (figure 122). I removed the clapboards and had the entire back reshingled. The nineteenth-century back door was not salvageable, so a similar modern door was installed. Unfortunately, its panes of glass are too vertical in orientation. (The fan seen in the window in

120 *East of ell and shed, 1970*

121 *East of ell and shed, 1975*

122 North side, 1970

123 Richard Bliss's wall and clothes poles, and west of chaise house, 1970

124 North side, 1975

figure 124 has served in every house I have worked on to draw out damp, dust, and paint fumes.)

I had intended to turn the shed into an eating porch by opening up the west wall (facing the bird feeder) with three or four French doors for the winter and screen doors for the summer. I wanted to eat with a sense of the out-of-doors and step onto the lawn through laurel and myrtle.

Drainage and Yard

When purchased, the ground behind the house sloped toward it and groundwater flowed into the basement. During one of his visits, Mr. Bliss recalled there had been a drain across the back lawn—a deep ditch lined with flat stones that went under the shed into the courtyard and carried off advancing water. When he put the concrete base under the shed, he eliminated the drain because he wanted an extensive grass lawn. To help prevent water from entering the cellar near the back doorway, he had moved the stepping stone aside, dug a giant hole, and filled it with rocks. These he covered with earth and then replaced the stepping stone. Contrary to what was intended, this acted like a dry well and allowed a freer flow of water into the house.

Moving aside the stepping stone again, I removed the rocks, packed the cavern with clay, then replaced the stepping stone. The back lawn was graded to slope away from the house. That pitch met the ground rising to the knoll and made a slight valley that moved water around behind the shed onto the driveway. Mr. Bliss said that he had always intended to put up a gutter across the back of the house, and had even called a contractor who never showed up. Although the house did not originally have gutters, I put up a wooden one with a V-shaped profile on wooden brackets across the back (figure 125). The gutter sloped to the right where a drainage pipe went into a wooden downspout of square section (figure 124). At the left, the gutter projects some eighteen inches beyond the roof and had an open end and no

downspout; what water spills out drops to the drive.

The large pole sticking up in the middle of the backyard in figure 122 was placed there by Mr. Bliss. His wife had clotheslines that ran from the house to this pole, passing in front of the bulkhead to the left of the rear door. (Clothes hanging on lines in this position are seen to the right in figure 203.) Mr. Bliss found that the lines interfered when he was delivering barrels of cider (which he hardened in the cellar) to the basement bulkhead. Therefore, he built a stone wall just about at the bottom right of figure 122 and put poles on the hill above the wall (figure 123). The clotheslines were then run between the new poles and that in the lawn. To hang clothes, Mrs. Bliss had to walk out to the stone wall, climb the stone steps, and go to the upper poles to reach the lines!

Windows

The 1740s house probably had only narrow 9 over 6 sash. The 1780s reworking added 12 over 12 sash on the first floor and 12 over 8 on the second, although a few of the 1740s smaller windows were retained. As the small paned sash began to rot and became unfashionable, they were replaced by larger pane 6 over 6 sash, and the earlier ones were used in the slaughter–chicken house and the shed. (That such homesteads were not always as carefully repaired and done up as restorations now present them is evidenced by the missing pane of glass from the upper sash in figure 95 and the look of the fence in figure 107.) The gable ends of the main house still retained small pane sash. The east end had an original 9 over 3 sash (figures 108 and 193), while the west gable had two windows, one in each of the small, nineteenth-century rooms.

I took the early sash from the shed and slaughter–chicken house and reused them in the main house. In the late nineteenth-century shed I put the 6 over 6 sash removed from the main house. This in fact falsified—turned inside out—the historic sequence where old and unfashionable features went to the lesser areas.

The only rear window not altered since the ell was added was that at the left of the second story. It had a cornice molding the width of the window integrated into the main house cornice. The larger, right-hand second-story windows had original cornices but they were one pane narrower than the present windows (figure 125). Clearly, these moldings once capped narrower and shorter 9 over 6 sash. I decided to shorten these large windows, to bring their bottom line level with the window over the back door but not to narrow them. (Figure 122 shows them as found and figure 124 as shortened.) This nonhistoric compromise kept a degree of light in a northern room.

The window over the rear door had no individual cornice (figure 126), although it had what was probably the oldest sash. Its muntins were nine sixteenths of an inch in width; all the other small pane muntins were narrower, dating from the 1780s rebuilding. It let light into the old but not original back hall (figure 181).

Most of the outside window sills had been replaced and did not have the large half-round molding remaining on a few early Bliss sills, and on the Carpenter House as seen in figure 113. Without replacing the sills I could have nailed on a large half-round molding. Some replaced sills were very thin and I fattened these with a strip along their lower edge. But some needed an entirely new outer edge. For these I used pieces with an unhistoric groove on the underside. The top face of sills slopes down to drain water away from the sash and some of it naturally laps around and under, heading toward the junction of the bottom of the sill and the clapboard. With the new design, the water hits the groove and drops off. (Figure 127 shows the groove in the section of the sill that comes out from the lower sash.)

I had wooden storm windows made and used small slide-in screens. Perhaps now I would use combination storm windows and screens. Some historic houses fill an entire outer or inner open-

125–126 Windows and gutter, north facade, 1975

127 New window sill from sash outward

ing of a window with one sheet of glass or plastic during the winter. If glass, it can be enclosed in a narrow metal edge and screwed into place or secured by metal catches that fix into a thin metal strip nailed inside the window trim. During the summer all that shows is the edge of that strip. Plastic can be pierced for screws. For the slaughter–chicken–guesthouse, I used glass storm windows with a thin metal edge inside the sash.

Roof

The front roof was reshingled with pressure-impregnated, fire-retardant wooden shingles. It is often said that using wooden shingles increases fire insurance costs, but I have not found this to be true. The roof at the rear, still sound, was left with its asphalt shingles. The vertical lines in the roof as seen in figure 124 show the location of the rafters. The boards between them holding the shingles have sagged to slight curves. There is usually *no* reason to correct this. Indeed, it should be prized as character developed over the years.

Chimneys

Often it is possible to strengthen brickwork by pointing it—cleaning out the mortar to a depth of about an inch, and filling in with new mortar. This is only necessary if there is danger of an opening developing through the bricks and let-

ting moisture in or sparks out. Part of the charm of old brick surfaces is that the mortar has moved back and the bricks project. When pointing *is* necessary, the mortar should match the old in color and texture, and be recessed at an angle that will shed the water and allow the bricks above to seem to stick out. A soft mortar that will move with seasonal climatic changes should be used. Portland cement is wrong for two reasons: it shrinks slightly when it dries, leaving thin openings; and it is so hard it will not adjust as the bricks move during climatic changes. (See Bibliography.)

It proved to be best to take the chimneys down to the roof. Much of the mortar between the bricks above this level was missing and sparks might have passed through the brick; also, as early chimneys were made without flashing, this allowed it to be added easily. I was fearful that the attitude of many modern workers, "I can do it better than they did," would produce unacceptable chimneys. Early bricks were in many instances harder than the mortar, and only a thin line was used. Nowadays mortar can be stronger than the brick, and the tendency is to put a thick layer between each course. The design of the main chimney of the Bliss House (figure 128) was very simple. It rose straight toward the top where it stepped out five eighths of an inch for two courses, then back to the lower dimension for the two final

128 Rebuilt center chimney, 1975

courses. That would not be hard to reproduce, but I wanted to be sure that the mason did not increase the amount of mortar, making it grossly visible. Also, thicker mortar with the original number of brick courses would make the chimney too tall.

Before the chimney was dismantled, I placed a stick against it and marked off the bottom and top of each course of bricks with the mason watching, and he understood that when the chimney was finished, I would check the spacing. He did excellent work and the resulting chimney was accurate (figure 128). In the middle of the front of the main chimney he replaced an eight-inch-square clay plaque which had fired into it the digits "17" and two digits scratched in after firing that probably read "42." Undoubtedly such plaques could be purchased and the year of the chimney completed by the owner. If the date does read 1742, it confirms the Bliss family tradition of the date

of the first building; but the upper part of the chimney stack must date from the 1780s. Therefore the plaque may have been reused in the rebuilding, or it might be a 1780s plaque given the earlier date.

Early chimneys did not have flue liners. They are not necessary if the bricks are properly pointed. Too many reproduction chimneys have flue liners which are allowed to stick up above brickwork. One indicator of an early house's visual strength is the massive chimney. To break its top edge with a bouncing edge of usually light-colored liners diminishes its power and looks silly. (In England, chimneypots were used from early times, but exposed flue liners lack their charm.)

Paint and Plantings

The unusual front facade fenestration of the Bliss House produces a lopsided effect (figure 129).

129 Daniel Bliss Homestead, 1971

130 Daniel Bliss House, 1972

*131 Daniel Bliss House, 1975
(*The Magazine Antiques,
*Helga Photo Studio); seen also
as plate* VII

The one window at each level west of the front door did not properly balance the paired windows to the east. I wondered for a long time how to unite the two halves. Further, I wanted to make the house appear more distant from the road. I knew dark colors make objects appear to recede. One evening while driving back to the house, I noticed that the setting sun made the window-panes dark green. The next day I saw an advertisement for paint in which an old barn had a ratty brown-green bronze color. It occurred to me that if one painted the clapboards a dark brown-green, it would unify the front facade because the windows would be less visible. This would also make the house recede from the road while infusing it into the vegetation I was planting. I mixed two parts rather bright green with one part bright red, which produced a rich, warm, dark green. Over the years the elements made the red dominant, and while the rest became a warm brown, the shadowed areas under each clapboard remained green. The result was a fabulously varied surface.

The rather distorted view produced by a wide-angle lens in figure 129 shows the house a year after purchase. The lilacs, taken from a friend's lane, look awful. Figure 130 shows the house the following winter. (It is easy to see the extra-width clapboards on the east wall of the main house.) Three years later, a fuller growth screened the house from the road (figures 131, and color plates VI and VII). (The plantings are discussed in greater detail in Chapter 2 under figure 57. See also Bibliography under Landscaping.)

5

Restoring the Bliss House — Inside

THE INTERIOR WORK

Basement

The interior work paralleled that occurring on the outside. The first task was to make sound all of the lower supporting members. Often because of rotting at a lower level there has been settling in the upper floors. If these changes happened early in the history of the house, as at Rehoboth, adjustment has probably already been made to plaster, moldings, and doors. If the sagging is recent, jacking to make things level should be done before anything is replaced. If jacking seems necessary, remember that altering one part can cause other features that are sound to crack or move out of plumb. In evaluating what you should do, you have to decide whether it is better to leave things as they are and enjoy the changes or begin what may be a long series of adjustments. In many early houses out-of-kilter parts have for years been supported by props; adding lolly columns may be a good solution to providing permanent additional support.

Before doing any reclapboarding or putting new shingles on the Bliss House, the bottom boards covering the sills and those over the corner posts were pulled off. The bottom three or four feet of the corner posts and areas of the sill had to be replaced and new parts were spliced into the old. However, most sills were either sound or retained sufficient wood to serve. The first-floor joists in the area of the damp basement were far gone but I decided not to remove them. (Probably because water had not gathered there, those in the crawl space at the west end were sounder.) One of the most destructive approaches to early houses is to assume that the timbers holding the lower floors must be pulled out if they show signs of deterioration, for this normally also removes the first-floor boards they support.

First I sprayed all the basement wood with Cuprinol wood preservative to kill bugs and dry rot fungi. Then new, similarly treated joists were run against and bolted to the old ones (figure 133).

Since the basement had at times flooded, a sump pump was installed below floor level. Instead of pouring a concrete floor I covered the earth with

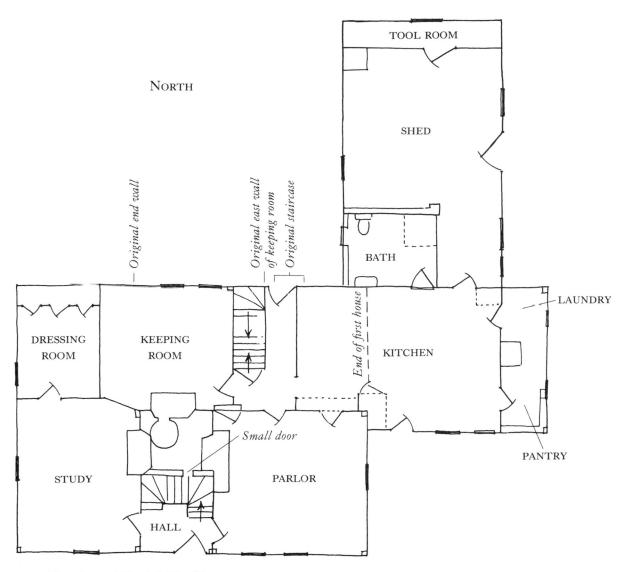

NORTH

TOOL ROOM

SHED

Original end wall

Original east wall of keeping room

Original staircase

BATH

End of first house

DRESSING ROOM

KEEPING ROOM

KITCHEN

LAUNDRY

STUDY

Small door

PARLOR

PANTRY

HALL

*132 First floor of Daniel Bliss House,
indicating original location of walls*

133 Basement: new joist bolted to original

heavy plastic, punching holes in it to allow venturesome water to flow, and put down a three- to four-inch layer of large pebbles. On these I placed boardwalks. The new furnace was set on a concrete slab with its top surface six inches higher than the level of the sump pump intake.

In some houses masonry walls, interior or exterior, draw water up from the foundations in what is called "rising damp"; in the upper walls this moisture causes paint and plaster to crumble away. Although it is difficult to stop this condition, a variety of remedies and literature on this problem can be found in the Bibliography.

Heating: Deciding what kind of heat to use in early houses is a major consideration. A hot-air system has the advantage of requiring only small openings in the floor, and humidity control and air conditioning can be added to the newer units. This heating may prove dusty, however, if the basement is not very clean and there are not adequate filters. Also, it means large ducts must be run to each room. Sometimes these can be hidden in closets or inside the walls boxing the chimney (see "Catalogue Your House's Secret Passages" under Electrical and Plumbing in the Bibliography). I find baseboard radiators impossible to accept aesthetically—they are much higher than early baseboards, except in grander nineteenth-century houses. They sweep too imposingly behind the furniture and radiate heat against everything. One of the charms of the Bliss homestead was the very narrow baseboard, mostly embedded in the plaster. It carried the horizontal wood of the floor up the wall in a minimal manner. I find that freestanding radiators painted the same color as the wall, and placed under the windows where they best counteract drafts, are the best solution, unless hot-air vents in the floor are used. Until the cost of electricity became exorbitant, I preferred to heat with electric wires in the ceiling, which I used in the guesthouse discussed in the last chapter.

If you decide on oil as a source of heat, consider very seriously placing the storage tank outside the house. One of the great Houston, Texas, collections of Eastern furniture was partially destroyed by a fire rushing up from the oil tank, and the owner was only just rescued from the stalled elevator. When using oil, be aware that during delivery it may get spilled onto adjacent buildings, lawns, or shrubs, killing whatever it soaks. At Rehoboth, I placed a two-foot-wide concave metal dish around the pipe, sinking it about four inches below ground. This directed any spills toward the center and away from neighboring bushes.

The furnace will need one of the old flues or a new one built for it. Normally, each fireplace has a separate flue, although it may be encased in one or more chimney stacks. Customarily one of these flues is employed and many builders believe this makes its fireplace inoperable—indeed, that fireplace is often sealed up. In fact, it is usually possible to bring the furnace pipe up through a closet or inside the walls boxing the chimney, and have it enter into a flue above the draft shelf of the fireplace. One owner in New Hampshire took down the left end of the keeping-room fireplace and moved it in four inches. This added sufficient room to what was already inside the paneling for the furnace flue to pass up between the new end and the boxing wall and turn into the fireplace above the draft shelf. In Rehoboth, I used the cooking stove chimney at the east end of the kitchen ell.

First Floor

General: The more you succeed in retaining an unbiased interpretation of what you are doing, the more satisfying the results will be. Stick to the evidence the house itself gives you. Restorers always make changes of which they are unaware and the only hope of approaching the truth is to follow every shred of evidence. When restoring a brick wall on the second floor of the John Brown House in Providence, we knew exactly where it stopped for the door openings because there were knife or chisel marks on the subfloor showing their extent. When the masons finished building the new wall, the verticals of the two doorways were half an inch to the west of where they should have been. The masons' explanation was "That's the size bricks we had." We could have sawn away the brick that extended too far and mortared out the other sides to the proper size. Instead, we planed down one side of the wood frames and fattened out the other. The final openings were properly located.

Have faith in what you do know and use early methods if they seem to make sense. When Faith Bybee was working on the group of houses she had moved to Roundtop, Texas, she knew that some kitchen floors were made of packed earth, hardened by the application of oxblood. When dry and polished, the floors look like tile. Asked how she should make such a floor, the only response could be: "Buy an ox, or get blood from a slaughterhouse."

Before you begin, if you are going to remove moldings temporarily to make repairs or changes, photograph each wall, for it is easy to forget what came from where. If it is not an original surface and you will paint over it, take a broad felt pen and put large numbers on all the moldings you are going to take off, then photograph the walls. If you want to clean up the plaster walls of a room temporarily, or even for years, it is possible to make a dramatic effect by covering them with unpatterned white ceiling paper.

Electricity: Run wires, even those for television aerials, telephones, and security system, before replacing anything. Take all precautions when wires are installed. Be sure they are grounded and that there are circuit breakers. Light plugs should be low. Some people like to place them in the baseboard (but check if local fire codes may prevent this). Others put them just above the baseboard in the plaster. For the electrician, this is easier than in the baseboard, and he or she may say the law will not allow outlets in the baseboard when this is not true. Still others put them in the floor, but these can be dangerous because spilled liquids can cause short circuits and dust accumulates in them. It is possible to use models with screw-in caps, which minimizes the problem. Sometimes the entire plate is recessed about a half-inch into the floor and a wooden piece put over them when not in use. I find it unsatisfactory to put outlets where most electricians seem to want them, two or three feet above the floor; you have an ugly wall and constantly dripping wires.

Switches to lights should be inconspicuously placed, certainly not in the center of a large area where you will want to hang a painting. These too can be placed in the floor and fitted with a tap switch that can be turned off and on by foot. Ceiling lights are always difficult unless you have a house from the gas or electric era. Seventeenth- and eighteenth-century houses, except of the grander sort, rarely had chandeliers. As in a museum, a strongly lit ceiling and upper wall will draw the eye away from the lower part of the room, and high indirect lighting is rarely satisfactory. Ceiling lights in halls and stair areas now seem logical. I have used both modern and electrified early lamps in these areas.

Parlor

WORKING JOURNAL

Tuesday, June 2. Took down mantel in parlor, breaking one metal bracket. The paneling was perhaps originally red with dark green over it. The red—if it is indeed there—may be first finish coat or a primer under green. Next coats are: blue, beige, white and white. Molding around "tall cupboard" [*glazed door in figure 135*] on north wall, both doors, and the remaining old sections of baseboard is the same. Casings of

134 *Parlor fireplace wall, 1970*

135 *West and north parlor walls, 1975*

corner posts seem to lack the early colors—research. Made hole in south wall—later lath and plaster cover remains of wallpaper, but no evidence of paneling. Probably originally a thinner plaster wall. Now, rough 2 × 4s between outer planks that make up sheathing of house and present lath [*figure 143*].

Thursday, 4. Following shape seen in plaster, opened plastered-up doorway between parlor and back hall [*right door in figure 135 and at left of figures 136 and 137*]; door casing intact minus most of trim. Removed moldings on doorway Richard Bliss put from parlor to kitchen [*right opening in figure 136*].

Monday, 8. P.M. Searched chaise house attic and barns, found original door from parlor to back hall, and most of the original trim moldings for doorways and windows of parlor and study—including window-sill trim. Also one 12 over 12 size window frame.

Tuesday and Wednesday, 9 and 10. Removed Victorian moldings from parlor, study, and dressing room, and can mount original moldings found in chaise house on present frames and sills. Took out the modern and nineteenth-century cupboards and moldings from keeping room.

SUMMARY

Parlor colors: The green I have just used is a good match of the original color in the bottom coat. First thought bottom layer was red but not so. Green matches areas scraped down to and clearly seen when removed the heavy coats on fireplace wall with paint remover. Second coat was a nineteenth-century powdery blue—sample square left in glazed cupboard. On door to hall it is lighter and more powdery (but this door had been further from the smoke of the fireplace and in the chaise house). Third coat a medium-light beige or ochre. Two whites above that.

The original green was on the fireplace wall, all door trim (including that of the "tall cupboard" at the left of the north wall, and the two eight-panel doors), and the original window moldings. Could not find any green paint on the sides of the window moldings; but there was blue detectable on the *sides* of the sills' astragal moldings. No green on the shelves of the "tall cupboard"; the blue was the bottom coat on those. The earliest coat on the interior of the small fireplace wall cupboards was the beige.

The floor and the surviving original baseboard and the equivalent distance up the paneling and door frames (but *not* across the doors) was a very blackish brown [*figures 135 and 145*], bittersweet chocolate with liquorice, which has been matched. No patch of the original color left as evidence for it was too worn to convey much except in the aggregate. (Most of the baseboards were replacements. Milled new to match the surviving original.) The top coat on the floor, when I took off the later narrow fir floor, was a light pumpkin, nineteenth-century shade.

Fireplace wall cupboard: The two cupboard doors over the fireplace are missing. There definitely were doors, because the paneling is recessed for them, and in paint-removing the paneling, found the original hinge holes filled with putty, *after* the blue paint stage. (Thus doors removed when room painted beige.) They had been affixed with screws, not nails, since the screws of small right-hand cupboard are still in place and half-covered by corner molding and their screws are the early non-pointed with the slot off-center type. This little door had a cast-glass

136 *North parlor wall: original doorway to back hall at left, later doorway to kitchen at right, 1970*

137 *North and east parlor walls, 1975*

(iridescent) mid- to late nineteenth-century doorknob on it. I am waiting to be sure I don't find the center cupboard doors in a barn and so have painted the cupboard recess the same green as paneling, which it never was. If I can't find them, will copy the right-hand small door.

Doors: The door into the back hall had been removed after first white coat. It had been in the chaise house attic and was in bad shape. I mended it and reinforced it with iron patches, found in large barn. It was red on the back, same as base coat of back hall moldings and keeping room. It always had HL hinges but had first swung from the east frame. Later (before being painted at the blue stage) it was made to swing as it now does, from the west frame [*figure 135*]. (Does this tell us something about the "tall cupboard" to its left?) [*Yes, it did. The exterior moldings of the tall cupboard had the first layer of green paint, but the cupboard interior had blue as a first color. As we will see, that cupboard filled what was once a doorway between the parlor and the keeping room, and the door to the hall was changed to swing open over it when it became a cupboard.*] Didn't hinge the door to back hall as it was first installed, but in its second guise. Swinging from that direction, the large wall space is kept clear. Mr. Bliss says he plastered up the doorway to the back hall as an adult, and opened up the new one into the kitchen. Can't recall but *think* he said door to hall was already off.

The "tall cupboard" had a 1900-ish door—low-waisted and four panels with almost no fielding. It had only the two white paints on it, and clearly was much later than even the shelves. The bottom part of the interior of the cupboard has never been painted, suggesting there was once a glazed door, or just sloppy painters. There is a hole at back right of second shelf from top for supporting a shelf at right angles. This shows the shelves were once used somewhere else. The glazed door I put in has no authority. Purchased it as it seemed suitable as a pure guess for what might possibly have been there at the early cupboard stage. If the door frame was once the main doorway into the keeping room, it presumably then had an eight-panel door like the others. The door I put in had been hung with one HL hinge below and one H hinge with shaped edges above, which I reused.

The HL hinges and latches of the other doors of this room had been removed and butt hinges installed. Found marks that indicated the eighteenth-century hinges and latches found in the barn were right and put them back. Certain about hinges, the exact type of latch is less sure—at least in the back hall. Size of paint buildup makes certain both parlor doors had oval end pulls [*figure 155*].

Moldings for parlor, study, dressing area: The basic 1780s window trim and inside window sills (all of which are identical in parlor and study) found in the top of the chaise house—they can be divided by paint history—turned out, on inspection, to be not quite complete for either front room. There seem to be only two parlor sill moldings. The east parlor window sill is 3¾ inches lower than other two parlor windows and one quarter inch wider. It also lacks the original green paint. This raises the problem of whether there was always a side window. If not, that would be without parallel in my experience; if so, why enlarge it so oddly? Since both rooms have incomplete moldings, should I lump the two lots together for a complete parlor, the most formal and elaborate of the two? The answer seems to be that I will have to do some milling to complete these rooms, so why not put back the old where it came from and add new where it is needed?

Floor: Original floor was under narrow fir floor and in *super* condition, even pale pumpkin paint over a dark red-brown, except for a band along the south edge which is all rotted. Will patch.

Brickwork: Fireplace not bricked up, just closed with tin with a stove hole through it. After removing narrow board floor, lowered hearth to wide board level and found the original height was as I have put it back—found one bit of powdery pink brick underneath which shows softer, probably earlier type of brick. Returned pattern as close to the other surviving hearths as possible in the space. Took down the later extra layer of brick at the back of the fireplace. The original back is there but too damaged and so put the extra layer back, exactly as it was.

The outer face of the fireplace bricks seemed originally to have had a very thin coat of plaster to smooth it and white paint, or perhaps just layers of whitewash. On this was bright red paint and then a later thick plaster (very ugly).

The parlor at first seemed heavily altered, which was, in fact, true; but the original floor, except for the southern end, was in good condition and most of the original moldings were found and grafted in. On the fireplace wall, a modern man-

tel was easily removed (shown by the dark line of early beige paint above the lower panels in figure 134). Two small doors were missing from the cupboard above. In the north wall—to the right of the fireplace—was a closet with a very late door (right of figure 134, where its door has been removed, and center of 135, where it shows the glazed door I added). It was once a doorway into the keeping room. To the right of that was a doorway Richard Bliss had closed when he made a new one directly into the kitchen. It is seen opened up but without the outer stages of its moldings to the left in figure 136 and as completely reinstalled at the left in figure 137.

The moldings of the door Mr. Bliss added between parlor and kitchen have been removed in figure 136, and the plastered-up wall is seen in figure 137. Here and in the study the window trim and most of the baseboard had been updated in the late nineteenth century with heavy moldings: I found the window trim and the door to the back hall and its trim stored in the chaise house. Upon seeing them returned to their original places, even to using some of the nails remaining of the door trim in their original holes, Mr. Bliss said gleefully: "I knew I shouldn't throw them away."

Hoping that the small doors to the cupboard over the fireplace would be discovered in the attic or one of the barns, I finished the room without them. About a year later, when finally convinced they would not turn up, two copies were made of the small door to the right. The fielding or raising of the panels on this fireplace wall, as with the vertical sheathing in other areas, is particularly deep, and the recessing edge is slightly curved—a plane with a curved blade must have been employed.

When copying parts, it is important to remove the paint where you are taking the design. Otherwise, it is not necessary to remove paint unless the layers obscure the form of the decorative shaping. If paint must be removed, do it with a chemical solvent, an electrically heated scraper, or a heat gun rather than a blow-torch. Too many

138 New three-part inside molding

*139 Two-part inside molding: hall side of parlor to
back-hall doorway*

houses have been lost because wood is so easy to
ignite. Also rats' nests and other combustible rub-
bish accumulate under paneling, moldings, and
floors. Although you may think you have everything cooled down when you leave for the night,
this may not be the case.

Moldings: The interior moldings employed three
basic shaped pieces of wood (figure 138). These
were joined either as a two- or a three-part molding (figures 139 and 138). The first is like the
exterior combination found in figure 116. The
remaining board surrounding the doorway to the
back hall had on its inner edge the simple bead
molding (left of figure 136), and was like the
lower board in figure 138. What was missing
from the parlor side was the second and third
stages that originally covered the dark, unpainted
area. These were found in the chaise house. The
broader of the two had a cyma, or reverse-curve
molding, and the narrow, a big cyma shape. The
fancier rooms of the house—parlor, front hall,
study, and the main bedroom—used this three-
part molding. Other rooms used the two-part
version, and the hall side of the door Mr. Bliss
closed in had a two-part molding, as seen in figure
139. (Moldings in early houses, as on early furniture, were usually built of several pieces. This
practice should be followed when copying them,
for it permits a slight variation in spacing which
gives them life.)

The old trim from one of the window sills is
seen from the rear in figure 140 and shows the
original nails and the return molding—the part
added to the end at a forty-five-degree angle and
run into the wall. The dark area is without paint
and was originally embedded in the plaster. When
the walls were studded in the late nineteenth century, the window frames were thickened and made
flush with the outer surface of the plaster. In reap-
plying the old moldings, I mounted them on what
was there, not in the plaster, and this made them
stick out further than originally. It was not clear
from paint evidence whether the sides of the

moldings, where they left the plaster, were painted white or the trim color. I decided to paint them white to diminish the sense of mass. I could not find the original green on the return of the sill molding but the blue coat was there so I carried the green around to the sides, as in figure 141. This may well be an inaccurate combination. The few missing sill moldings for the front rooms were reproduced (as seen in figure 142).

When applying new parts, countersink the nails and put putty over them. Do not let yourself be seduced into using copies of large-headed, hand-made nails and leave them showing on the surface. The original intention was to have a smooth, painted molding, not a surface studded with iron-work.

Floor: The view of the south wall of the parlor (figure 143) shows the rotten ends of the floor-boards removed and partly patched. I sliced away about fourteen inches, making the cut above the

141 1780s window molding reinstalled

140 Back of 1780s window-sill molding

142 New molding for window sills

center of the first joist. Instead of piecing each board to follow the line of the original board, I ran a long board across the end, supporting the near side on half the original joist. The further side rests on a new strip nailed to the sill. Such repairs are standard in early houses and I saw no reason for not doing this rather than adding little ends to each of the old boards.

It is possible sometimes to understand the original movement of people within the house by studying the wear patterns on the floor. When walls have been taken down, this can show where doorways and other major features were placed.

The new wide baseboards were replaced with narrow boards that looked, when installed, like the lower stage of the standard indoor composite molding (figure 138). The boards were in fact one inch thick, but when embedded in the plaster they appeared thin (figure 136).

Floor paint: There is strong evidence that most eighteenth-century floors were not painted but left natural and scrubbed very clean. Lye water was used to produce a beautiful white, smooth surface (but not the high gloss often found today). Sometimes the boards were covered with loose sand, which at times had elaborate patterns scratched into it. Probably, in most houses, the painting of floors began in the nineteenth century.[1]

Evidence of the attention paid to eighteenth-century floors is shown by a passage in Lydia Huntley Sigourney's *Sketch of Connecticut Forty Years Since* (1824). This account also documents the scarcity of carpets. Here one is thought to be a bed coverlet accidentally placed on the clean floor:

Mr. Larkin, at entering the apartment, seemed desirous to make his way on that narrow strip of the floor which in those days was always permitted to surround the carpet. At length a large table, which he doubted whether it were decorous for him to move, obstructed his course, and he exclaimed with some perplexity,—

"I *must* [there was no way around it] tread on the kiverlid." The lady supressing a smile said,—

"I beg, good Mr. Larkin, that you would step on the coverlet. It would save Beulah some labour, who

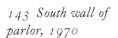

143 South wall of parlor, 1970

prides herself on the whiteness of the floor, which she daily scours."

Thus assured, he made one or two strides towards a chair which she placed for him, walking on tiptoe, and murmuring with some regret, as he rested his heels upon the hearth,—

"Your ha-ath [hearth] too, is clean as a chenny tea-cup, Ma'am. I hate to put my coarse huffs on it. But I ha'nt been used to seeing kiverlids spread on the floor to walk on. We are glad to get 'em to kiver us up with a nights. This looks like a boughten one," he added, examining the figure, and feeling its texture. "'Tis exceeding curous. They must have had a pretty many treadles in the loom that wove this."

The Lady remarked that the use of carpets, like other luxuries, was gaining ground too rapidly among those who were often deficient in real comfort. "Silks and satins put out the kitchen-fire, as a wise man has said."[2]

In figure 134, three pieces of floor covering found in the house rest on shelves over the fireplace; they are described in figures 198 through 200.

Heating pipes: The studding, added when most of the first-floor walls were replaced, meant that the early split lath with its uneven widths (figure 163) had been replaced by sawn lath of regular dimensions (figure 143). By this photograph the nineteenth-century baseboard has been removed and the sash are those moved in from the shed. The copper pipes ran to the radiator above. All the radiators were fed from one large pipe that circled around the edge of the house near the outside wall, and a pipe for returning the water accompanied it. If I were doing the house now, I would have two or more heating zones with separate thermostats. One set of pipes from the furnace would serve the lower story, another the upper story, and perhaps a third certain rooms that were virtually never used. The main pipes and those in the walls were carefully insulated, for there is little between them and the elements. Water expands as it freezes and frequently cracks the pipes; to repair them, the walls or floor would have to be reopened.

Fireplace: The fireplace opening had been covered with a metal sheet with a hole for the stove pipe. The fireplace crane was in place behind it. The lower part of the back had a brick facing (figure 144). I started to remove this and found that the original bricks behind had been so eaten away by fire that either they had to be replaced or the area filled with mortar. Mortar would have produced a very unsatisfactory appearance, and to eat out the remains of the old bricks and replace them could be done at some later date, so I chose the visual effect that someone, probably in the nineteenth century, had created by facing this part. The effect is rather like using an iron fireback.

The hearth had been raised about an inch to bring it level with the new floor. The bricks were laid in straight courses, which did not accord with hearths that had not been reworked. When relaying the hearth at the original level, I followed the pattern of the undisturbed examples: each course of bricks turned at the ends and went toward the fireplace. I do not like early hearth bricks laid up in visible mortar, for it is usually an unacceptable color and always visually intrusive. In relaying the hearth I first put a layer of mortar, then a half inch of loose sand with a slightly uneven top surface, then the bricks. The uneven sand allows the top of the bricks to undulate slightly and appear less newly laid. I poured sand on the bricks and broomed it back and forth until it filled the crevices. Loose sand near the top gets on the floor and scratches it, so after the sand had settled, I vacuumed the top: the upper eighth of an inch or so disappeared and the hearth looked fine. (If your house calls for a brick hearth and you do not have enough depth for full bricks, do not use marble or slate or something inappropriate. Have the back half of old bricks sawn away by a professional.) The outer face of the fireplace brick had been mortared over a painted surface. I removed the mortar and painted the brick, thus allowing the unevenness of the surface to show.

In the hearth to the right of the fireplace opening was a circular-shaped depression, seen in

144 *West wall of parlor, 1975 (*The Magazine
Antiques, *Helga Photo Studio); seen also as plate* VIII

145 *Depression in parlor hearth for fireplace tools*

figure 145, which probably held fireplace equipment from sliding. During the eighteenth century it was possible to obtain pieces of stone for this purpose about six to eight inches square and approximately an inch thick, with a circular hollow on one side. This depression in a brick was a local response and is found in a few other New England houses.[3]

Early fireplaces did not have dampers. These are essential if you choose not to heat your neighborhood. The first winter at Rehoboth there were no dampers and no door to the attic. Before I added a door and stuffed the flues with pillows (garbage bags full of leaves work as well), the oil truck visited almost as frequently as the postman. I watched a professional put in one tip-and-slide damper for $200 and then, following his method, I installed them in the other fireplaces—except for that in the guesthouse. Large chimneys often attract birds and allow mosquitoes to enter. You may wish to screen against these, but if you use the fireplaces, soot will close a fine mesh screen. A close-fitting damper will control the mosquitoes; chicken wire across the top will stop birds.

Ceiling: In figure 134 the ceiling has a large hole in it. There was an opening between this and the room above to allow heat to pass to the bedchamber. It was covered each side by an iron grill. I had found that the keeping room originally had exposed rafters, so I opened the parlor ceiling near the vent to see if this ceiling had been similarly exposed. There was "summer beam" construction (the cracks in the plaster of the ceiling, seen in figure 144, show the line of the large beam as it moves out from the edge of the present fireplace paneling), but the wood under the plaster showed no sign of paint, dirt, or molded edges to suggest it was ever exposed.

Doors and hardware: The doors in the house were of three basic dates. Five were probably from the 1740s half-house and were hung on strap hinges. Four of these five had two panels (figure 188) and their pulls had triangular-shaped ends (figure 189). The fifth was a batten door of vertical molded boards (figure 174) decorated like the related sheathing in the keeping room and kitchen. The doors from the 1780s rebuilding had between four and eight panels depending on the importance of their location. The raised sides of the panels faced the more elaborate room (just as clapboards rather than shingles faced the road) except when both sides were of equal importance; then the panels were raised on both sides—for example, the doors from the front hall to the parlor (figures 144 and 154). These doors originally had HL hinges and the pulls had rounded ends (figure 155). The door between the hall and the study had three original HL hinges (figure 156). The lower story of the ell used four late eighteenth-century doors (in far wall of figure 179). Those of the upper story had shallow field-

ing from the late nineteenth century. Similar doors were moved from the keeping room to the kitchen (left of figures 176 and 179).

All the hardware was painted the *same* color as the woodwork and was originally fixed in place with the nails clinched over on the other side. (The tips were turned at an additional right angle so they could be driven deep into the wood.) The clinched prong was bent to follow the grain so it would sink and be less visible when clinched in and painted. (The early latch in figure 189 has been reattached with screws.) Some hinges had small bits of leather under the head of the nails to tighten the fit when the nail was clinched over on the other side. The strap hinges of the front door I added had bits of textile under their nail heads. Some of the keepers had shaped tails that entered the wood, preventing the main part from moving downward (figures 146 and 147). I had a blacksmith add tails to standard reproduction ones for places that needed a new one.

146–147 Latch and keeper

When hanging a door with nailed-on hinges, push it toward the hinge side and up against the head molding. To hold it there, use shingles at the latch side and bottom. Their wedge shape allows you to push the door as far as you want. After the hinges are attached, the door will sag slightly and should not bind at the top or hinge side. Doors can be extended if they are not the right width or are too short by glueing and nailing on a strip. Many early doors were refitted to adjust to the altered shape of the old opening. The 1740s door in figure 188 was reused in the 1780s third of the Bliss House. After that section sagged, the bottom was cut and the top gained a new wedge shape. A door filled out with an extra piece usually looks better than one heavily trimmed, for then the stiles or rails have an overly narrow appearance.

Paint: The final understanding of the colors of the parlor is detailed at the beginning of the journal summary on page 114. It is advisable to leave layers of paint unless they obscure details. Newly stripped woodwork can look raw. If you try to save a lower layer, it will usually look scraped or muddy if you use a solvent, since it has become soft and taken on particles from other layers. Also, the layer you are trying to save probably had areas worn down to the wood. Such regions should have a beautiful mellow wood color, but messed-about paint will tint them as though washed with watercolors.

If the layers have different bases—oil as opposed to milk, for example—certain solvents can separate them easily. The standard way to find the original colors has been to dry scrape an area, leaving in an obscure location a square of each layer as evidence of the paint history. Such research should be done in the dimmer areas, where light will have faded the colors least. This is often behind a normally open door. The scraped areas, however, may not show the original color. It is now known that paint that has been covered may be lighter or darker than it

was originally; further, in scraping, particles of other coats can leave a false impression on the patch. It is possible to cut through with a sharp knife or sand instead of scrape, using a fine wet and dry sandpaper with mineral oil to float away the unwanted particles. This may leave a good sense of the color.

Today, an accepted method is to have chips of the paint professionally analyzed and a recipe formulated (see Bibliography). In selecting *new* paint colors, I have found the most helpful sources of inspiration to be the covers of museum catalogues and detailed colorplates in art books. They often feature carefully selected colors in a way I find more inspiring than little paint samples. Even if they are not historically accurate for your house, they often provide an array of sensitive tones. For example, the color of the trim in the first-floor hall on Beacon Hill was inspired by the dull grayish green of the architectural details of the vestibule of Michelangelo's Laurentian Library in Florence, found in a full-color tourist guide to Michelangelo's works in Italy.

Many of the houses I have worked on have been nineteenth century in date, but I tend to think in eighteenth-century colors. I "earlied up" the 1830s Providence house by introducing wood colors that were darker than historically correct. In the room that was to hold the earliest furniture, I painted the area between the chair rail and the baseboard the same color as the darkened woodwork, as though it were a dado. This helped pull down the height of the nineteenth-century ceiling. The lines left by a brush are part of early texturing. Therefore, when painting, use a brush or go over roller-applied areas to eliminate the stippled effect a roller produces. Many early paints were glazed to give them a high sheen. I have seen streaky glazing used over a painted wall in an attempt to produce an aged surface. The result seemed to me messy rather than poetic.

The validity of wallpaper should be considered. White walls help to provide clarity and a sense of light but they are often quite wrong historically. There are fairly good reproduction wallpapers available (see Bibliography). The two fireboards that remained in the attic of the Bliss House (seen in figure 194) had mid-nineteenth-century wallpapers. (The base of one is cut to slip over the horizontals of the andirons.) The entire room in which each was used must have had the same paper on the walls (as seen in figures 184 and 31). It is possible to "patch" early wallpaper by painting in the missing parts—if properly done, this is difficult to discern. If, when patching paper with paper, you tear rather than cut the edges, they will be thinner and when applied, less noticeable. As noted earlier, I have temporarily cleaned up many dirty houses by covering the walls with white, unfigured ceiling paper.

Do Not Over-Restore

The floorboards that ran in front of the parlor fireplace hearth had been replaced by three narrow boards (figure 148). I chose to leave them rather than replace them with wider boards. Such changes, like the roughening of plaster, are part of what creates the difference between an early house and a reproduction. When plastering, I sought to create a surface like that nearby on early walls. I used undercoat plaster so it would not be too smooth, and where appropriate made it as rough as seen on the back hall wall in figure 149. I do not mean pseudo-Italian restaurant wall texture patterned by great C-shapes. What you want is a plasterer's apprentice doing the best he or she can.

Often when applying plaster I worked the surface with my hands wearing rubber gloves. Such a varied wall effect is part of the reason I love cities like Venice. There the scaling medieval plaster creates a personal, intriguing surface over variously colored brick. I am glad the shortage of funds keeps them from being freshened up.

148 Patched parlor floor

149 West wall of back hall

150 Front hall, 1970

151 Front stairs and "peek-hole" door to area between chimneys

First-Floor Hall

WORKING JOURNAL: SUMMARY

Antoinette Downing says open string bannisters are usually later than 1740, but not unparalleled (Cocumscusset). But that is an early limit and should denote the 1770s or 1780s. She is a little suspicious of the molding along the edge of the treads, but the drops, rail, balusters, placement, etc., are all fine. [*A detailed review of Downing's analysis is included as Appendix 3.*]

A later floor was removed and a good early floor exposed. Between these I found the floor cloth from about 1860 shown as figure 198. Like the west side of the house, there is only a crawl space under the front hall, although it is probably part of the original half-house. Since there was no room in the crawl space for the plumbers to work, floorboards all around the uncellared section were lifted to install the heating pipes. A small radiator was put to the right of the front door.

The probably 1840s front doorway was replaced by an unusually wide door with a paneled exterior (figure 151) and a sheathed inner face (figure 155). The doors joining the hall and the two front rooms have eight panels and are fielded on both sides.

The balustrade (figure 151) is a local variant, for it is like that in the 1780s Carpenter House, figure 153. (The exterior of that house is seen in figures 112 and 113.) The differences are that the staircase in the Bliss House begins at the right and swings to the left; the door to the closet under it is not as dramatically paneled; and above the fourth step that winds to the straight flight, there is a small, paneled "peek-hole" door (figure 151) that gave access to the back of the oven and the area between the chimneys (figure 152—also located on the diagram as a "small door," figure 132).

Looking up between the chimneys, one could see, about every five feet, the staging boards embedded in the bricks on which people stood as they built the next section of chimney. Many of the bricks showed soot on the outer face, indicating they were reused. Undoubtedly, the half-house was served by two fireplaces on each floor, and when the western part was added, the chimneys were taken down, leaving only the oven, part of the cooking fireplace, and perhaps the parlor fireplace.

Study

WORKING JOURNAL

Wednesday, May 27. Investigated the fireplace in study a little. There is clearly something behind the present bricked-up fireplace, maybe two rebuildings—the ceiling of the room has been made level, so it shows none of the dramatic slant equivalent to the floor of the bedroom above, although the joists themselves should give this same dramatic slant.

Thursday, June 4. Most modernized room of all. New, late nineteenth-century heavy, coarse moldings around the windows; baseboards wide; large, square "archway" between study and dressing room. [*In eighteenth-century terms: the southwest parlor and a small first-floor bedroom.*] Modern floors here and in dressing room—1½" *lower* than front hall's later floor so maybe old floor was removed. Eight-panel doors into front hall and keeping room and their architrave trim all original. Hearth floored over or removed. Mostly new plaster—wallpapered.

Fireplace bricked up around stove hole. Fireplace mantel [*figure 158*] seems to be the molding and one panel from a floor-to-ceiling paneled fireplace wall—like the one in the parlor.

This remaining woodwork has been perched on crude square "pilasters" set into the baseboard to make an ugly, taller than wide fireplace. It has a modern triangular pedimental capping—like the one in the kitchen—and a modern mantel shelf with metal bracket supports. There is a vertical seam in the plaster at the right edge of this concoction. From it to the front hall door is old plaster on split lath; going left from this seam is new plaster on sawn lath. Between the left edge of the mantel and the keeping-

152 *Area between chimneys, seen through "peek-hole"*

*153 Front hall of Carpenter House, 1780s
(Society for the Preservation of New
England Antiquities)*

154 Front hall, 1970

155 Front hall, 1975

room door is a hollow space behind the plaster which seems, peeking through, to be brick and plastered up to the height of a cooking fireplace. There is mixed sooty and clean brick above that. In there are either damaged shelves or boards put in to nail the new lath to. This may be either the old cooking fireplace or one rebuilt when the east half of the house was added. [*I still thought this west end was older.*] Either way it has been patched up somehow and then bricked up 1870-ish. Corner posts on outside walls are about half-buried in plaster as in parlor so walls were originally much thinner.

Thursday, 11. Opened study fireplace [*figure 157*]. The bricked-up area inside the ugly mantel was vertical in proportion, 40″ × 30″ and cut up through the original line of the lintel. That is, the original horizontal opening was filled in at the sides and increased in height. Then the fireplace mold-

ing and one panel were stuck up on new plinths. Even later, this was closed in with brick around a stove hole. Removed new sawn lath left of vertical seam: above and left of fireplace (at first reluctantly). Found slanting plaster cupboard above fireplace. Clearly, this area was later studded up with pieces that had once been used elsewhere. Opened up tall vertical cupboard to left of fireplace. One of the vertical studs for the new lath was once part of an early baseboard. Put other split boards that had been used as studs back together [*shown piled on floor in figure 161*]. Proved to be part of original paneling of the fireplace wall: shows red under dark yellow paint; edge of one had quarter-round molding and mortises in it for paneling rails. Hearth of fireplace missing; was originally 1″ *above* new floor. Crack in back of fireplace to left and above height of original lintel proved not to be opening to oven.

156 *Study to front-hall door with three original* HL *hinges*

(The new ones in the left cupboard were painted white to distinguish them from the originals.) I covered the left cupboard with a nineteenth-century textile and kept the shelves above the fireplace open, as seen in figure 159. In time, I would have taken details from paneling within the house, and perhaps other Rehoboth houses, to complete the woodwork: a paneled door on the bottom three quarters of the left-hand cupboard, a fixed panel above it, and paneling with doors over the fireplace.

The fireplace crane was purchased locally with a history of use in a Rehoboth house. It fit without changes into supports still in the brickwork. The lower brick of the back had been eaten away by heat and is covered with a probably late nineteenth-century layer. Under the new floor was evidence of the size of the original hearth. Fol-

As seen in figures 157 through 159, the paneling above and to the left of the fireplace was missing. The proportions of the fireplace opening had been changed: probably in the late nineteenth century, it had been made narrower and three bricks higher. Later it had been closed around a stove hole. The metal horizontal in figure 157 shows the original height and width of the fireplace. (If the house has early stone lintels and one is cracked, do not throw it away. Cover the lower and rear edge with an angle iron embedded in the side brickwork. Then if necessary put another support behind it.)

All that was left of the paneling is seen in figure 158. Above the fireplace, the brickwork slants as the chimney moves toward the main vertical. The plaster had marks where shelves were once set against it and the cupboard at the left retained three shelves (figure 157). The top fourth of that opening had no plaster and must have been covered with a fixed panel—as at the left of the parlor fireplace wall (figure 134). My immediate solution was to put back shelves over the fireplace and new ones at the top of the cupboard to the left.

157 *Study fireplace wall, 1970*

158–159 Study fireplace wall, 1975

160 North wall of study; keeping room through right door, dressing room through left, 1975

lowing that line, I cut away the new floor and on the original hearth support put a layer of concrete, then sand, and finally bricks, following the pattern of undisturbed hearths in other rooms. When they were in place, I broomed sand between them.

That much of the ceiling was lower than it had originally been was proved by the difference in height between the top of the cupboard over the fireplace and the present ceiling. At first they were the same level. The doorway from the study into the hall (figure 156) shows the degree of slant toward the front of the house the original ceiling obtained. The top of the door and the lower board of the trim molding still follow that line, but when the new horizontal ceiling was installed the outer two moldings were adjusted to follow. The sloping was caused mainly by the sagging of the floor joists. Perhaps the wood used to make this east end was too green or too light and bent out of shape soon after construction was finished. I could have jacked everything back to level and readjusted the molding and floor, or reinstalled a sagging ceiling. Instead, I chose to accept all these changes as character. (The door to the hall, unlike others in the house, had three original HL hinges, figure 156. This illustration shows clearly the dark red-brown color of the floor carried onto the baseboard and doorway trim but not the door itself.)

The left of the keeping-room ceiling joist seen through the right door in figure 160 was at the end of the original half-house (see drawing, figure 132). That doorway in the north wall of the study was placed at an angle. This permitted the study to be deeper while keeping the right edge of the doorway level with the keeping-room fireplace wall.

At the time of purchase, there was a large rectangular "archway" between the study and the dressing room. My method of closing that opening was perhaps the least satisfactory of restoration choices. Undoubtedly, there was once a door that matched the two eight-panel doors with an architrave using a three-part molding. What I used was a batten door found in the barn and minimal surrounding moldings.

Floor: The original floor and its subfloor had been replaced by a single narrow oak floor. Over this I placed boards taken from a nearby eighteenth-century inn that was being torn down. (That wonderful inn should not have been touched. The site now sports a gas station. It was said that a local historical society which might have fought to save it did not do so because a member had disliked the building since her husband had kept a woman there. Such are the more personal factors that can condition what is preserved.)

One of the most common mistakes in restoring old buildings is the use of wide, attic floorboards in lower rooms. Wide boards were once the cheapest boards available, and the degree of a room's grandeur was commensurate with the narrowness of the boards used. Those purchased for the study were ten to twelve inches wide.

In lifting up old boards, be sure to mark the *back* with their sequential order. If you mark the fronts, it will show when you relay them. Even chalk leaves a mark. Putting boards down in the original order keeps together the color pattern and edges that have received the same wear. Knots affect wear and heavily trafficked areas will be thinner.

When laying a floor of old or new boards, do not use large-headed nails unless that is really correct for the period and region of the house. Easily obtainable cut nails, or hidden nails driven into the sides of the boards, may be more correct. Bring the boards into the house after the new plaster, and anything else that is damp, has dried out—this may take as long as two or more weeks. Otherwise the wood, adjusting to the dampness, will swell, and if fixed in place then it will shrink as everything dries out, leaving gaps. (Boards, like other wooden parts, are largest during the dampest period and smallest during the driest season. In New England, with or without central heating, the driest months are usually January and February, with August the dampest. Doors and other wooden parts should be fitted when they are at their greatest size.)

Old floors with an early surface should not be sanded or even buffed with heavy steel wool, for you will eliminate the variations that make old boards look old—where knot areas stand up and worn areas recede. If for some reason you must sand, sand with the grain, for sanding across it even with a circular sander causes marks that are virtually impossible to remove. The treatment of new boards to look old is discussed with the guesthouse in Chapter 6.

Dressing Room

The east wall of the dressing room was of vertical boards covered with individual pieces of split lath. The dark stripes on the boards at the right of figure 161 were the areas left when the lath was removed. The lath was probably applied when the wall was moved westward as part of adding the new third of the house in the 1780s. Before the change, this 1740s sheathing was probably against the inside of the exterior wall of the half-house. Since the back of the wood had never been seen, it was rough and without paint or molded decoration. Unhistorically, I chose to expose it and paint it white. As with most of the first floor, the north wall (left of figure 161) had been cut away and studded late in the nineteenth century. The inner face was covered with sawn lath and plaster. (The piece of fireplace wall paneling seen to the right of figure 161 is the one returned to the study.)

Closets: Modern living in early buildings demands new spaces for closets and bathrooms. Usually, the best solution is to sacrifice an entire room. Kitchens may be put in original locations, but bathrooms and a modern quantity of closets cannot. I have seen front halls on first and second floors used as bathroom spaces, completely alter-

161 *Dressing room. Sawn lath at left on north, outside wall, shadows of split lath at right, 1970*

162 *Dressing-room cupboards and bookshelves, 1975*

ing the natural flow and aesthetic impact of the building. Too often new bathrooms and closets are abruptly inserted into corners of rooms. Far better are those that take up an entire wall or run from a door to a distant corner (see figure 190).

I covered the entire north wall of this room with clothes closets faced with old wood, using plain vertical boards run up to one horizontal board, and HL hinges (figure 162). I have never used sliding doors because they clank; further, it is impossible to expose all of the interior space at one time and I never know which to open first. Behind the left door I built in a chest of drawers found in the attic. Most of the other wall space was covered with bookshelves. The tops of the end boards were shaped to reverse curves. To make these ends, I used sixteen-foot lengths and cut them in the middle to an eight-inch double curve. The resulting length of each board was four inches longer than if I had cut them straight across. Following a Shaker practice, I did not

recess the shelves into the uprights. Each shelf is secured at either end with two good-sized common nails. The end boards were nailed to the edges of door moldings, studs, or the board wall. If the ends are not lined up against anything to which they can be secured, you can nail at an angle through the shelves into studs.

Keeping Room

WORKING JOURNAL

Friday, May 22; a Mr. Bliss Visit. Richard Bliss was his grandmother's favorite; she was his grandfather's third wife and had no children. She spent her old age in a rocker at the west end of the keeping room and kept a sugarbowl in the cupboard opposite and every so often she would get up and eat a spoonful of sugar—she ate a pound a day. There was a cast-iron cookstove there at the time. He thinks the "Franklin" there now was never used but only the latest decoration around the stove hole. He recalls his father's saying the cooking hearth with oven was open when he was a child, before the Civil War, and was in the study. [*This proved not to be the case and is a cautionary example of the dangers of overdependence on oral history.*] It took four-foot logs and it was part of the evening routine to pass the logs through a window of the keeping room for use overnight and the next day. The wood came from the woodshed out back as wood was not stored in the house. Mr. Bliss's children believed Santa Claus came down the chimney and out the peek hole in the front stairs [*figure 152*] and used to look there for extra presents.

Sunday, May 31. Keeping room was not used in Mr. Bliss's time and so has no twentieth-century additions. Old floor, though a few places need repair. One fine eight-panel door into study and six-panel into back hall—both with good early doorway trim. Fireplace bricked up. Much simpler, flatter molding around fireplace than any other fireplace—different proportion. Only a little wider than high. Small old hearth still there. Plaster of west wall shows no signs of a door into dressing room, but has marks of a hanging cupboard, 2' tall and 4' wide along ceiling in the center. Plain nineteenth-century floor-to-ceiling cupboard with door and shelves in northwest corner. Windows in north wall have been enlarged—crude flat boards surround. East wall occupied by nineteenth-century dry sink with metal liner and shelves above [*lines of shelves seen on plaster in figure 168*], door below; and a big, plain nineteenth-century floor-to-ceiling cupboard with shelves to its right. The two cupboards (and even conceivably the sink) should be removed but built into the kitchen in ell. Back of parlor "tall cupboard" projects, part into keeping room, part into back hall: plastered and corner molding.

Tuesday, June 2. Found cooking fireplace and oven! Went into keeping room and began with cold chisel opening bricks inside "Franklin," which seems to have been a surround for a small fireplace—top and bottom shelves and sides bowed. Each side with crane. Surfaces have classical leafage cast into them. Bricks inside this close around a stove hole.

Removed stove hole and brick inside "Franklin." Space beyond *full* of soot, bricks, dirt. Got boxes for bricks, wheelbarrow for soot. Three full loads of soot. At bottom a foot of sand—obviously put there as protective filler. Removed metal "Franklin" and then brick around its outside to edge of fireplace opening. Took plaster off left of mantel and couldn't find oven. Measured, checked. Realized it must be belt high and at right of back. So steel-brushed back of fireplace and found irregular bricks—removed them. They were filling a slightly damaged arch [*figure 164*] but most of opening and oven floor intact! Oven contains turkey's wings—must have been for cleaning it out. Left end of fireplace has holders for crane. Bottom one a big hunk of metal secured with nails. Crane from attic fits! Realized should have known big fireplace was here, since hearth visible and its "returns," after I swept, clearly not complete. Center of hearth's brick *pattern* is far left of center of present hearth. It once went much further left, and fireplace too. The oven being at the back (an early idea) and conjectured original size of fireplace and hearth denote they were part of early half-house. Flue beautiful. Two metal cross bars for lug pole. Took modern top board off lighter, original mantel shelf. Rest seems original to *present* 1780s fireplace. Nails securing mantel to wall driven into pegs mortared into brickwork.

Friday, 12. Set out to clean up keeping room, but in doing so saw through a small hole in the plaster in the west wall a bit of wood with a molded edge. With great amazement thought it could be "feather-edged" paneling. Grabbed tools and took off plaster and split lath. Sheathing is all across west wall! There is no sign of any door through it to dressing room. Considerable signs of whitewash, except 45″ of north end, which was *not* whitewashed and bore signs of shelves [*figure 172*]: an upright about 63″ high and shelves—three, lowest about 35″ from ground. Decided to take plaster off other side, in dressing room.

Then discovered that the plaster ceiling of keeping room is over beams which, since they show early whitewash (much more left than on paneling), also heavy grease and smoke in front of fireplace, were unquestionably exposed even though not carefully finished. Then made holes in the ceilings of parlor and study and saw the "summer beam" type ceiling construction in the first, but all visible beams clearly too rough for exposure and had not been whitewashed or painted—clearly not meant to be seen.

Exposure of wood ceiling in keeping room and south wall of back hall (found when opening the plastered-up door between the parlor and back hall) reveals the original east wall of the keeping room was further east, probably as far east as the west edge of the parlor to hall door.

Keeping-room floor in very bad condition—much rot and beetle, and different sag of different sills has made floor too slanted for a main room, even for me, which is very slanted.

When I was looking at the house before purchase, it was impossible to get into the keeping room because the doors would only open a crack. That from the back hall was blocked by a variety of things including stacks of newspapers and magazines. The door from the study was held shut by the swelling of the floor; eventually, it was forced open and the room cleaned out.

The room had a series of cupboards and a dry sink that had been installed in the nineteenth century. I could have kept it as a nineteenth-century farm kitchen reusing eighteenth-century space, but chose instead to return it to an earlier configuration. The fronts of the tall cupboards were moved to the kitchen. (They are the two dotted-in cupboards on the drawing, figure 132, and those at the left in figures 176 and 179.)

The fireplace was bricked in and those bricks held an iron surround. In 1970, a stove hole held the flue pipe from a kerosene heater. The fireplace, as opened in figure 163, showed supports for a crane and the one found in an attic fit. Its horizontal bar was curved dramatically at the right end, suggesting that it was once in a bigger fireplace and had been shortened by curving for the fireplace when it became this size. Inside the flue, about six feet from the hearth, were iron bars running from front to back. These would have held a lug pole from which dropped trammels for supporting large pots—a practice that continued well into the eighteenth century. I thought this large fireplace might be within a still larger, typically 1740s fireplace, but this proved not to be the case.

Clearly what was from the 1740s house was part of the hearth, the back and right end of the fireplace, the oven, and the bottom few feet of the flue. When the new third of the house was added, the left end of the fireplace and its hearth were pulled in and the crane bent to fit the new space. The chimney was taken down to the lug pole supports and the study and study chamber fireplaces added. The present pattern of the hearth bricks supports this theory. Each course of the bricks across the front turns at the right and goes back (figure 165). At the left, some of the courses do this but not in a regular pattern (figure 167).

The mantel, seen in figure 172 and installed in room views, is the date of the present fireplace configuration. It uses the three-part molding found elsewhere in the house but with a wider spacing. These are crowned by an original narrow shelf. (At the time of purchase a broader one had been placed on top.) The boards supporting the lath over the fireplace are visible in figure 163, and above the plaster in figure 171. These are of the 1780s reworking and carry split lath, as used on the front and back of the sheathed wall when it was pushed westward at the same date.

To the left of the fireplace is the back of the parlor cupboard, which extends into the hall be-

163 Keeping-room fireplace with split lath, 1970

164 Opening to oven, 1970

165 Keeping-room hearth; 1975

166 *South wall of keeping room, 1975*

167 *East wall of keeping room, 1975*

yond. Undoubtedly, this was originally the doorway between the parlor and the keeping room. At that time, the east keeping-room wall that runs into that cupboard was about a foot and a half further east, toward the kitchen. The exposed corner post at the right of the window in figure 167 had original whitewash. When purchased, it had a casing with the same paint history as the 1780s mantel. The casing dated from the time the ceiling was closed in, the board wall moved west, and the fireplace made its present size.

The windows in the keeping room were bigger than when the house was in its half-house stage; probably they were then narrow 9 over 6s, or even smaller. Since this wall had been cut away when the whole lower floor was studded, it was impossible to be certain about the original fenestration. Now the windows had a simple board trim. I left them the large size as any change would be conjectural and the amount of light they allowed into this north room was important.

Since there was no cellar under this part, it was easy to adjust the extremely uneven floor. It was not made too level: the room still slants about three inches from one side to the other. The western end of the floorboards had rotted (some up to

three feet). I sawed away individual rotted ends and pieced out the floor, running the boards in the same direction as the original parts (figure 173). These were secured with a few screws so they could be lifted to make the crawl space accessible. While the floor was open, I ran pipes from the cellar under the east end to the dressing room in case I should want to turn it into another downstairs bathroom. This was not in fact necessary for it is not difficult to lift floorboards that lack tongue-and-groove joints, and pipes could have been installed at any time.

As seen in figure 168, I replaced some of the outside boarding before reshingling, and much of the sawn lath and plaster on the interior which was in very bad condition. Before replacing the lath, electrical wires and pipes for radiators on the second floor were run between the windows.

Removing the plaster ceiling revealed the original wooden ceiling—whitewashed and greasy near the fireplace—and the pinned joint between the original building's rear girt and that of the 1780s addition (figures 169 and 170). The 1740s joists are square in section and finished with an adz—a tool like an ax, but with the blade turned at a right angle to the handle. The two joists that come

168 North wall of keeping room, 1970   *169 North wall of keeping room, 1975*

170 *North girt joint and differing joists*

171 *Joining of 1740s and 1780s parts along southern wall of keeping room*

from the new girt are narrower and deeper and show saw marks. The south end of the new joists are housed in a 1780s member over the angled doorway (figure 171). (This view shows the upper end of the boards that held the 1780s lath over the present fireplace. These were not there when the larger 1740s fireplace was in place and would not have been seen when put there in the 1780s for the new plaster ceiling hid them.) In the 1740s joists were handmade nails, tapered and whitewashed for hanging kitchen items. When I added additional nails for my convenience, I used modern wire nails so the discerning can locate the

original ones (both kinds are visible in figure 170). Exposing joists and boards meant noise passed more easily between upper and lower rooms; also more dust filtered down and it was harder to run hidden wires.

The vertical sheathing that made up the west wall was part of the 1740s house. Quite likely it finished the original west wall when it was a few feet further east, although it may have been in some other part of the house. (Probably it was not a thin board wall separating two rooms, for the back—as seen at right in figure 161—was rough and unpainted.) In 1970 both sides had hand-split 1780s lath. Under it, the keeping-room side had traces of early whitewash, except for the right forty-five inches. That section was originally covered by shelves. In the sheathing, hidden by the later plaster, were the tapered shanks of four maple pegs. Every other board of the sheathing had concave shaping on both edges; the alternate boards had quarter-round moldings and were slotted to receive the intermittent boards. The dramatic angle of the board centering the wall resulted from both economic and aesthetic pressures: it preserved the width of board as sawn from a tree and is an attractive variant. A similar use of tapering boards is found as a decorative feature in the back of some contemporary fireplace settles.

My desire to use early materials led me to re-whitewash the paneling and ceiling. For the next year and a half it snowed whitewash, particularly

172 West wall of keeping room, 1970

173 West wall of keeping room, 1975

174 Cellar door in back hall

ends of the boards above the fireplace. But a designer said it was the best room in the house—the most interesting. Equally eclectic were the objects within, ranging from the seventeenth to the mid-twentieth century.

Back Hall

WORKING JOURNAL: SUMMARY

Floor bad condition but old. Two wooden strips with hooks along east wall—not let into the plaster. Fine early batten door to cellar. New plaster areas on wall between hall and parlor confirm a door originally there. Trim of door to ell of crude flat boards but door frame inside and door heavy enough to be outside door—probably moved from original east end of house. Hall door to outside is glazed nineteenth century and in bad condition. Stairway to second floor worn very thin, as is floor of upstairs hall, but with wonderful worn dark blue-green paint. Floor not salvageable without many coats of paint, but at least can try to match color.

when somebody walked across the floor above. Eventually, this was scraped off and a water-base white paint used.

This is the most eclectic room in the house. An architectural historian did not like its mixture of periods: the 1740s ceiling, uncased post, wall of vertical sheathing, part of the hearth and oven; the 1780s fireplace size, mantel, present location of the boarded wall, and the cupboard back jutting in from the parlor; the never-before-exposed

Part of what made the color of the floor interesting was the worn oak showing through the blue-green paint. I tried matching the color and ended with a terrible aqua—and of course the color of the wood was gone. I should have realized that the aspect of thin paint on worn grainy wood cannot be produced with heavy paint. Eventually I covered the aqua with the same red-brown color used elsewhere.

The west and east walls, and the stairs within them, had once been further east (see diagram, figure 132). The batten door to the present basement stairway used tapered molded sheathing like that on some walls, and strap hinges, figure 174. Undoubtedly, it was part of the 1740s house, but its original location is uncertain. It may have been the door to the original cellar stairs.

At the time of purchase, the east wall had a series of mismatched hooks for the hanging of outdoor coats and hats on two narrow boards nailed to the wall. Since these were not embedded into the plaster they were not early, and in a neo-Shaker mood I replaced them with a series of wooden pegs fixed through the plaster into the wood beneath. I used nicely turned handles from nineteenth century chisels, which looked very like early pegs and were beautifully worn.

Kitchen

WORKING JOURNAL: SUMMARY

Nothing built in except big glazed cupboard made by Richard Bliss—looks 1920s—between back window and door of future bathroom. Glass on left end to let window light in. Doilies thumbtacked to shelves. Aqua wall phone and frilly curtains. Plaster bad and in some places patched with odd boarding. Wainscoting of horizontal boards. Except for modern door to parlor and heavy door to back hall, nice plain late eighteenth-century doors in nineteenth-century door frames. Everything grained yellow-brown, probably imitating oak, perhaps yellow pine. Date of graining uncertain. Might conceivably be nice with white walls.

Molded vertical sheathing on kitchen side of wall between kitchen and parlor. The parlor side is rough and clearly never meant to be exposed—like the back of the paneling of the west wall of the keeping room.

A nineteenth-century mantel with triangular pediment-shape back board on east wall between doors to pantries. Cooking stove chimney in pantries. Enameled iron cookstove. Ancient electric stove and modern refrig on west wall. Round oak table, oak dresser on castors with linoleum on top. Molding, crumbling linoleum squares on floor. Can't tell about floor underneath yet. [Bob] Mende found in cellar the marks of the original stair steps which went down where there is at present the wall between kitchen and hall.

The wall between the kitchen and parlor, seen covered with open shelves in figure 176, was originally finished on the kitchen side with molded vertical chestnut sheathing. Through this Mr. Bliss made the new door to the parlor. To fill in the opening, I took similar boards from the second-floor closet that became a bathroom. Also from that closet came the open shelving I placed across the kitchen paneling. These were early shelves and had been moved into that second-floor closet from somewhere else in the house. I kept the full extent of the shelves and placed to their left a floor-to-cciling kitchen closet. This I faced with the door from one of the nineteenth-century closets found in the keeping room. The front of the other floor-to-ceiling kitchen closet (seen to the left in figure 179) came from the same room. (The shelving and the closets are shown with dotted lines on the plan, figure 132.) The cabinets around the sink area were made from old wide boards. For door pulls I usually chose plain white porcelain knobs of a nineteenth-century shape.

The original half-house had ended to the east along the dash-line shown on the plan. The lower story of the addition is of heavy oak members, and the second story of lighter, nineteenth-century construction. The original staircase went down where the wall with the kitchen sink is now placed. The back wall of the old part had not been cut

175 *West end of kitchen, 1970*

176 *West end of kitchen, 1975*

tile flooring, although the subflooring had rotted away. You could see between the boards if a light was turned on in the basement: this distressed some guests who suddenly glimpsed through boards the area lit beneath them. But the oak boards and the new supporting joists (figure 133) made a sound floor. In the cooking area I replaced the oak boards with a plywood and dark mottled brown vinyl floor. If you do extensive cooking, it is difficult to keep aged boards with shrinkage cracks clean.

When found in the house, the "island" in the center of the room (figure 176) had a worn linoleum top. Its many small drawers faced in one direction and the piece probably was the base of an early twentieth-century baking counter, perhaps with an upper section now removed. I decided to store cooking utensils in it. The

177 *Original vertical planking with whitewash*

away and studded like the rest of the first floor; it retained heavy, vertical, whitewashed planking under later lath and plaster, which was, therefore, the original exposed interior surface. Perhaps other outer walls, particularly in the keeping room, were once similarly rudimentary. The remaining whitewashed planking is directly behind the new stove and I boxed around part of it to keep this early practice visible (figure 177).

There were sound wide oak boards under the

new Formica top made the handiest working surface.

The other end of the kitchen, as seen in figures 178 and 179, had a mantel with a triangular cap under a stove hole. I used the chimney in the pantry area for the furnace flue (in it were the three clay pipes described earlier and seen on the table in figure 82).[4]

The wide horizontal boarding below the south windows was probably original to this addition. The narrower boards on the opposite wall were added later. These and the ceiling light were left. A modern light was put over the sink; another came with the vent over the stove. Between the two front windows I used what I consider one of the handiest lamps for early houses: a simple pin-up lamp painted white, or a color that helps it retire into the wall. The windows near the eating table (figure 179) and the front ell door let onto the lawn. Birds at the feeder, the growing hedge screening the road, and the morning sun made it one of the most pleasing morning spots I have known.

Pantries

WORKING JOURNAL: SUMMARY

East end of kitchen. Behind right door, shelves and a chest of drawers—they and window carefully grained to match kitchen. Back of door has more open—rosewood-like—mid-nineteenth-century graining. Chest a late addition since shelves had been removed to make room. Behind left door ancient porcelain sink, running cold water, and lead drainpipe running out to barnyard. Chest of drawers along shed wall, cupboard above with sliding doors, one with mirror. Sink and cupboard seem 1920ish. Towel rod for roller towel.

178 *East end of kitchen, 1970*

179 *East end of kitchen with doors to pantries, 1975*

In the left pantry I replaced the sink with a washer and dryer on a new plywood and vinyl floor. There was no cellar under the pantry area and during one cold spell the pipes to the washer froze. I used a heater with a fan to thaw them, and later rerouted them to come in above the plywood.

The pantry to the right contained shelving of various dates. Figure 180 shows perhaps the earliest part with its ends shaped to reverse curves. Some shelves had been removed to make way for

180 Nineteenth-century shelving in right pantry

a chest of drawers; these I restored, following lines on the plaster.

Bathroom

WORKING JOURNAL

Saturday, May 30. Cleaned out large pantry, actually a small room projecting into the shed; nine-inch-thick walls to keep it cool. Shelves all around of no distinction. Small, old, 6 over 6 window. To be bathroom with shower.

It is often difficult to decide where to put bathrooms without sacrificing a hall or chopping into a larger room. Like closets, bathrooms that take a corner from a room always produce an awkward L-shaped space. Fortunately this house had a large pantry and nearly immediately above it a large closet. Both made good bathrooms. Also, they were near the kitchen and laundry, keeping all the plumbing in one area. This cut down on expenses and the unsightliness that may result from running new pipes.

I went to a salvage yard and purchased second-hand toilets and sinks of good porcelain and nice shapes. Using second hand plumbing materials can be aesthetically and monetarily advantageous, but it is often difficult to keep the faucets from dripping without regrinding the seats under the washers. New castings of old metal fixtures are available. Although many are all brass, some come with a chrome finish, and one need not be part of the brass-everywhere aesthetic. (Some suppliers are listed in the Bibliography.)

In the lower bathroom, I built a tiled stall shower. The plumber installed the pipes and the shower base. I insisted on a solid, poured one rather than plastic, which might wobble and when stepped on produce cracking sounds. Most of the wall space needed replastering. I used undercoat plaster over plaster board. Wearing rubber gloves, I finished it by smearing the surface to appear similar to what remained of the old plaster. The floor received plywood and the same mottled brown vinyl as the pantries and cooking end of the kitchen.

Second-Floor Bathroom

WORKING JOURNAL: SUMMARY

Upstairs bath to be put in large cupboard located in hall over the northwest corner of kitchen. West and south walls of plain boards, which seem never to have been painted on sides facing hall but always to have had wallpaper [*right of figure 181*]. Inside, the other two walls have early, 1740s, molded vertical sheathing. The boards on the north wall do not reach up past the plaster ceiling and were probably placed there sometime after the room was completed. The inside of all four board walls, as the shelves, have a dark "Victorian" varnish. Took the paneling from the north wall to close the doorway between kitchen and parlor. Set of open shelves has been moved to the kitchen.

181 Part of upstairs back hall, 1971

182 Upstairs back hall, 1975

I grained the inside of the bathroom door although I had not intended to do this. The door was taken onto the back lawn for repair and paint. After giving it a coat of water-base dark red over an old cream color layer, I left it out overnight to dry. In the morning the dew was keeping the dark color wet and I took paper to rub it off and start again. Large grain patterns emerged, so I completed them across the entire surface. I twisted pieces of newspaper into large corkscrew shapes and rolled them over the surface with my palms. To achieve a complex grain pattern, I rolled in different directions on different parts of the door.

The claw and ball foot tub used in this bathroom was found in the room further to the east, where it had a drain although it needed to be hand filled by bucket. Since I like to read in the bathtub, I placed a light over it with a string pull rather than metal chain, to prevent electrocution. Most of the plumbing pipes for this bathroom (as seen in figure 181) are run against the west board wall with the remnants of wallpaper and the toilet-paper holder. (Next to this stood the potty stool.) To hide the pipes, another board wall was built over them, edging the rear window (figure 182). To maintain access to the pipes, these boards could be slid up and the bottoms pulled out over the narrow baseboard.

Across from that wall is a door to the attic. When the house was purchased, there was no door here. Rather, a late door had been placed at the beginning of this narrow jut of the hall. Changing the location of the attic door kept the new pipes from freezing and allowed light from the back window into this northern area.

Chambers

(Following early practice, I have used the term "chamber" to designate a sleeping room, and as a prefix, the name assigned to the room below it.)

The detailing of the second floor of the main block of the house was from the 1780s, and except for the four two-panel doors moved there, showed no vestiges of the earlier stage. This suggests that the original 1740s house may have been only one and a half stories, which would account for the presence of an 1780s front staircase. The parlor chamber had the most complicated woodwork in any second-story room and the window trim was like that found below. The simple fireplace wall paneling (figure 183 and plate x) was a standard local design, also used in the Rehoboth Carpenter House (figure 184—the mantel shelf dates from about 1840–50; the exterior is seen as figure 112) and the nearby Old Parsonage (doorway shown as figure 114). The Carpenter House fireboard is papered the same as the walls. The Bliss House retained two papered fireboards in the attic (see figure 194).

The study chamber, in the 1780s end of the house, had the dramatically sagging floor that caused the ceiling in the study to be straightened. It is this slant that makes the back posts of the slat-back chair at the right in figure 185 and plate XI seem to angle forward; on a flat floor, they are perpendicular. The pitch is part of what caused one visitor to call the house "spooky" and my father to comment that he would have to be tied with a rope to get across this room. I saw no reason to alter the floor. Clearly, it was not dangerous. The sagging developed soon after this end was added and has not moved sufficiently in recent years to crack the plaster. To jack it up now would throw the study floor and ceiling out of kilter, crack the plaster, and so on.

The door trim used the bottom and top layers of the three-part molding as found elsewhere (figure 138). The fireplace surround, figure 186, replaced the second and third stages with the molding used on the fancier window sills (figures 141 and 142). It is slightly simpler than the molding around the parlor chamber fireplace in figure 183. Since the second-story walls did not have later studding, the casings over the corner posts were more exposed than on the first floor.

The door to the dressing-room chamber was a

*183 West wall of parlor chamber, 1975
(*The Magazine Antiques, *Helga Photo
Studio); seen also as plate* X

*185 North wall of study chamber, 1975; seen also as
plate* XI

*184 Carpenter House chamber, 1780s (Society for the
Preservation of New England Antiquities)*

186 Study-chamber fireplace molding

187 Ceiling hooks in small northwest dressing-room chamber

188 1740s doors between keeping-room chamber and southwest and northwest chambers

simple batten door. (This encouraged me to do the same immediately below, figure 160, but that first-floor doorway should have had a fancier door and a three-stage architrave.) In the ceiling of the dressing-room chamber were three wrought-iron hooks (figure 187) and a hole for a fourth. Together they mark the corners of a large rectangle. What these originally held is uncertain. Many eighteenth-century beds did not have high posts to hold curtains, so sometimes they were hung from the ceiling. In other cases, provisions were suspended from hooks. One now amusing quote defines this type of storage, as well as suggesting how people of earlier times smelled:

In the simpler houses the chamber remained a semi-storage area for foodstuffs as it had been in the seventeenth century, and as late as July 22, 1791, the Rev. William Bentley of Salem, recording a conversation on the subject, observed "that the effluvia from the human body by fair experiment did render cheese, butter, &c. rancid, & that the custom of lodging in chambers with cheeses, &c. was detrimental to the cheese, &c."[5]

The regularity of the spacing and location of the Bliss House hooks imply that they were for bed hangings. The eighteenth-century beds found in the attic were of the low post variety, although one was a high pencil-post type later cut down to low post level.

The three doors of the keeping-room chamber were from the 1740s half-house and had two deep panels, triangular-end pulls, and strap hinges (figures 188 and 189). The angled top and lower edge of the door into the front room (figure 188) show how much it needed to be changed to compensate for the slope of the floor. This room was used as another study and dressing room. I put a closet wall between the west door and the back wall made of new eight-, ten-, and twelve-inch boards and used HL hinges (figure 190). There are shelves for clothing behind the left door. The two windows in this room were originally narrow and short and probably had 9 over 6 sash. In

189 *1740s latch reattached with screws*

container half-full of kerosene. One wooden barrel with bark hoops ⅓ full of nineteenth-century bottles, some still with patent medicines. Bushel basket full of probably early cane for caning chairs. Hat blocks—for bowler hats? Two log barrels, one full of deceased and matted feather pillows. Other full of unidentifiable substance looking like reddish beetle backs. Attic extension over ell: Windsors, nineteenth-century grained slat-back chairs, Boston rockers, all in pieces but may be salvageable. Yellow "schoolmaster's" desk out of ell attic—full of leath-

1970 they were the size of 12 over 12 windows and from the inside looked far too big for their wall. They were shortened to hold 12 over 8 sash but not narrowed. Their wall had vertical boards to the dado level. As seen in figure 191, I filled in with boards where the shortened windows left a space.

Attic

WORKING JOURNAL

Sunday, May 31. Endless piles of piles. Array of bottles—medicine, beer, canning, etc.; car tires, etc., dirt. Found swing bench for front porch. Large crane—so there was once a big fireplace somewhere. Maybe eighteenth-century coat. Horsehide covered domed trunks. Corner shelf—triangular with gros point hanging with Gothic pointed lower edge and tassels. Drawer full of pillows and baby mice. Found a lidless

190 *Cupboard wall, west end of keeping-room chamber, 1975*

191 *North wall of keeping-room chamber, 1975*

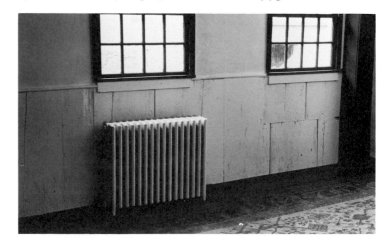

er. Ditto cobbler's bench. To make logical place to put things, sorted two small "monk's rooms" at west end—their walls of nineteenth-century sawn lath (like over study fireplace) and nails. Moved pile of early beds from under south eaves into right room [*figure 195*]. There are various trundles and low post eighteenth-century beds. Only one painted—red. Early loom or something among beds. Wasp sting. Put in left room [*figure 194*]: two fireboards—one with slits for horizontals of andirons has 1840–50 paper with borders over several layers; other from 1825–30 is again over layers. One with slits salvageable. Other's wallpaper too far gone. Papers, books, piles of pictures—photos, tintypes, and prints, and one charcoal on sandpaper, all nineteenth century.

Monday, June 1. Cleaned off above two small rooms. There batten door painted white and many whiskey and gin bottles! Sweeping and vacuuming—put stuff to be auctioned in northwest corner and pile in southwest corner for dump. Completed brooming and vacuuming attic except under stoves east of staircase—found painted floor cloth under one stove.

Best things in attic: Queen Anne table [*figure 60*], pig-scraper, large and small log barrel, yellow "schoolmaster's" desk, various beds, especially one hewn headboard. (N.B.: Leg of one trundle has an extension added and strapped in place with leather, the wheel having been removed.) Map may be interesting—roller at base—ironstone platter.

The four views of the attic seen in figures 192 through 195 show it after days of sorting and cleaning. A possible approach to this farm would have been to retain everything, even to the hundreds of mason jars in the attic. It would have provided an important picture of eighteenth-, nineteenth-, and twentieth-century life in rural Massachusetts. A university did consider accepting everything I did not wish to keep, so graduate students could evaluate the collections, but this did not go further than the initial discussions.

The most obvious things in figure 192 are the press at the left, cobbler's bench, log barrel holding a wooden crutch, and other household items. A detail of the upper shelf (figure 193) shows this eastern window's 9 over 3 sash. The two small nineteenth-century rooms to the west (figures 194 and 195) hold a variety of items, including the two papered fireboards. I thought I might eventually want heat in these rooms, so pipes were run up inside a fake corner post casing on the second floor. The pipes stop just where they came through the floor. To keep these empty of water until I should want to use them, I put turn-off handles inside the fake casing. There is a small door in the casing that allows access to the turn-offs.

Mr. Bliss remembered a highboy in the house and during one visit said one of his wives who did not like old things sold some, notably a table on which she had placed strawberries for sale near the edge of the road. This had upset Mr. Bliss for he thought it might be valuable. There were in the attic three mid-nineteenth-century turned-leg tables and the eighteenth-century "Queen Anne" table seen in figures 137 and 60. One of Mr. Bliss's daughters and her husband had taken a variety of items when they built a house on part of the Bliss land, and many are seen in figure 196. The slat-back armchair at the back left of that picture had been converted to an upholstered chair in the nineteenth century. Among the items they retained were handmade shoe lasts, one initialed A.B., perhaps for Asaph Bliss who died in 1857 or his son Asaph L. Bliss who died in 1861. (His inventory is included in Appendix 2.) The variety of chairs in the house and barns is arranged in front of the barn in figure 197.

192 West wall of attic of main house, 1974

193 Detail of west wall of attic of main house, 1974

194 Southwest attic room, 1974

195 Northwest attic room, 1974

196 *Bliss objects remaining with one of Richard Bliss's children*

197 *Chairs remaining with the Daniel Bliss Homestead in 1970*

198 *Floor carpet found between original and later floor of first-floor front hall, about 1860*

199 *Floor carpet found under a stove in the attic, about 1860*

200 *Strip of ingrain carpet found in the attic, 1850s*

Some of the rarest items to remain from earlier times are floor coverings. The one in figure 198 was found in the first-floor front hall between narrow boards and the original wide boards. It is painted on a burlap back. The piece in figure 199 was under one of the stoves in the attic. It, too, was painted on burlap, but of a tighter weave than figure 198. Both date from about 1860. It is not surprising that linoleum soon became popular for it has much the same texture as painted floor cloths. The 1850s strip of ingrain carpet in figure 200 was in the attic. Mr. Bliss recalled tacking down strips of carpet each winter and rush mats each summer. The attic also contained rolls of slightly padded paper printed on one side with a pattern of narrow oak flooring.[6]

6

Bliss House Outbuildings and Guesthouse

THE BARNS

WORKING JOURNAL: SUMMARY

Seem basically sound, but ugly gray asbestos shingles on slaughter–chicken house and south side of main barn—the latter has gaping modern windows at east end. Wood shingles in various stages of decrepitude elsewhere—worst on big barn whose north wall needs boarding and shingling. Small chicken house [*formerly corn crib*] in woods probably salvageable to be opened into screened gazebo. All roofs will do at least for now. Walled barnyard in front of barn grown up in thistles, etc. Would make a rich vegetable garden.

Outbuildings originally shingled except front of chaise house and large barn. Mr. Bliss opened front of far end of large barn for chickens, then closed it in and put in present windows, which were given to him by the road supervisor. He said, about doing jobs for people—shingling a roof, straightening a silo—no money passed. "An obligation was incurred."

The view of the back of the house in figure 201 is taken from partway up the knoll. Just beyond the peonies where the lawn begins, Mr. Bliss had placed a wall and above it, clothesline poles (as seen in figure 123). To the right of the building in figure 201 is Perryville Road and to the left, behind the house shed, a flower garden I added. When purchased, the ground in that area was part of the gravel-packed barnyard. A bulldozer dug a five-foot-wide trench a foot deep and I filled it with local peat. Beyond this garden is the circular base of the silo.

Moving down onto the lawn and turning to the left (figure 202), the building at the center is the chaise house and to its left, the slaughter–chicken-guesthouse. Between them is the giant oak cabled

201 View from north, 1971

202 Looking east across backyard, 1971

203 *Left building—probably the "wood house"—was gone by 1970; the child is Phyllis Waite, 1920*

204 *West end of chaise house with door to privy*

205 *Privy*

immediately after the tree on the knoll collapsed. There had been a building on the light area in the foreground and it is seen in figure 203. (Mr. Bliss recalled it as a woodshed and his story of the pre–Civil War practice of passing firewood in through the keeping-room window had the wood stored in a nearby woodshed. The 1807 will of Jacob Bliss listed a "wood house.") Beyond this building is the roof to the chaise house, and between that and the main barn, the frame of the windmill which also appears in figures 206 and 207. To the extreme right of figure 203 is a pole holding the clothesline which then still ran to the house. From the line hangs a pair of longjohns.

The west end of the chaise house, figure 204, had the door to the three-hole outhouse seen in figure 205. Each hole was roughly triangular and they varied in size. The attic of this building contained a variety of farm equipment, including seeders and wagons. This is where I found the eighteenth-century moldings and door that were reinstalled in the south rooms of the main house. The extension to the rear was added by Mr. Bliss so he could put the school bus in during the winter and keep its motor warm with a coal fire. Beyond the chaise house and the windmill was the

206 *Walter D. Bliss in barnyard, chaise house at left, corn crib at right, 1920*

207 Barnyard, about 1911

corn crib mentioned in eighteenth-century records (figures 206 and 207). In early photographs, it is still raised on stone posts to discourage rats from climbing to the corn.

By 1970 the windmill was gone and the corn house lowered. It had become a chicken or turkey house. There was also a group of early twentieth-century chicken houses beyond this which were so collapsed I hauled them to the dump. In the woods behind these was the twentieth-century household dump. With the aid of a power scoop and dump truck it was moved to the town dump. I watched each scoop in hope of reaching a level with objects of interest. Except for a few 1920s and 30s milk bottles I did not see any. It was not, however, a very systematic investigation!

The view of farmyard, chaise house, corn house,

windmill, and large barn seen in figure 207 evokes an atmosphere that is normally impossible to re-create as an area for modern living. Chickens destroy most vegetation—perhaps this contributed to the fact that early houses had so little planting. This degree of raw beauty results from a day-to-day quest for survival. (Figure 208 shows the space as it appeared in 1971.) The beauty and mood of workers naturally using the land as in figure 100, where Richard Bliss sharpens his scythe, and figure 209, are suggested at such villages as Sturbridge and Williamsburg where oxen pull wagons accompanied by costumed, long-haired youths. But such attempts, although necessary, cannot repeat early times when for financial reasons camera-clicking T-shirted tourists must be the focus. As a young scholar I visited Williams-

208 *Barnyard, 1970*

209 *Haying, about 1911*

burg and commented to the president of Colonial Williamsburg that I missed animals, manure piles, and other evidence of real folk. I was told that Williamsburg had had thirty-two lawsuits against it by people bitten by animals, particularly the peacock that used to strut in the Governor's Palace garden. Because of the implied criticism, I was sent to Coventry—not spoken to by the curatorial staff about anything pertaining to furniture—for the rest of the week.

The large barn is seen from the south in figure 210 and from behind at the left of figure 214. To the left of the first is the base of the silo. This barn was originally two thirds of the present length, and the line of the original right end of the roof can be seen over the left second-story front window. In the nineteenth-century photograph, figure 88, an earlier cupola centers the original part of the building. In the twentieth century, Mr. Bliss opened up the front of the right third and, in reclosing it, put in modern windows. Those in the original building still have eighteenth-century frames that probably once held 9 over 6

210 *South side and west end of large barn, 1972*

sash. Mr. Bliss recalled that, like the other main buildings, this too once had clapboard facing the road.

The ground at the rear and left is higher than the barnyard and the front of the barn sits on piers—animals could walk under it. I was never certain whether I would eventually take off the new third and restore it to its original size or leave it as it stood. The ground inside the silo base made a rich herb and vegetable garden.

THE SLAUGHTER–CHICKEN– GUESTHOUSE

WORKING JOURNAL

Saturday, September 12, 1970. Mr. Bliss visit—says the "chicken barn" was originally a two-story slaughterhouse with hoist. It was then twice as long—went to oak tree across second, open, three-sided foundation.

Mr. Bliss's father reduced it to present size and had doors on back for driving in equipment. Mr. Bliss converted it to brooder house. Mr. Bliss also had turkeys when it was realized they stayed healthy if kept away from chickens and raised up on wires.

In 1970 the former two-story slaughterhouse appeared as in figure 211. It contained chicken-brooding equipment, had two vents on the roof and two on the front. The stone foundation to the right was for another section of the building, which Richard Bliss's father had removed. I decided to convert this to a guesthouse, naming it the "Dower House"—the building to which the widow used to retire so the eldest son could occupy the manor. Mr. Bliss had added the asbestos shingles and supported the center of the front with a piece of telephone pole. Unlike the more imposing main house, chaise house, and large barn, all four sides originally had wooden shingles.

159

211 *Slaughter–chicken house, 1971*

OUTSIDE

I decided to make the remaining part of the original building a "seventeenth-century keeping room," and add on the *back* line of the old foundation, to the right, a kitchen, bathroom, and a bedroom/study. (See drawing, figure 212. This plan was done on graph paper but only the horizontal lines of the grid show in the photocopy.) I did not follow the original front line of the missing part for several reasons: placing the new front facade in line with that of the remaining building would have rendered the building's mass long and narrow; I wanted the roof of the new part to step back and down; and I wanted to keep the old foundation area as a nestled garden, part of the enclosing nature. Earlier in the century the woods behind the building had been cleared, except for the large trees, as pasture. I cleared out the brush but left the encroaching woods (figure 214).

I built the stone foundation for the addition as I had learned while work camping in El Salva-

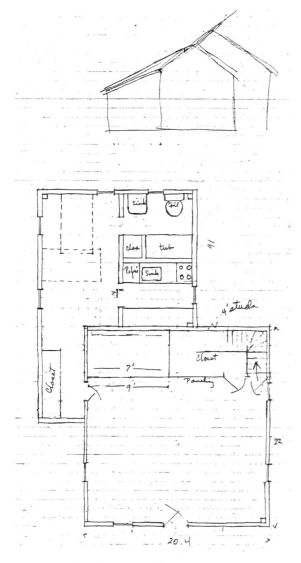

212 *First thoughts on graph paper, 1972*

213 *Beginning work, 1972*

214 *View from the north—left: large barn; center: chaise house and distant main house; right: slaughter–chicken house; 1972*

dor: dig a narrow trench, throw in stones, and pour in concrete around them. Above this I laid large rocks in a way that would have pleased Boston's 1870s Romanesque-style architect Henry Hobson Richardson: the mortar was deeply recessed and seemed worn away over the centuries. On this was placed a sill. The Mende firm did the structural part and I the finishing work.

In arranging the fenestration I employed a New England practice that seemed particularly appropriate. The main buildings normally have balanced windows while additions such as kitchen ells often do not. In many instances, windows are surprisingly close to doors and there are long stretches of clapboard or shingle. To achieve this "feel," the keeping-room block had paired windows on the south and west, but the south face of the addition has one window and an expanse of

shingles. Many people looking at the plans suggested the bathroom window be put in the same wall to balance the design. I wanted the creative tension of dissimilarity. For the same reason I moved the door from the center of the west wall (figure 215) to the west end of the north wall. (The drawing seen as figure 212 is an early working plan in which the outside door is still located in the west wall.) I brought two giant flat stepping stones from a neighboring early house site and stacked them to make two steps to the new door.

The fireplace is off-center but its chimney slants to come through the ridge pole. Its exterior shape follows the pattern of the large main house chimney: near the top two courses step out five eighths of an inch and then return to the original size for two more courses.

215–218 Views, 1972–1973

162

INSIDE

Not many early features remained inside, and none was consistent with my vision of the room. The east end, figure 219, would gain a fireplace, a closet with a paneled wall and door, and to the right a staircase door (figure 228). To the north, about where the left window is in figure 219, a doorway would lead to the hall of the new part. To design the fireplace, I studied published seventeenth-century fireplaces and looked at several firsthand. With only a few changes, I based my design on the one Roger Bacon partially rebuilt in his house as seen in figure 36. I measured it and on graph paper laid out each brick. I also photographed it.

Figure 220 looks up from under his lintel. To the right is the inside part of the lintel cut at an angle and covered with mortar to keep it from scorching. For my lintel I acquired an old yellow pine beam from a mill and slanted the inside. Roger Bacon had closed in his flue with a sheet of asbestos, leaving within it a smaller hole sufficient for the draft. This he closed by hand with another sheet of asbestos when the fireplace was not in use. I had the mason put in dampers—he could not get one long enough for the opening, so he placed two end to end. Some people have wanted to line these reconstructed chimneys—or, in this case, totally fake chimney—with ceramic flue lines. Perhaps it is possible to get one large enough, but I know of a case where two were run side by side. Instead of drawing the fire, the draft came down one flue and up the other without taking much of the smoke. I did not think a flue liner necessary.

The mason who had accurately rebuilt the chimneys on the main house built this one. I had considered using stone but he informed me firmly that there were no early stone fireplaces because stone shatters under heat: a stone fireplace had just been built at Brown University and when lit peppered the room with bits of stone, like shrapnel. Certainly many early stone fireplaces were used,

219 East wall of slaughter–chicken house, 1972

220 View up Bacon House fireplace

221 Clinton D. Baer building fireplace, 1972

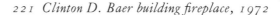

222–224 Views of fireplace, 1975

but one has to know the appropriate kind of stone. The lintel was placed on thin pieces of tulip poplar above the brickwork; this allows the lintel to shrink and expand during seasonal changes in humidity. The slender pieces of wood are crushed rather than cracking the plaster above or the bricks below.

Doing the outside corners of the fireplace, where the front faces turn to the slightly canted sides, was tricky. As seen by the shadows on the headers of the bricks turning the corner in figure 225, there can be an overdramatic dovetail effect. This would be appropriate if you wanted the fireplace to look colonial revival, but in most earlier fire-

places the angle of the bricks was subtly adjusted so the misalignment of the headers was not noticeable (figure 221), and often the front face was smoothed with plaster. I played colonial revival tricks within the fireplace, putting recesses to the left (figure 224) and to the right an arch closed in with bricks (figure 225). This was to give the illusion that there was an oven behind the paneling and that its opening had been closed at a later date.

When everything was dry, I built small fires along the back and right faces to add the soot of ages. Roger Bacon, perhaps more realistically, whitewashed his and concentrated the fire in the center (figure 36). The fireplace and chimney above the roof were of reproduction brick fired to look old. The attic part of the chimney was to be plastered and there I used concrete blocks.

For the hearth, I put a concrete foundation and over this a layer of sand about an inch and a half thick. I gave the sand a dramatically rolling top surface and the bricks placed on it followed the undulation (figure 226). I wanted to create the kind of movement found in the keeping-room hearth seen in figure 165. The bricks were laid in the same pattern as that found in the main house and followed the same procedure described for relaying the parlor and study hearths there.

The floor was of new ten-inch boards. To give it a worn surface, I threw on quantities of sand. Then, using a circular floor sander with steel wool pads, I spent hours grinding the pine wood in a logical use pattern. This took away the soft parts and allowed the knot areas to stick up. It did leave hard-to-remove circular scratches. Most of these

225–226 Views of fireplace, 1975

I worked out by hand, sanding and scraping with the grain. Several coats of paint removed any further traces. The keeping room combined a mixture of old and new woodwork. The summer beam is from a seventeenth-century Rhode Island house. The paneling to the right of the fireplace is mid-eighteenth century, as are the doors. (If one were consistent, the summer beam should have been boxed by the date of paneling and doors.) All the casing of the girts (around the top edge of the room) and the corner posts are new wood with a half-round molding—similar to that seen in figure 110. (Most of the casings contain nothing inside.) The woodwork was painted a dark green and the disparity between the old and new surfaces was not too evident.

I installed as much insulation as space would allow before the floors, walls, and ceiling were begun. For heat, I placed electrical wire on the ceiling before it was plastered. (Also before plastering, some wrought-iron hooks were added, figure 228.) The problem with this type of heat is that if part of you is under a table or obscured from the rays, it is colder than the exposed areas; and, of course, electrical heat is now exorbitantly expensive. I did not put any heat upstairs, but there was a stove hole in that part of the chimney in case I wanted to add a stove. Today I would use a small furnace, perhaps located in the bathroom/kitchen area along with the hot-water heater, or in the back part of the open area below the building (seen in figure 211), provided it could be kept from freezing. If this were recessed and boarded on its outer faces, anyone looking at the building would read it as a useful cupboard and not a furnace.

The windows were made like those in the dressing room and kitchen chambers in the main house and have very few parts (figure 227). Nine over 6, 6 over 6, and 4 over 4 sash are held by removable beaded boards within a narrow frame. That frame is of boards run toward the wall and these have half-round moldings run on their outer edges.

227 *Window construction in loft looking east*

To obtain inclusive photographs of the keeping room it was necessary to use a wide-angle lens, which makes it seem larger and sparser than it was. Figure 228 shows the fireplace, paneled wall, cupboard door, and staircase door. At the left is the north wall door leading to the hall and bedroom/study. Figure 229 is the south wall through which one looked at the main house. Figure 230, of the west and north walls, includes the exterior door that had been moved from the center of the west wall. Now it is nestled in the northwest corner.

228–229 Views of keeping room, 1975

230 *View of keeping room, 1975*

Going through the door near the fireplace, one entered the far end of the hall seen in figure 231. Immediately, there was a board cupboard for clothing. Past the corner of the old building—which now encloses the end of the fireplace—was the door to the kitchen (in figure 232 it is exaggerated by the wide-angle lens). It was done in tones of dark brown-red: floor, cupboards, window, Formica surfaces, stove, and refrigerator.

Past the kitchen was the bathroom (figure 233). It contained the hot-water heater in a closet, a plastic one-piece bathtub/shower, and a toilet and sink purchased from a building salvage business. There were problems replacing the leather valves of the toilet tank but it was accomplished. (Reproduction toilets are available—see Bibliography.) The giant oak tree and rocks provided a dramatic view through the windows in the bathroom, the

end of the bedroom/study, and the upper room (figures 218 and 227).

When creating the upstairs, my mind continually returned to the sleeping loft of the Rhode Island, Israel Arnold House described in the Preface. I wanted a stringent, heavily faceted white space with a giant chimney flanked by a small window and confronted by a staircase. The stairs twisted up through the closet and come out at the chimney stack. I realize that the upstairs I created was an overly lean Danish modern/neo-Shaker vision of the past with new woodwork and plaster. To make the steps look old and full of character, with thin edges and knots rising, I ground them with a hand-held electric sander and finished them with hand sanding. It is difficult to produce logical and convincing wear—ideally one wants people with sandpaper on their shoes

231 Study–bedroom, 1975

232 Kitchen, 1975

233 Bathroom, 1975

234

234–236 *Stairs to loft, 1975*

236

235

237 *Detail of staircase railing, 1975*

running endlessly up and down the steps. But I studied the wear in other houses and sought to reproduce it.

The simple railing, figures 235 through 238, was inspired by that in the sleeping loft of the Israel Arnold House, but uses two rather than three rails. There are bead moldings on the corners of the rails and the posts (figure 237). The latter were attached to the sides of the boarded staircase with screws so the railing was removable when furniture went up or down. I used real plaster, but when the plasterer put in the ceiling of this area, he rounded the corners between the slanting sides and the flat top. I did not discover this until after it dried. I wanted a sharp edge between the angles so, with a sharp tool, I scraped away the rounding area, creating a distinct, hard break between the sides and top. I put cupboard doors on one side so those eaves were available for storage. (The wide-angle aspect in figures 238 and 239 makes a rather intimate space seem to have cavernous proportions.)

The final statement, both inside and out, is a romantic 1970s vision of an ideal little house in the woods as guided by certain earlier ideas. As with the work on the main house, this building was the product of a series of choices that resulted from training, advice, and personal vision. During the entire Rehoboth project, other choices would have been as interesting and at times more historically

238–239 Loft, 1975

correct. I hope that I knew when I was deviating from historic precedent. But one is inevitably of one's time and it is impossible to return totally to the mentality and procedures of another age.

Appendix 1

Furnishing the Joseph Lloyd House Using the 1793 John Lloyd II Inventory

Although refinements have since been made to the Joseph Lloyd House, I have reproduced the divisions established at the beginning to demonstrate the process. To assist the modern reader, furniture, pictures, fireplace equipment, and informative textiles have been italicized. As the most helpful items indicating differing rooms are bedsteads (referring to the wooden frames; "bed" refers to a mattress) and fireplace equipment, these are singled out with single and double asterisks in the margin.

The Estate
Inventory of John Lloyd
of Queens Village
June 3, 1793

An Inventory of the Goods, Chattels, & Credits,
of John Lloyd, Jun.ʳ, of the Town of Oysterbay,
Queens Village, in Queens County, and State of New York

	£	s	d
One white hat 10/, two black ditto 9/	0.	19.	0
One white broad cloth Coat & Jacket 40/, one bottle green dᵒ 29/	3.	9.	0
One Coat dᵒ 8/, one Surtout 16/, one bearskin dᵒ 16/	2.	0.	0
One stamped vest 6/, one streaked dᵒ 2/, one black dᵒ 4/, blue dᵒ 4/	0.	16.	0
One white dᵒ /6, four waistcoats 2/, one old Coat 1/	0.	3.	6
Seven pair of old Breeches 6/, black pair of dᵒ 8/, white dᵒ 2/	0.	16.	0
Two pair of drawers 2/, one pair of Overhalls 4/	0.	6.	0

	£	s	d
Two pair of Shoes 5/, one pair of Shoe Buckles 3/, knee d.º 6/	0.	14.	0
One pair of boots 40/, one pair of d.º 6/, one pair of Shoes 2/	2.	8.	0
One pair of lead colored breeches 4/, one d.º Coat & Vest 40/	2.	4.	0
One Stock buckle 4/, one pair of gold sleeve buttons 16/	1.	0.	0
Ten neck Stocks 16/, one Jane Coat 8/, two white Jackets 1/6	1.	5.	6
Thirteen Jacket patterns 65/, two linnen Jackets 4/	3.	9.	0
Three pair of linnen breeches 12/, five pair of trousers 14/	1.	6.	0
Two pair of breeches 2/, three Jackets 9/, one pair of drawers 1/6	0.	12.	6
One Birdseye Coat 8/, one great Coat 8/	0.	16.	0
Four holland shirts 60/, eleven old d.º 77/, five linnen d.º 30/	8.	7.	0
Four handkerchiefs 12/, one pair of silk stockings 8/	1.	0.	0
Four pair of woolen d.º 8/, ten pair of linnen d.º 20/	1.	8.	0
Two pair of hemp d.º 4/ one pair of cotton d.º 3/	0.	7.	0
One pair of mittens 2/, one pair of leather gloves 3/	0.	5.	0
One watch 40/, one walking cane 1/6	2.	1.	6
One ink stand 1/, tooth brush /3	0.	1.	3
	£35.	14.	3

Amount brought forward	£35.	14.	3
One great Bible 16/, one d.º 5/, a number of pamphlets 2/	1.	3.	0
Johnson's Dictionary 2 vol.ˢ 9/, Bragge's Sermons 3/	0.	12.	0
Elements of agriculture 2 vol.ˢ 9/, practical farmer 1/6	0.	10.	6
Tillotson's Sermons 8/, paradise lost & regain'd 1/	0.	9.	0
Spelling Dictionary /3, Calamy's Sermons 1/, history of Engl.ᵈ 8/	0.	9.	3
Prayer book 1/, Essay on crimes & punishments 3/	0.	4.	0
Sherlock's discourses 2/, Comparitive view 2/, french Gramm.ʳ 1/	0.	5.	0
Free Mason's history 2/, Country Gentleman's Companion 2/	0.	4.	0
Treatise of detraction 1/6, West on the Resurrection 5/	0.	6.	6
Salmon's Grammer 8/, Baileys Dictionary 2 vol.ˢ 12/	1.	0.	0
Royal Dictionary 9/, Anson's Voyage 3/, small bible 1/	0.	13.	0
Gordon's Grammer 1/, Robert Nelson's true devotion 1/	0.	2.	0
Sherlock's Sermons 2 vol.ˢ 2/, Military discipline /6	0.	2.	6
Family Physician 6/, money scales &c 8/	0.	14.	0
Forty nine pair of Sheets	53.	18.	0
Sixty towels 180/, twenty pair of pillow cases 156/	16.	16.	0
Thirty table cloths 360/, *two square* [rectangular?] *cherry tree tables* 80/	22.	0.	0
One looking glass 60/, one oil cloth [floor cloth] *2/, six chairs 18/*	4.	0.	0
** *Tongs, fire slice, & hand irons* [andirons] *20/, bellows 2/6*	1.	2.	6
A number of old gimblets 1/, one pair of spurrs, 4/	0.	5.	0
One two foot rule 1/, Horse phlemes 1/, Spy Glass 60/	3.	2.	6
Two brooms /6, one pruning knife 1/, one muslin bed quilt 80/	4.	1.	6
Four Counterpanes 80/, one Cradle blanket 8/	4.	8.	0
One set of woolen curtains 40/, one calico bedspread & curtains 20/	3.	0.	0
Eighteen yards of linnen check 36/, *one easy chair & c* [cover] *60/*	4.	16.	0
Two double rose blankets 16/, *six chairs 24/*	2.	0.	0

		£	s	d
* One bed [mattress] 60/, one old d? 30/, *one set of calico curtains bedstead* [bed] *& c* 80/	. . . .	8.	10.	0
One toilet [dressing] *table & apparatus 6/, one piece of carpet 2/*	. . .	0.	8.	0
Oval looking glass 20/, large gilt looking glass 60/	. . . . .	4.	0.	0
		£174.	16.	6

Amount brought forward £174. 16. 6

		£	s	d
One brush 3/, *sixteen pictures 30/,* one bed pan 12/	. . . . .	2.	5.	0
Two stone pots 2/, *one earthen d? /6, one toylet* [dressing] *table &c 6/*		0.	8.	6
Three chairs 12/, one old bed 30/, one old bed quilt 12/	. . . .	2.	14.	0
* One dutch blanket 12/, *one bedstead, & curtains, &c 30/*	. . . .	2.	2.	0
* *Small trunk 2/,* old iron 2/, *small bedstead &* bed 30/	. . . .	1.	14.	0
One stand 2/, two pistols, 16/, one sickle 1/	. . . . .	0.	19.	0
A number of seed horns & shells 2/, thirteen bags 13/	. . . .	0.	15.	0
** Three sacks 6/, one gun 16/, *one pair of handirons 6/*	. . . .	1.	8.	0
* *One bedstead 10/,* four bed blankets 20/, old bed quilt 4/	. . . .	1.	14.	0
Old square tea table 2/, one old desk 20/, looking glass 20/	. . . .	2.	2.	0
* *One rocking cradle 3/, two chairs 3/, bedstead 10/, curtains 15/*	. . .	1.	11.	0
** Two dutch blankets 8/, one coverlid 10/, *one fire shovel 2/*	. . . .	1.	0.	0
One picture /6, one warming pan 6/, two dutch blankets 13/	. . .	0.	19.	6
One stove [footwarmer?] *1/, ten candlesticks 15/, one gageing rod 2/*	. .	0.	18.	0
One old carpet 3/, one d? 3/, eight smoothing irons 4/6	. . . .	0.	10.	6
One old bed 20/, two old blankets 6/, one old bed 10/	. . . .	1.	16.	0
One chair 2/, one old bed 20/, one bed quilt 18/	. . . .	2.	0.	0
One dutch blanket 6/, two d? 12/, one counterpane 15/	. . . .	1.	13.	0
* Two blankets & *a bedstead 10/, two Chests 3/*	. . . . .	0.	13.	0
One Saddle bridle &c 60/, *one marking iron /9*	. . . .	3.	0.	9
Sixteen razors & a case 9/, seven pair of sheep shears 9/	. . . .	0.	18.	0
Four old books 1/, *two old chests 2/, three window curtains 1/*	. . .	0.	4.	c
One looking glass 10/, one old table 2/, two chairs 6/	. . . .	0.	18.	0
One bed 20/, two dutch blankets 12/	. . . . . .	1.	12.	0
* *Bedstead & cord 8/, great wheel 6/, one reel 2/*	. . . .	0.	16.	0
One cloath horse 2/, one meat Jack 40/	. . . . .	2.	2.	0
One brush 1/, ten chairs 40/, one stand 10/	. . . . .	2.	11.	0
One carpet & looking glass	. . . .	20.	0.	0
** One case of knives & forks 40/, *one pair of hand irons 40/*	. . .	4.	0.	0
One pair of snuffers 1/, pewter platters & plates 60/	. . . .	3.	1.	0
Five sickles 5/, two hetchels 4/, two augers 2/	. . . . .	0.	11.	0
Old iron 4/, old lumber 16/, one cradle [farm?] 3/	. . . .	1.	3.	0
Thirty weight of feathers 60/, small wheel 8/, one rope 1/	. . . .	3.	9.	0
One hetchel 4/, twenty two weight of wool 30/, eight sides of leather 64/	.	4.	18.	0
Three calves skins 18/, six sheep d? 4/ one cradle & scythe 8/	. .	1.	10.	0
One side saddle 30/, one great wheel 3/	. . . . .	1.	13.	0
Small trunk 2/, one old desk 30/, one chest 6/	. . . . .	1.	18.	0
		£256.	3.	9

	£	s	d
Amount brought forward	£256.	3.	9
One Soupspoon 35/, two Silver cans 80/	5.	15.	0
One doz.ⁿ of teaspoons 40/, nine table spoons 54/	4.	14.	0
One pair of sugar tongs 6/, one pair of snuffers /6	0.	6.	6
Knives & forks & box 6/, earthen ware 30/	1.	16.	0
Teaboard [tray?] & set of china with a Cadee 70/	3.	10.	0
Thirty china plates 15/, seven d.^o dishes 7/	1.	2.	0
Eight cups & saucers 5/, sugar pot and milk d.^o 2/	0.	7.	0
Ten tumblers 5/, eleven foot glasses 3/	0.	8.	0
Plate warmer 8/, four stonepots 4/, candle box 3/	0.	15.	0
Five earthen pots 2/6, candle box 1/6, two sugar d.^o 1/ . .	0.	5.	0
Tea board [tray?] & canister 2/, one case & bottles 4/ . . .	0.	6.	0
Two decanters 5/, two demi Johns [bottles] 16/	1.	1.	0
Twenty square bottles 5/, ten round d.^o 1/6	0.	6.	6
Two jugs 2/, one jarr 1/, two earthen vessels 1/	0.	4.	0
Twenty four casks & sixty barrels of cider in d.^o . . .	16.	0.	0
Two Casks & four barrels of vinegar in d.^o	1.	0.	0
Forty five weight of tallow 22/6, a number of old casks 8/ . .	1.	10.	6
Apples & casks 20/, a number of glass bottles 9/, stone pots 1/ .	1.	10.	0
** *One frying pan 1/6, four iron pots 12/, two gridirons 5/* . .	0.	18.	6
Two dish kettles 4/, three trammels 12/	0.	16.	0
Tongs & fire slice 4/, old table 2/, one d.^o 5/ . . .	0.	11.	0
Copper tea kettle 4/, large iron kettle 12/, one copper d.^o 40/ .	2.	16.	0
Fish d.^o 18/, two brass kettles 12/, three cedar tubs 12/ . .	2.	2.	0
One churn 2/, cheese 40/, six flour barrels 6/	2.	8.	0
Bake pan 1/, tea kettle 6/, 24 milk pans 12/	0.	19.	0
Two stone pots 1/6, one pair of scales & weights 3/ . . .	0.	4.	6
One hand saw 4/, six pails 6/, steelyard* 5/	0.	15.	0
Six butcher knives 3/6, Bullet moulds 8/, one ax 4/ . . .	0.	15.	6
Smoaked meat 120/, fifteen barrels of apples 45/ . . .	8.	5.	0
	£317.	14.	9

	£	s	d
Amount brought forward	£317.	14.	9
One pair of old red oxen 300/, one pair of young d.^o 260/ . . .	28.	0.	0
Two pair of four year old Steers	24.	0.	0
One red pied cow 90/, one d.^o 80/, one red white fac'd d.^o 80/ . .	12.	10.	0
One dun d.^o 90/, one black d.^o 80/, one brindled d.^o 80/ . . .	11.	10.	0
One black pied d.^o 70/. one red pied d.^o 80/	7.	10.	0
One pair of two year old Steers, one red white fac'd y̆ other white 120/	6.	0.	0
Two pair of two year old Steers 240/	12.	0.	0
One pair of yearling brindle Steers 80/, a pair of black pied d.^o 80/	8.	0.	0
One brown Steer 40/, one two year old Bull 60/	5.	0.	0
Three yearling Bulls 120/, four two year old heifers 200/ . .	16.	0.	0
Six yearling heifers 240/	12.	0.	0
Salt hay at the hundred merefield 160/, english d.^o at d.^o 160/ .	16.	0.	0
Wadsworth mare 60/, black horse 80/, taint eye Mare 240/ . .	19.	0.	0

	£	s	d
Bay d? 240/, two year old horse 260/, Horse colt 90/ . . .	29.	10.	0
One brindle cow 60/, red white fac'd d? 90/, black white fac'd d? . .	11.	10.	0
Red pied d? 80/, red d? 90/, dun d? 90/, red d? 80/	17.	0.	0
Red pied d? 90/, Brown pied d? 90/, red d? 90/	13.	10.	0
Red pied d? 80/, brown Steer 30/, two waggon horses 160/ . .	13.	10.	0
One colt 90/, one two year old mare 240/, two half bushels 3/ . .	16.	13.	0
One Chaise & Harness	26.	0.	0
English hay in the old Barn 80/, Salt d? in d? 70/ . . .	7.	10.	0
Five Calves 150/, two d? 40/, two stacks of sedge 140/ . .	16.	10.	0
Two crackels 8/, two pair of waggon wheels 24/ . . .	1.	12.	0
Part of a fish net 80/, one hundred bushels of corn 300/ . .	19.	0.	0
Five & a half barrels of pork 400/, two barrels of Beef 120/ . .	26.	0.	0
One hundred & fifty weight of hogs lard 70/, one ox chain 8/ . .	3.	18.	0
Sorrel Mare 300/, Stallion 1200/, old funning mill 30/ . .	76.	10.	0
One d? 120/, two hundred weight of flax 100/	11.	0.	0
Hay & stalks in the barn at home	9.	0.	0
One waggon & harness 160/, four scythes &c 20/ . . .	9.	0.	0
One grindstone 4/, two pair of geers 4/, two shovels 3/ . .	0.	11.	0
Two chissels & one Auger 2/6, five old axes 20/ . . .	1.	2.	6
Eight rakes 8/, one ox chain 10/, one horse sled 12/ . .	1.	10.	0
One Cart 80/, three yokes &c 12/, one ox chain 8/ . .	5.	0.	0
One Sleigh & Harness 100/, four barrels of vinegar 20/ . .	6.	0.	0
	£816.	1.	3

	£	s	d
Amount brought forward	£816.	1.	3
Three hides 24/, six hoes 12/, one pair of geers 2/ . . .	1.	18.	0
Three plows 50/, two harrows 20/, two bush scythes 8/ . .	3.	18.	0
One harrow 4/, three corn baskets 6/, two dung forks 3/ . .	0.	13.	0
Five pitch forks 5/, two shovels 6/, one crow bar 4/ . .	0.	15.	0
Ten hogs 117/6, fourteen small d? 140/	12.	17.	6
One old Cart 40/, cross cut saw 20/, four iron wedges 4/ . .	3.	4.	0
Six hundred sheep at 8/ p? head	240.	0.	0
Four Hundred d? at 6/ p? head	120.	0.	0
Four hundred & fifty bushels of wheat at 8/ p? bushel . .	180.	0.	0
One horse 80/, one pocketbook 6/, 23 pieces of dutch lace 8/ . .	4.	14.	0

Negro Servants

	£	s	d
Three old Negroes, Viz.—John Potter & His Wife Judith, and old Hannah, which being nearly past labor, we think of no value, but neither as an encumbrance to the Estate	0.	0.	0
Boston, & Benjamin, two younger Negroes, to whom it appears by the Books of the deceas'd, he had verbally given their times, & paid them wages as other hired Men, for near two years past, which we supposed therefore, were to be considered as no part of the Estate of the Deceased	0.	0.	0

	£	s	d
Negro Man Jupiter	16.	0.	0
D.º Samuel	16.	0.	0
D.º Edward	32.	0.	0
Negro Girl Sarah	20.	0.	0
	£1468.	0.	9

Bonds & Notes due to John Lloyd Jun.ʳ dec.ᵈ

	£	s	d
One penal Bond, given by James, & Mason F. Cogswells, principal, & interest due on the same is . . .	1171.	11.	5
One d.º given by James Cogswell, principal, & interest due on y.ᵉ same .	408.	1.	3
One d.º given by Lemuel Douglass, principal, & interest due on d.º . .	19.	18.	5
Sundry bonds, & Notes, given by John Lloyd, due on the same . .	4274.	15.	1¾
One Note given by Mary Soper, interest, & principal due on d.º .	31.	1.	0
One Note given by Ledekiah Morgan, principal & interest due on d.º .	11.	19.	0
One d.º given by Isaac Rogers & Stephen Brooks due on d.º . .	8.	0.	0
	£7393.	6.	11¾
Cash in the house, at the death of the deceased	352.	11.	3
	£7745.	18.	2¾

Queens Village January 28.ᵗʰ, A.D. 1793,

The above & foregoing inventory taken, & appraised

by   Joseph Barker
                [signature]
                                        Appraisers
             Matthias Abbott
                [signature]
             Amelia Lloyd   Administratrix
                [signature]

Queens County ——— Be it Remembered that on the third Day of June Seventeen Hundred and Ninety Three Personally came and appeared before me Joseph Robinson Surrogate of the said County aforesaid Amelia Lloyd Administratrix of John Lloyd Jun.ʳ of Queens Village deceased and being duly sworn on her Oath declared that the within writing Signed by her The Deponent Contains a true and Perfect Inventory of all and Singular the Goods, Chattels, and Credits which were of the said John Lloyd Jun.ʳ as far as had Come to her hands Posession or Knowledge or into the Hands Posession of any Person or Persons in Trust for her to her knowledge

                                    Joseph Robinson Surrogate
                                    [signature][1]

A list of furniture and some textiles in the John Lloyd II 1793 inventory, preserving the original sequence. A possible fireplace room division is shown. Values are given in shillings unless otherwise indicated.

		Value (Shillings)
2	square cherry tables	80
1	looking glass	60
1	oil cloth [floor cloth]	2
6	chairs	18

FIREPLACE

1	set woolen curtains	40
1	calico bedspread & curtains	20
1	easy chair & c [cover]	60
6	chairs	24
1	bedstead calico curtains, &c.	80
1	toilet [dressing] table & apparatus (textile skirt?)	6
1	piece of carpet	2
1	oval looking glass	20
1	large gilt looking glass	60
16	pictures [prints?]	30
1	toylet [dressing] table, &c.	6
3	chairs	12
1	bedstead & curtains, &c.	30
1	small trunk	2
1	small bedstead & bed	30
1	stand	2

FIREPLACE

1	bedstead	10
1	old square [rectangular as opposed to round] tea table	2
1	old desk	20
1	looking glass	20
1	rocking cradle	3
2	chairs	3
1	bedstead (listed with curtains, bed or window?)	10

FIREPLACE ?

1	picture	6
1	stove [footwarmer?]	1
10	candlesticks	15
1	old carpet	3
1	ditto [old carpet]	3
1	chair	2
1	bedstead	10

		Value (Shillings)	
2	chests	3	
2	old chests	2	
3	window curtains	1	
1	looking glass	10	
1	old table	2	
2	chairs	6	
1	bedstead & cord	8	
10	chairs	40	
1	stand	10	
1	carpet & looking glass	20	(pounds)

FIREPLACE

1	small trunk	2
1	old desk	30
1	chest	6
1	Teaboard [tray?] & set of china with a caddy	70
1	Teaboard & cannister	2

FIREPLACE

1	old table	2
1	ditto	5

Furniture in the John Lloyd II inventory, arranged by form. Value given in shillings unless otherwise indicated.

	Number	Value
BEDSTEADS:	?	[20 (bedspread and curtains—probably in storage)]
	1	80 (and calico curtains)
	1	30 (and curtains, etc.)
	1	30 (small)
	1	10
	1	10 (and curtains: bed or window?)
	1	10
	1	8
	7?	
CANDLESTICKS:	10	15

	Number	*Value*	
CARPETS:	1	2	(piece of)
	1	3	(old)
	1	3	(old)
	1		(listed with a looking glass for £20)
			(see also floor cloth)
	4		
CHAIRS:	6	18	(3 each?)
	6	24	(4 each?)
	3	12	(4 each?)
	2	3	(1½ each?)
	1	2	
	2	6	(3 each?)
	10	40	(4 each?)
	30		
CHESTS:	2	3	(1½ each?)
	2	2	(1 each?, old)
	1	6	
	5		
CRADLE:	1	3	(rocking)
DESKS:	1	20	(old)
	1	30	(old)
	2		
DRESSING	1	6	(and apparatus)
(toilet)	1	6	(etc.)
TABLES:			
	2		
EASY CHAIR:	1	60	(and cover)
FLOOR CLOTH:	1	2	
LOOKING GLASSES:	1	60	
	1	20	(oval)
	1	60	(large, gilt)
	1	20	
	1	10	
	1		(part of £20)
	6		

	Number	*Value*	
PICTURES:	16	30	(prints?)
	1	6	
	17		
STANDS:	1	2	
	1	10	
	2		
STOVE:	1	1	
[footwarmer?]			
TABLES:	2	80	(40 each?) (square [rectangular] cherry)
	1	2	(old square [rectangular?] tea)
	1	2	(old)
	1	2	(old)
	1	5	(old)
			(see also dressing tables)
	6		
TEABOARDS:	1	70	(with a set of china and caddy)
[trays?]	1	2	(with cannister)
	2		
TRUNKS:	1	2	(small)
	1	2	(small)
	2		

Furniture as placed in the Joseph Lloyd House in 1980.[2]

PARLOR

Fireplace, andirons, tongs, etc.	Ten chairs
Carpet	Square [rectangular?] cherry table
Looking glass	Old square [rectangular] tea table
Picture	Teaboard and set of china with caddy
Some of 16 prints	Stand

OFFICE

One pair of andirons	Three chairs
Floor cloth	Old desk
Looking glass	Old desk

OFFICE (cont'd.)

Small trunk
Small trunk
One case bottles
Two decanters
Ten tumblers
Eleven foot glasses
One pair of snuffers
One foot rule
One gauging rod
A number of old gimlets

One pruning knife
One spy glass
One pair of spurs
Twenty square bottles
One brush
One saddle and blanket and c.
Two pistols
A number of seed horns and shells
One gun

KITCHEN

Two chairs
Two old tables
Candle box
Ten candlesticks
One pair snuffers
Tongs and fire slice
One fire shovel
Three trammels
Two grid-irons
One frying pan
One meat jack
Two dish kettles
Four iron pots
One warming pan

Four stone pots
Five earthen pots
One jar
Two demi-johns
Earthenware (30 shillings)
Stone pots
Two earthen vessels
Two jugs
Ten round bottles
One clothes horse
One stove [footwarmer?]
Two sugar boxes
Pewter platters and plates (60 shillings)

FRONT PASSAGE

Some prints

REAR PASSAGE

Six chairs

UPPER FRONT PASSAGE

One old table

PARLOR CHAMBER

One pair andirons
One carpet
One looking glass
One oval looking glass
Two chairs
One easy chair and cover
One dressing table covered with a skirt

One chest
One rectangular tea table
One stand
Bedstead
Candlebox
Pot

OFFICE CHAMBER

Three window curtains
Looking glass
Two chairs
One bedstead with curtain

One small bedstead
One stone pot
Four old books

MIDDLE CHAMBER

One looking glass
One dressing table
Bedstead with curtains

Small bedstead
One chair

NORTHWEST CHAMBER—STOREROOM

Rocking cradle
Thirty weight of feathers
One rope

Three calf skins
Eight sides of leather
Six sheepskins

STILL UNSPECIFIED

Two carpets
Two chests

Two old chests
Two bedsteads

DINING PARLOR
(This is now absorbed in the non-historic, multipurpose area, and objects judged to have been used here are not in the house.)

Six chairs
One square cherry table
One case of knives and forks
Knives, forks and box
One pair of sugar tongs
Two silver canns

Thirty china plates
Nine tablespoons
One soup spoon
Twelve teaspoons
Seven china dishes
One plate warmer

CELLAR
(Not shown to the public; objects judged to have been here are not in the house.)

A number of glass bottles
A number of casks
Twenty-four casks and sixty barrels of cider
Old iron
One iron

One marking iron
One side saddle
Apples and casks
Two casks and four barrels of vinegar
Eight smoothing irons

BARN
(The barn is no longer standing and these items are not on the property.)

Two augers
Five sickles
Old lumber
Twenty-two weight of wool
One cradle (farm) and scythe
Seven pairs of sheep shears

One cradle (farm)
Forty weight of tallow
Three sacks
Thirteen bags
One sickle

Choosing office furniture was assisted by a Southold, Long Island, inventory:

Inventory of the office of Ezra L'Hommedieu
Southold Long Island, 1811

1 Desk (pine)
1 Desk and bookcase
6 Chairs (flag [rush] bottom)
1 Chair (rocking)
1 Arm chair
2 Looking glasses

1 Cabinet and bookcase
1 Table (maple)
1 Chest
1 Trunk (traveling)
1 Pr. Fire dogs [andirons] & tongs

Appendix 2

The Descent of the Daniel Bliss House, and Its Furnishings

The October 28, 1751, deed between Daniel Bliss and Ephraim and Hannah Chaffee reads in part:

> Beginning at a Stake & heap of Stones being ye South west Corner Standing Thirteen rods Northerly from Wolf Plain Brook or Run (so called) from thence till it Comes to a Stake & Stones being ye South west Corner of ye Land of Nathaniel Butterworth son of Noah Butterworth Deceased from Thence Running with said Nathaniel Land about one hundred and fourty Rods till it Comes to a Highway; and then Turning & Running Westerly and bounding northerly . . . also two Sixteenth part of a Certain Tract of Land Containing two acres Laid out for a millot Lying on Both sides of Palmer River Laid out to John Butterworth & Doctor Richard Bowen. . . . Also ye privilege of a Cartway through ye Land of John Jones from ye above Bounded tract of Land till it Comes to ye millot. [This land lay south of Homestead Avenue.][1]

In a deed of February 28, 1759, Daniel Bliss gave to his son, Jacob Bliss:

> In consideration of ye value of thirty pounds lawfull money paid me in Labour for me after he arrived to ye age of Twenty one years . . . Two Certain Tracts or Parcells of Land Situate in Rehoboth Mass lying Westerly of ye west Branch of Palmer River, and partly on both Sides said River, one of said Tracts of Land Containing Three Acres and a half & four Rods Lying on ye Northerly Side of ye Highway [now Homestead Avenue], Going Easterly Toward the House of Uriah Bowen. . . . Also a Dwelling House Standing on ye above Tract of Land.[2]

This is the first mention of the Dwelling House and this land above Homestead Avenue, where it was later joined by Perryville Road (see map, figure 86). Evidence has not been found as to when Daniel acquired this land to the north of Homestead Avenue, nor whether there were any buildings on it prior to his purchase. The family tradition is that Daniel Bliss built this house north of the road in 1742. Clearly, son Jacob was occupying buildings on this site in 1759 and his father Daniel must have been living elsewhere, probably on a neighboring property, just to the northwest. At his death in 1780, Daniel gave his son more land. Jacob died in 1807 and his heirs were his widow, two sons, and four daughters. The share his widow received is typical of the time:

> I give to my Beloved Wife Judiath Two thirds of my Dwelling house & one half of my wood house and one third of my Barn & one third of my [corn] Crib & half of my Chaise and half of my Chaise house & one half of my Cider Mill Also to my Wife I give the horse I am then Possessed of & a Privilege to my Well and third of my garden & all of my land Upon the North side of the Road. Excepting part of the house lot & ground where the [blacksmith] Shop Stands Likewise to my Wife. Twenty three acres of land Upon the east side of the home lot Upon the south side of the highway Also to my Wife Thirteen Acres & a half of land Joining to & lying Upon the North side of an Eight acre lot That I Shall hereafter name to my son Asaph. . . . I give to Beloved Wife one Cow two Sheep and all the Indore Moveables Except my Desk Also to my Wife all my Produce then on hand.[3]

Such a division ensured that the main heir did not dispossess his mother or keep her from using a fair share of every necessity of life. In some wills, the wife was even guaranteed a percentage of the fireplace and oven. Daughter Lucy received the remaining third of the Dwelling house with privileges to the well "and one half of my Chaise & half of my Chaise house and one Cow & two Sheep," along with some land. Daughters Bethiah, Chloe, and Rachel each received parcels of land.

An inventory of Jacob Bliss's estate was taken on October 27, 1807, and recorded on March 1, 1808. It reads:

An Inventory of the Estate of Jacob Bliss late of Rehoboth in the County of Bristol Deceas[e]d . . .

	$	cnt
(viz) About 137 Acres of Land with the Building there on Standing at 4521 $	4521	--
Two yoak of Oxen $126, 2 Cows 36 $2 two year old 34	196	--
Sundry Articles wearing Apearel $15	015	
Three Beds and furniture, 66$ 1 Desk 8,$ 1 Table 3$	77	
2 Tables 1.50, 6 Green Chairs 6$ a number of old d[itto] 4$ . . .	11	50
1 Case 50cnt 1 Looking Glass 50 cnt 1 Chest 75 cent	1	75
A number of old Casks 10$ weaver, lombs & Tacklen 6$ . . .	16	--
2 Spining wheals 1$ 2 Brass Grittles 10$ Cider Tubs 3 . . .	14	--
Sundra Artiles [Articles] Hollowware 5,$ puter [pewter] 4$ . . .	9	--
Tinware 2$ Sundra Articles Crockery and Glass 1	3	--
Meal Chest and Seives 2$ a Quantity of Lining [Linen] 13.50 . .	15	50

	$	cnt
Rie Seive 50 cnt 2 meal Bags 75 cent hand Iron [andiron] shovel & tongs 3.50	4	75
Sunrea farming utentials 60$ one Chaise & Harnes 30	90	--
Black Smith Bellow and Tools 20$ 2 woolin Coverled 8	28	--
Steel Yard [weighing scales] 2$ Knives and forks 1.50—Book 4$ . . .	7	50
Some Leather 4$ about 1400 Whiteash Planks 49$	53	--
a Quantity of Wood and Timber 100$ house plank 3	103	--
About 15 Cord of wood Corded in the Wood	30	
	675	0
one Swine	10	50
4 Sheep	8	--
Rehoboth 27 Dec^{ber} 1807	693	50
	4521	--
	5214	50$^+$

Jacob, Sr., had two sons, Jacob, Jr., and Asaph. In the father's will Jacob, Jr., received land and half of his father's wearing apparel. Son Asaph had previously received land, and a different house with barn and orchard which he was already occupying. Now he was given more land and on his father's house lot, the use of the well, two thirds of the barn, the stable barn, two thirds of the corn crib, the "Shop that Blacksmiths work in and tools," half the cider mill, "half my Wearing Aparel and Desk and all my Farming Tools," and "all the Right I own in the School house." In addition he was to receive on his mother's death her widow's portion, which included two thirds of the house.

Asaph consolidated the house by gaining the widow's two thirds after his mother's death, and purchasing in 1813 the third bequeathed to his sister, Lucy. At his death in 1857, he left his widow, Sarah, the "improvement of [use and income from]" one third of his property during her lifetime, "except that part that I have here in given to my son Asaph Leonard Bliss," including "wood sufficient for one fire and more if she should need for her own use or repair on the premises. Also the use and improvement of all my Household furniture. . . . Also one cow and one hundred dollars in money. . . ." Two daughters, Abby and Rosina, each received $200 and some furniture. His son, Asaph L. Bliss, received, along with land, two thirds of the house during his mother's lifetime and the remainder at her death; also the house lot and half his father's wearing apparel. The other son Georgie was given a lesser share. Asaph L. Bliss died in 1861. The inventory of the estate reads:

	Dolls.	Cts.
Settee .50, 4 Chairs $1.00, Stand $.50	2	00
lot of plates $.50, glass lamp $.50, Clock $1.50	2	50
2 picture frames $1.50, Bureau $3.00, case of drawers $1.50 . . .	6	00
writing Desk $1.00, old table $.50, small bed $3, ...	4	50

	$	cnt
best bed $4, top bed & bolster $3.00, bedstead as $2, ...	9	00
old Draws $1.00, Chairs & glass $.50, library $2, ...	3	50
3 bedsteads $2., 4 picture frames $.50, Looking Glass $1, ...	3	50
Wash stand, bowl & pitcher $1.00, stand $.25, table & cover $1.50 . .	2	75
6 chairs $1.50, stove $2.00, brass kettle $.50, coverlets $.75	4	75
2 comforters $1.00, 2 bed quilts $1.00, bed & under bed & [one word		
unclear]	6	00
bedstead $.50, Map of Bristol County $2.00	2	50
Note signed Wm B. Chase, Amount Due	19	11
Money		20
Wheels & Iron bar $.75, 2 muck forks $.50	1	25
lot of hoes $.50, lot of wheels $.50, old stove $.50	1	50
Old Iron $.50, wood saw & axe $.50, one pig $7.50	8	50
wrench $.50, weighing scales $.25, harness $.25	1	00
Lumber wagon $5.00, chaise $2., plough $.50	7	50
cabbage & potatoes $2.00, small black trunk & contents, 75	2	75
lot of pen holders $.50, 2 small bells $.25 [two words unclear] 25 . . .	1	00
razor & strap $.25, pocket rule $.25, Syringe $.50	1	00
6 pr forcips $3.00, lot of small tools $1.00	4	00
lot of tools & vice $.50, Galvanic Battery $3.00	3	50
black trunk & contents $.50, square box & contents $1.00	1	50
Small trunk $.50, Gold watch $15.00	15	50
	Amt. $115	31

Part of House, Barn & about ½ acre of land	450	
about 45 acres of Wood Land	1250	
	Amt. 1750[5]	

Through the years, sales and bequests separated much of the original land from this Bliss house. Nearly all was reunited by J.[ames] Walter Bliss. He deeded most of it to Richard P. Bliss on March 2, 1921, leaving his daughter, Mildred E. Waite, a small section with a "Bungalow" to the left of the main house and some additional land.

Appendix 3

Dating Parts of the Bliss House

Summary in the Working Journal made after a visit from Antoinette Downing

1) There was a nucleus house here surviving in the exposed ceiling, the molded vertical sheathing of some walls, and the batten cellar door and the oven, the original part of the keeping-room fireplace. With this go the four two-panel doors upstairs, one of which has clearly been moved. 1742 is a very *late* date for these features. Mr. Bliss says the house is not mentioned in Daniel's 1741[1] purchase of "100 acres more or less," and appears only later, he thinks in "Old Dan'l's" 1759 gift to son Jacob, and recorded in 1780. But Antoinette says this first house could have been a very small one, primarily one room each floor. On the other hand, the four early two-panel and batten doors suggest at least that many interior doors, so it can't have been too small. The oven is of a style, placement, and size earlier than the existing fireplaces, as is the use of bars for a lug pole in keeping-room flue. This suggests we may have the old stack from head height down—(N.B.:

Must check if those bricks look mixed—used and unused—below that). She says if I took down the plaster on the keeping-room fireplace wall (it is later: but on split lath nailed to boards some of which are broken bits of molded vertical sheathing), I might see a joint. It is hard to imagine any reason for dismantling almost the whole central chimney (except the oven) and rebuilding, except if it was not a complete, five-fireplace house—if the idea was simply to get smaller, later size fireplaces, one would simply fill in.

2) The fireplace woodwork of all five fireplaces (including the keeping room) is late colonial, i.e. 1770–1780s. (I note in her book similar ones marked 1750.) So it is a 1780s house with odd vestiges.

3) In the hypothetical early house all windows would have been small 9 over 6 of that special flatter muntin kind of which one survives (in the second-floor back hall). The 12 over 12 and 12

over 8 are the 1780s when windows were enlarged.

4) She resists the idea of "faking" the fireplace of the keeping room to get a 1740s size.

The Daniel Bliss House was built in at least four stages. Faced from the road [*figure 129*] the right or eastern two thirds of the main block was probably built about 1742, although it may then have been only a story and a half. [*The possibly original plan of this half-house is shown in figure 132.*] The left or western third was added, probably in the 1780s. At that date the right front room or parlor received new moldings and fireplace wall paneling. The door from that room into the keeping room became a cupboard. To make space for a shifted back staircase, the east wall of the keeping room moved west and runs into the cupboard. The west wall of the keeping room, made of molded vertical sheathing, was pushed further west. The front hall staircase was updated, or if it had been a story and a half house, there may have been no early front steps. In adding fireplaces to the new west

rooms, the brickwork was almost entirely taken down and rebuilt. The brickwork remaining from the half-house is: the keeping-room fireplace (but it was shortened on the east end), the oven and what is left of the keeping-room hearth and possibly the parlor fireplace. Probably in the nineteenth century the ell was added. Its lower story had heavy timbering and eighteenth-century doors; the upper floor, lighter structural members and late nineteenth-century doors. The lower level may first have been a 1780s one-story addition. The shed dates from the mid- to late nineteenth century.

The original east end of the main house and the probably nineteenth-century ell have joined cellars. The west end had only a crawl space. (A similar arrangement was found nearby on Rocky Hill Road. Molly Fuller, widow of Timothy Fuller, received in 1810 through her husband's will, "Also the West end of the dwelling house, viz the new part and one third part of the Cellar under the old end of the house.")[2]

Notes

Chapter 1

1. Most of my historic information is taken from Richard C. Nylander's "The Jonathan Sayward House, York, Maine," *Antiques* 116 (September 1979), pp. 567–77. In addition, I am grateful to Mr. Nylander for discussing the house and its contents in even greater detail.

2. Taken from Abbott Lowell Cummings, *Rural Household Inventories* (Boston, 1964), pp. 190–1.

3. Departmental file, Paintings Department file, Museum of Fine Arts, Boston.

4. In 1792, for example, Charles Carroll ordered from England for one of his Annapolis parlors "'a floor cloth of the pattern following, let it be handsomely painted and very strong.' The pattern given was that of the rug's dimensions not design." William Voss Elder, III, "The Carroll Family: An English Lifestyle in America," in *"Anywhere So Long As There Be Freedom, Charles Carroll of Carrollton, His Family & His Maryland"* (catalogue for an exhibition organized by Ann C. Van Devanter, The Baltimore Museum of Art, 1975), p. 282.

5. I am indebted to Jane C. Nylander for discussing the contents of this room, particularly the rugs.

6. Elizabeth Stillinger, *The Antiquers* (New York, 1980), pp. 8–16.

7. Trumbull White and William Igleheart, *The World's Columbian Exposition, Chicago, 1893* (Chicago, 1893), pp. 518, 519, and 521.

8. Richard C. Nylander in conversation, March 1983.

9. William Seale, *The Tasteful Interlude, American Interiors Through the Camera's Eye, 1860–1917* (2nd ed., Nashville, Tenn., 1981), fig. 164.

10. The best publication on Beauport is Paul Hollister's "The Building of Beauport, 1907–1924," *American Art Journal* 13 (Winter 1981), pp. 69–89.

11. Hollister, p. 72.

12. Stillinger, pp. 27–34. See also Josephine P. Driver, "Ben: Perley Poore of Indian Hill," *Essex Institute Historical Collection* 89 (January 1953), pp. 1–18.

13. Samuel Chamberlain and Paul Hollister, *Beauport at Gloucester* (New York, 1951), p. 10.

14. Richard C. Nylander in conversation, March 1983.

15. *From Y to A—Letters from Isabella Stewart Gardner to Abram Piatt Andrew* (privately printed by Andrew Gray, New York, 1967), p. 7. Letter dated September 5, 1908, Green Hill, Brookline, Mass.

16. John Cornforth, "Beauport, Gloucester, Massachusetts-1," *Country Life* 172 (October 1982), p. 1319.

17. I am grateful to Abbott Lowell Cummings and Richard C. Nylander for reviewing these two rooms with me.

18. Stillinger, pp. 222–3.

19. John A. H. Sweeney, *Henry Francis du Pont—Observations on the occasion of the 100th anniversary of his birth, May 27, 1980* (Winterthur, Del., 1980), unpaged, facing page with portrait of Mrs. Henry Francis du Pont and her daughter, Pauline Louise, 1921. Quote given in Stillinger, p. 225, but with different wording.

20. Letter to Thomas T. Waterman, May 5, 1939. Filed: Stamper/Blackwell House, Winterthur Archives, Winterthur Museum, Winterthur, Delaware.

21. For a detailed biography of Elsie de Wolfe, see Jane S. Smith, *Elsie de Wolfe* (New York, 1982).

22. Letter to Henry Francis du Pont from Thomas T. Waterman, undated. Filed: Stamper/Blackwell House, Winterthur Archives.

23. Same letter cited in note 20.

24. There are two versions of Mrs. John Powell (1764) and a portrait which is possibly of Mrs. Michael Gill (1770–71). See Jules D. Prown, *John Singleton Copley, In America*, 2 vols. (Cambridge, Mass., 1966), vol. 1, figs. 143, 146, and 276.

25. Sweeney, unpaged, facing page with photograph of Mrs. Henry Algernon du Pont with her children Louise Evelina and Henry Francis.

26. Mary Allis in conversation, 1965.

27. For a more complete description of the Oak Hill rooms, see Wendy A. Cooper, Jonathan Fairbanks, and Wendy Kaplan, (working title) "The Oak Hill Rooms in the Museum of Fine Arts," *Museum of Fine Arts Bulletin* 81 (Boston, 1983).

28. I am indebted to Graham Hood for bringing this article to my attention and providing me with a copy.

29. When I asked Richard C. Nylander whether he had seen a reconstructed room he found convincing, he suggested the Fitch House, which led me also to the Freeman Farm.

30. Richard C. Nylander reminded me of this connection. See Alice Winchester, "Living with Antiques, Time Stone Farm in Marlboro, Massachusetts," *Antiques* 59 (June 1951), pp. 460–4.

Chapter 2

1. Abbott Lowell Cummings in conversation, March 1983.

Chapter 3

1. I am indebted to Morgan Phillips for discussing these materials with me.

Chapter 4

1. The transaction was not recorded until June 29, 1741. Bristol County Registry of Deeds, Taunton, Mass., book 30, page 166.

2. I am grateful to Susan Montgomery for researching these pipes. She reports that the McDougall company in Glasgow made TD pipes throughout the nineteenth century. The general shape of the bowls, the angle of the bowls where they meet the stems, and the bore diameters of the

stems indicate that these examples were made between 1820 and 1860. See Ivor Noël Hume, *A Guide to the Artifacts of Colonial America* (New York, 1978), pp. 301–3.

3. Barbara Franco reported to Susan Montgomery that it was common in seventeenth-century England to use objects as good-luck talismans for a new house, fireplace, and hearth, apparently a carryover from earlier ritual sacrifices. For example, the London Museum includes a display of whole chickens, shoes, candlesticks, bits of grass, et cetera, sealed inside a chimney from the Cauderdale House (c. 1700), Highgate, Greater London.

Chapter 5

1. Jane C. Nylander, "The Early American Look: Floor Coverings," *Early American Life* 14 (April 1983), pp. 12–18.

2. Quoted in William Lamson Warren, "The New England Bed Rugg," in *Bed Ruggs 1722–1833* (catalogue for an exhibition, Wadsworth Athenaeum, Hartford, Conn., 1972), p. 12.

3. Abbott Lowell Cummings in conversation, March 1983.

4. See notes 2 and 3 of Chapter 4.

5. Abbott Lowell Cummings, *Rural Household Inventories* (Boston, 1964), p. xxv.

6. The floor coverings and the wallpapered fireboards were given to the Society for the Preservation of New England Antiquities.

Appendix 1

1. John Lloyd II inventory transcribed by Miriam S. Silverman.

2. Lists of objects placed in each room compiled by Hope Alswang.

Appendix 2

1. Recorded October 4, 1752: Bristol County Registry of Deeds, Taunton, Mass., book 39, page 181.

2. Recorded November 6, 1780: Bristol County Registry of Deeds, book 60, page 136.

3. Docket labeled "Jacob Bliss 1807," Bristol County Probate Court, Taunton, Mass.

4. Same file as note 3.

5. Docket labeled "Asaph L. Bliss, 1862," Bristol County Probate Court.

Appendix 3

1. Richard Bliss often cited 1741 as the date of this purchase. The Bristol County Registry of Deeds, Taunton, Mass., records it as October 18, 1751.

2. Will of Timothy Fuller, dated April 3, 1810. In docket labeled "Timothy Fuller 1810," Bristol County Probate Court, Taunton, Mass.

Bibliography

by Ann Faubion Armstrong

The Bibliography is divided into two sections. The first deals with general topics, including buying a house, analyzing its condition, and researching its history. It begins with three helpful catalogues. The longer second section covers specific rehabilitation topics.

Many of the publications are pamphlet size and best obtained directly from sponsoring organizations whose addresses are given. A large number of articles cited are from *The Old-House Journal*, which is published by The Old-House Journal Corp., 69A Seventh Avenue, Brooklyn, N.Y. 11217. Subscriptions to this useful magazine are at present $16.00 per year and individual back issues are now available for $1.50 each. A number are produced by Technical Preservation Services Division, Office of Archeology and Historic Preservation, U.S. Department of the Interior. These are usually two sheets in length and have good bibliographies. They may be ordered from the U.S. Government Printing Office, Washington, D.C. 20410. All books cited are available in paperback with the exception of the *Reader's Digest Complete Do-It-Yourself Manual* and *Wallpaper in America*.

Catalogues

The Old-House Journal Catalogue, 69A Seventh Avenue, Brooklyn, N.Y. 11217. The most complete available.

The Renovators' Supply, Inc., Millers Falls, Mass. 01349. Mainly hardware and fixtures.

Restoration Works, Inc., 419½ Virginia Street, Buffalo, N.Y. 14201. Hardware, mantels, plumbing fixtures, cleaning and restoring products, plus some tools.

Architectural fragments, from entire walls of paneling to a single pane of old glass, can be obtained from special salvage companies or from your local salvage yard or wrecker. For the addresses of local salvage companies, consult your local preservation organization or state Historic Preservation Office.

General

R. C. Biesterfeldt, T. L. Amburgey, and L. H. Williams, *Finding and Keeping a Healthy House* (Washington, D.C., 1974). Order from U.S. Department of Agriculture, Forest Service, Miscellaneous Publication #1284, U.S. Government Printing Office, Washington, D.C. 20410. Particularly good on termite and water problems.

Richard Day, George Daniels, Clarence Martin, and Robert Scharff, *Reader's Digest Complete Do-It-Yourself Manual* (Pleasantville, N.Y., 1978). Hardback. Soup-to-nuts book for the homeowner, discussing everything from tools through repairs to new construction projects.

Clem Labine, "How to Research and Date Your Old House," *Old-House Journal*, vol. 4, no. 10 (October 1976), pp.

1, 8–11. Basic introduction to using locally available sources of information.

Charles Hall Page and Associates, *Rehab Right* (Oakland, Calif., 1979). Order from Planning Department, City Hall, 6th Floor, 1421 Washington Street, Oakland, Calif. 94612. Good coverage of styles from mid-nineteenth century. Full discussion of rehab work with diagrams.

Morgan W. Phillips, "The Eight Most Common Mistakes in Restoring Historic Houses (—And How to Avoid Them)," *Yankee*, vol. 39, no. 12 (December 1975), pp. 46–56. Commonsense guide to planning and implementing the restoration of historic buildings.

Homeowners Glossary of Terms (Washington, D.C., 1974). Order from U.S. Department of Housing and Urban Development, 451 Seventh Street, S.W., Washington, D.C. 20410. Basic data for those with little or no vocabulary in the field.

Inspection Checklist for Vintage Houses (Brooklyn, N.Y., 1975). Order from Old-House Journal Corp. (for address, see introductory note). As useful and necessary to a good evaluation process as a flashlight—don't go house inspecting without it.

Settlement Costs and You: A HUD Guide for Home Buyers (Washington, D.C., 1977). Order from U.S. Department of Housing and Urban Development, 451 Seventh Street, S.W., Washington, D.C. 20410. Everything you need to know about buying a house from the role of the broker to securing a mortgage to closing costs (complete worksheets are furnished), plus a list of other HUD publications on related topics.

Wise Home Buying (Washington, D.C., 1974). Order from U.S. Department of Housing and Urban Development, 451 Seventh Street, S.W., Washington, D.C. 20410. Good first book on subject.

Electrical and Plumbing

Clem Labine, "Co-Existing with Old Piping," *Old-House Journal*, vol. 9, no. 2 (February 1976), pp. 1, 9–11. Basic guide to understanding your old plumbing and its problems.

"Catalogue Your House's Secret Passages," *Old-House Journal*, vol. 2, no. 1 (January 1974), p. 1, 10. Valuable article relevant to electrical and plumbing. Helps you locate existing voids and tunnels inside walls that extend through from floor to floor and can carry new wiring or pipes.

"How to Make an Electrical Survey," *Old-House Journal*, vol. 2 no. 11 (November 1974), p. 2. Brief but basic article on surveying your electrical system prior to planning repairs or increasing service. Issue also contains part II of "Preventing Rot in Old Houses."

Exterior Masonry

Anne E. Grimmer, *Preservation Briefs #6: Dangers of Abrasive Cleaning to Historic Buildings* (Washington, D.C., 1979). Order from Technical Preservation Services Division (for address see introductory note). Definitive article.

Robert C. Mack, *Preservation Briefs #1: The Cleaning and Waterproof Coating of Masonry Buildings* (Washington, D.C., 1978). Order from Technical Preservation Services Division. Thorough discussion of the topic.

———, *Preservation Briefs #2: Repointing Mortar Joints in Historic Brick Buildings* (Washington, D.C., 1977). Order from Technical Preservation Services Division. Good advice on major projects and repointing a chimney.

Exterior Siding

John H. Myers, *Preservation Briefs #8: Aluminum and Vinyl Sidings and Historic Buildings* (Washington, D.C., 1979). Order from Technical Preservation Services Division. All the sound reasons why you should not put such siding on your house, from aesthetic considerations to the possibility of unseen structural damage.

Heating and Insulation

Sally E. Neilsen, *Insulating the Old House* (Portland, Me., 1977). Order from Greater Portland Landmarks, Inc., 165 State Street, Portland, Me. 04101. Thorough treatment of the topic.

Baird M. Smith, *Preservation Briefs #3: Conserving Energy in Historic Buildings* (Washington, D.C., 1978). Order from Technical Preservation Services Division. Extensive discussion of utilizing the inherent energy-saving characteristics of the older house; passive measures as well as retrofitting.

Interior Decoration

A number of companies produce paints they advertise as "historic." Turco paint was used at Rehoboth—it has since been renamed Old Village Paint, and is located at

Stubb Paint and Chemical Company, 618 West Washington Street, Norristown, Penna. 19404. It also makes Old Sturbridge Village paint in a slightly different palette.

Catherine Lynn Frangiamore, *Wallpapers in Historic Preservation* (Washington, D.C., 1977). Order from Technical Preservation Services Division. Brief but authoritative coverage of wallpaper technology, history of styles, preservation of early paper, etc.

Nina Fletcher Little, *American Decorative Wall Painting: 1700–1850* (enlarged 2nd ed., New York, N.Y., 1972). Covers interior decorative paint, graining, marbleizing, architectural japanning, freehand and stenciled wall designs, etc. Bibliography.

———, *Floor Coverings in New England Before 1850* (Sturbridge, Mass., 1967). Order from Old Sturbridge Village, Sturbridge, Mass. Covers Turkey carpets, British and European carpets, painted floor cloths, stenciled floors, home-woven rugs, and small homemade rugs. Numerous period illustrations. Bibliography.

Catherine Lynn, *Wallpaper in America: From the Seventeenth Century to World War I* (New York, 1980). Hardback. Definitive work with hundreds of illustrations, many in color.

Denys Peter Myers, *Gaslighting in America: A Guide for Historic Preservation* (Washington, D.C., 1978). Order from Technical Preservation Services Division. A definitive work including period photographs.

Jane C. Nylander, *Fabrics for Historic Buildings* (enlarged 2nd ed., Washington, D.C., 1980). Order from The Preservation Press, National Trust for Historic Preservation, 1785 Massachusetts Avenue, N.W., Washington, D.C. 20046. Thorough coverage of fabrics from the eighteenth and nineteenth centuries; a catalogue of reproduction textiles; list of manufacturers, glossary, and bibliography.

Richard C. Nylander, *Wall Papers for Historic Buildings* (Washington, D.C., 1983). Order from The Preservation Press, National Trust for Historic Preservation, 1785 Massachusetts Avenue, N.W., Washington, D.C. 20046. Careful coverage of the subject; a catalogue of reproduction papers from 1750 to 1900; list of manufacturers, glossary, and bibliography.

William Seale, *The Tasteful Interlude, American Interiors Through the Camera's Eye, 1860–1917*, 2nd ed., (Nashville, Tenn., 1981). Order from American Association for State and Local History, 1400 Eighth Avenue, South, Nashville, TN 37204. Two hundred fifty-six interior photographs of homes from coast to coast.

Interior Plaster

John Obed Curtis, "How to Save That Old Ceiling," *Old-House Journal*, vol. 8, no. 10 (October 1980), pp. 131, 142–6. In same issue as painting guide, part I.

"Major Repairs to Plaster Surfaces," *Old-House Journal*, vol. 2, no. 1 (January 1974), pp. 5–8. Basic article. In same issue as article on locating secret passages for pipes and wiring.

"Minor Repairs to Plaster Surfaces," *Old-House Journal*, vol. 1, no. 3 (December 1973), pp. 5–10. Basic article on subject. Also good article on dealing with smoking fireplaces.

Interior Wood Surfaces

(see also *Interior Decoration* and *Paint*)

"Creative Use of Wood Mouldings: Early American Wall Treatments with Wood Mouldings," *Old-House Journal*, vol. 3, no. 10 (October 1975), pp. 8–11. Discussion of basic molding profiles (historic and modern), how to match, duplicate, replace, etc. Issue also has article on Victorian exterior gingerbread work.

Frederick Herman, "Refinishing Floors: Think Twice Before Sanding," *Old-House Journal*, vol. 9, no. 2 (February 1981), pp. 27, 44–5. Also contains article on repair of old floors. In same issue as a roof article.

Clem Labine, "Restoring Clear Finishes: Reviving Is Easier and Cheaper than Total Stripping," *Old-House Journal*, vol. 10, no. 11 (November 1982), pp. 221, 238–41. How to revive clear finishes. Contains a chart covering cleaning and reviving plus how to strip for refinishing if necessary.

"Refinishing Clinic," *Old-House Journal*, vol. 9, no. 10 (October 1981), pp. 229–31. Refinishing discussion plus stain removal and bleaching guide.

"Refinishing Clinic," *Old-House Journal*, vol. 10, no. 1 (January 1982), pp. 16–18. Discussion of filling compounds, interior stains and finishes (penetrating and surface).

Landscaping

Rudy J. and Joy Putman Pavretti, *Landscapes and Gardens for Historic Buildings: A Handbook for Reproducing and Creating Authentic Landscape Settings* (Nashville, Tenn.,

1978). Order from American Association for State and Local History, 1400 Eighth Avenue, South, Nashville, Tenn. 37204. Definitive coverage of the subject, including exhaustive lists of plants authentic to various historic periods.

Paint

(see also *Interior Decoration* and *Interior Wood Surfaces*)

Sara B. Chase, *Preserving Your Old House: Stripping Exterior Paint* (Boston, 1982). Order from Society for the Preservation of New England Antiquities, 141 Cambridge Street, Boston, Mass. 02114. Inexpensive balanced discussion of all stripping techniques, their advantages and problems.

David Hardingham, "Hints on Painting," *Old-House Journal*, vol 8, nos. 10, 11, and 12 (October, November, and December 1980), pp. 135–6, 155–62, 185–8. Basic discussion of subject. October issue also has article on repairing ceilings, including dealing with calcimine paint; November issue includes article on sanding parquet floors; December issue contains an article on painting techniques for doors and windows and one on old oil furnaces.

Matthew J. Mosca, "Historic Paint Research: Determining the Original Colors," *Old-House Journal*, vol. 9, no. 4 (April 1981), pp. 81–3. Exterior paint issue with seven articles on paint.

Roger Moss, *Century of Color: Exterior Decoration for American Buildings, 1820–1920* (Watkins Glen, N.Y., 1981). Order from The American Life Foundation, Watkins Glen, N.Y. 14891. Period color illustrations.

Roof

Clem Labine, "Roofing: Repair or Replace?" *Old-House Journal*, vol. 9, no. 2 (February 1981), pp. 29–32. Roof evaluation and repair. In same issue as a major article on floor refinishing.

Sarah M. Sweetser, *Preservation Briefs #4: Roofing for Historic Buildings* (Washington, D.C., 1978). Order from Technical Preservation Services Division. Types

of historic roofing material, their use, analysis of problems, repairs, etc.

Rot (see also *Windows*)

L. O. Anderson and G. E. Sherwood, *Condensation Problems in Your House: Prevention and Solution* (Washington, D.C., 1974). Agriculture Information Bulletin No. 373, U.S. Department of Agriculture, Forest Service, Washington, D.C. 20410. Thorough treatment of the subject.

"Detecting and Defeating Rot," *Old-House Journal*, vol. 2, no. 10 (October 1974), pp. 6–8. Also articles on Gothic revival architecture of A. J. Downing.

"Preventing Rot in Old Houses," *Old-House Journal*, vol. 2, no. 11 (November 1974), pp. 1, 5–6. Companion to article above. Also contains article on electrical system survey.

"Rising Damp in Walls," *Building Research Establishment Digest*. Order from Her Majesty's Stationery Office, Post and Trade Department, P.O. Box 569, London, SE1 9NH, England. What it is and how to deal with it.

Windows

Alan D. and Shelby R. Keiser, "Demystifying Epoxy: Using Epoxies to Repair Damaged Wood," *Old-House Journal*, vol. 10, no. 5 (May 1982), pp. 103–6. What you will need to know about using epoxies to solve your wood repair problems. Good photographic illustrations.

James McConkey, "Rotten Window Sills," *Old-House Journal*, vol. 8, no. 1 (January 1980), pp. 7–10. How to deal with major window-sill repairs.

John H. Myers, *Preservation Briefs #9: The Repair of Historic Wooden Windows* (Washington, D.C., 1981). Order from Technical Preservation Services Division. Full discussion.

Patricia Poore, "Replacing Old Windows," *Old-House Journal*, vol. 10, no. 4 (April 1982), pp. 71, 89–91. Entire issue on windows including guide to further reading and a list of new products.

Index

A Note About the Author

John T. Kirk, recognized as one of the leading authorities on American furniture, is Professor of Art History and Artisanry at Boston University. He has been Assistant Curator of the Garvan Collection, Yale University; Director of the Rhode Island Historical Society; Director of Boston University's American and New England Studies Program; consultant on restoration projects; and has personally restored six houses. He is the author of *Connecticut Furniture* (1967), *Early American Furniture* (1970), *American Chairs (1972)*, *The Impecunious Collector's Guide to American Antiques* (1975), and *American Furniture & the British Tradition to 1830* (1982).

Mr. Kirk was born in Newtown Square, Pennsylvania, was graduated from George School and Earlham College, and received an M.A. in art history from Yale. He has studied cabinetmaking at the School for American Craftsmen, Rochester, New York, and furniture design at the Royal Danish Academy of Fine Arts, Copenhagen. He lives in Massachusetts.

A Note About the Type

This book was filmset in Caslon (Old Face no. 2), so called after William Caslon (1692–1766), the first of a famous English family of type designers and founders. He was originally an apprentice to an engraver of gun locks and barrels in London. In 1716 he opened his own shop, for silver-chasing and making bookbinders' stamps. The printers John Watts and William Bowyer, admirers of his skill in cutting ornaments and letters, advanced him money to equip himself for typefounding, which he began in 1720. The fonts he cut in 1722 for Bowyer's sumptuous folio edition of John Selden, published in 1726, excited great interest. A specimen sheet of typefaces, issued in 1734, established Caslon's superiority to all other letter cutters of the time, English or Dutch, and soon his types, or types modeled on his style, were being used by most English printers, supplanting the Dutch types that had formerly prevailed. In style Caslon was a reversion to earlier type styles. Its characteristics are remarkable regularity and symmetry, as well as beauty in the shape and proportion of the letters; its general effect is clear and open. For uniformity, clearness, and readability, it has perhaps never been surpassed. After Caslon's death, his eldest son, also named William (1720–1778), carried on the business successfully. Then followed a period of neglect of almost fifty years. In 1843 Caslon type was revived by the firm of Caslon for William Pickering and has since been one of the most widely used of all type designs in English and American printing.

Composed by Graphic Composition, Inc., Athens, Georgia. Printed and bound by Murray Printing Co., Westford, Massachusetts. Color separations by Colotone, North Branford, Connecticut. Color insert printed by Mideastern, Inc., Brookfield, Connecticut.

Designed by Virginia Tan after a design by Earl Tidwell.